4 DAYS

A JOHN TESTAROSSA NOVEL

JD CARY

Published in the United States of America

Cover design: Bruiser Designs

This book is a work of fiction. While reference might be made to actual historical events or existing locations, the names, characters, places and incidents are either the product of the author's imagination or are used fictitiously, and any resemblance to actual persons, living or dead, business establishments, or locales is entirely coincidental.

ACKNOWLEDGMENTS

My mom, Rosemary Vail Smith, didn't live to see the publication of my first book, Testarossa. She read a rough draft and told me it was good, to keep going, that I 'had something'. With the completion of every new book, she is the first one I thank.

These are the people in my life who make me better:

Editor extraordinaire, Benee Knaur. Stripping it bare was hard; dressing it again was harder. Thank you for holding my feet to the fire.

My publicist Heather Roberts and her company LWoods PR, you make me look good.

Veronica Larsen at Bruiser Designs for the awesome cover.

My beloved, Steve, for handling my business and me with equal efficiency. Baby I love your way.

To my boys: You inspire the laughs, every minute of every day. I must have done something extraordinary to deserve you both. You're magnificent men.

To my mother-in-law, Mary
The next best thing

"Welcome to your new home, your home away from home. This is not just a profession, but a life style." ~ *LAPD Police Chief Michel R. Moore, addressing the 2018 LAPD Academy graduating class*

PROLOGUE

I'm no hero.

In fact, I'm not sure I'm even a good guy. I've seen too much, and I've done too much. I don't apologize, I just do, and hope things turn out. We got called in on this because a few of the girls know me. Sometimes that works in a cop's favor. Sometimes not.

"I want this muthafucka," Big Tommy said.

Two street whores stood shoulder to shoulder in the doorway of the flop hotel where they sucked dick for less than they were worth. The trannie lay bunched up in a corner like a throw-away towel. The short skirt she wore—yellow pleather—was bunched up around narrow hips. Blood pooled in her lap; some of it gathered under twisted legs. Her face was beaten beyond recognition, and her dick had been sliced off at the root and stuffed into her mouth. She was still alive. Another whore lay face down on a bed that was covered in a thin, cum-stained sheet. She was nude. Stripes crisscrossed her back, ass and legs. A bullwhip sat curled in one corner of the room. A lamp lay on the floor next to the bed, bulb busted. The base, made out of cheap metal, was dented and bloody; shade elsewhere. Blood oozed from her head. She was alive, too. The stench of blood, stale cigarettes, cheap perfume, paid-for sex, and general hopelessness permeated the walls, the bed, the window blinds, the carpet, the primed-only walls. A siren screamed in the distance.

I knew who'd done this; he'd done it before. He'd done far worse, but I couldn't prove it—yet. Big Tommy was down two money-makers now, and he was looking for some compensation. The man he wanted was a cop. Given his size, Big Tommy usually got what he wanted. I wanted to give him what he wanted; in fact, it would have been my pleasure. But cops don't rat out other cops.

Alex stood just inside the door, foot up on the wall, a toothpick rolling around in his mouth like he expected Lauren Bacall to walk by. He didn't want to be here, but then again, he wasn't the one who got the call. We rode as a team, bottom line. This shit-hole wasn't in our part of town. We'd leave soon, and let the local dicks take this on. I wanted no part of that.

"You know who he is. Talk to the cops or go after him your-self." I pushed the girls out into the hall and closed the door behind me.

"Get him to call the cops," I said to Ladera, the one who called me. "And we weren't here. Got that?"

"Thanks, baby," she said with a nod, slipping the Jackson I gave her down her bra.

This was what we did. This was who we were.

1

*J*ust when you think you have all the answers, life comes along and gives you a good smack in the head, getting you right back on track again. I'm a Detective third grade, along with my partner, Alex Ortiz. I've got the rank and the years. In terms of life and death, all of us under the LAPD banner are the same. We smell the same shit; we breathe the same dust of death and destruction; we cry the same tears.

I've been with the department a lot of years; before that with the NYPD. I have a few years on my partner in age and experience, but alone we're nothing. It ain't rocket science, police work. Here's what I've learned over the last twenty-five years in this business: answers come disguised, dressed up as something else. They're right there; you just have to see it. It's when you don't see what's right in front of you that you get burned with a bullet through the heart, either literally or figuratively. The literally, I have yet to experience, but I'm an expert on the figuratively. Some of that's my own fault, and some's just bad, dumb, shitty luck. Whatever.

Alex and I sat outside a coffee joint on Main Street in

Santa Monica. It was a sunny Monday in late March. We had a caseload going and not many leads. Cases tended to get dropped or put to the bottom of the pile when leads grew cold or we became uninterested. We sat on three cases now that looked like they were headed in that direction. Chatting with Cletus Dietz was getting us there quicker.

"...an' Henry, why, he tol' me 'bout the time the virgin *herseff* came to him with a bouquet a poppies, and she tol' him dat his day was drawin' near. She tol' dat fool ta get hisseff ready, cause it was comin'...*his time*, you get me? He tol' me...he tol' me she said when he come, he be wearin' white...I said, 'no shit, i-di-*it*.' Hahahaha." Cletus rubbed his generous stubble, then stroked his mass of matted hair. And then his eyes filled.

"He came, oh yes he did, *ohyeshedid,*" Cletus moaned, remembering the condition of his friend. He grabbed hold of his matted hair with a pair of filthy hands, moisture pooling in his yellow eyes. "Ohyesohyesohyesohyesohyes... my yes. My yes."

"Cletus. Cletus, c'mon now," Alex said, patting the man on the back of his soiled sport coat. Tiny things flew off in a mass exodus, causing my partner to take a few steps back. I thought he knew better.

"Did you see ol' Henry? Did you see him, *Officer Ortega*?"

I rolled my eyes and chuckled.

"Yeah, Cletus, we did," answered Alex, shooting me a nasty glare. "That's why we're here, remember? You said you saw something."

"I *did*?" he said, shocked as could be.

"Christ," I muttered. I was in no mood. I sipped my coffee and stared at the round and beautifully proportioned backside of a way-too-young-for-me woman as she exited the coffee joint and stopped in front of me to gab on her cell.

All women looked like trouble from the rear; this one was no exception. Alex stood in front of me, his suit jacket slung over a chair on top of mine, his white shirt glowing in the bright sun in contrast to his navy pants. The suit was new, recently bought for his son—and my godson—Steven's first communion. Alex's dark hair, freshly cut, was glistening with the shit he put in it to keep it from standing straight up like a porcupine on crack, and his eyes, usually brown and warm, had that tired-and-worn-to-a-nub look today. His body language warned that the patience he'd exhibited at the beginning of this interview was deteriorating.

I was about to get up myself and end this, when Cletus gasped loudly, clapped his raw, filthy hands together, and exclaimed, "I *DID*, didn't I?"

"Yeah, Cletus, goddammit. You said you saw something. Now, let's get on with it, could we?" Alex said, patience now gone. "Can you tell us what you saw?"

"Henry."

"Yes, Cletus, Henry was killed, remember? Did you see who did it?"

"Uh huh," he nodded vigorously. His yellow eyes got that wild look that could mean just about anything, or nothing at all.

I stood and stretched while we waited for the morsel that was about to fall out of Cletus's rotting hole. His large, rheumy eyes shifted from me to Alex, and then back to me again.

"Jesus," he said hoarsely. "It was Jesus." Then Cletus Dietz began to pace in a circle, muttering to himself.

I sat down, defeated. Alex thanked him and handed him a fiver, something we did all the time and never got reimbursed for. We might want Cletus to speak to us again, and he'd do it if he knew he could buy a beer after. As soon as the bill touched his hand, he became transformed. His eyes brightened as he bowed, tipped an imaginary hat, and thanked Alex in a Cockney accent. They clouded over again as he turned and walked off with his pants hovering somewhere south of his ass-crack, trailing fumes behind him like Pepe Le Pew.

"Shit," said Alex as he sank down into the chair and took a sip of his now-cold coffee.

"Yeah," I chuckled, not amused in the slightest. "Sometimes you're the windshield and sometimes you're the bug."

Henry McLaren turned up dead two days ago, next to a Dumpster in Venice. His head had been caved in by something blunt. I was going with the baseball bat. Alex took the tire iron. Henry'd been done up good where we found him, and we knew this because of the skull frags, gray matter and blood splatter found at the scene. I usually leave endearing forensic terms like blood splatter to the experts, but this one was a no-brainer.

Anyway, that was all we had at this point—that, and 'Jesus'. No matter. Dead is dead, and our job, as homicide detectives with the LAPD, was to find out why, then find out who, then arrest their ass.

"Why the hell can't that crazy lunatic ever remember my name, but yours is on the tip of his tongue—a name like Testarossa, for fuck's sake?" my partner asked. "How long have we known that sonofabitch?"

"Dunno, *Officer Ortega*. Last time we talked to him, you were Sergeant Friday."

"Yuck it up, *pendejo*," he grumped. "I've spent the last ten minutes talking to a guy who smells like feet." He sighed. "Not even fuckin' noon."

"Let me get you a fresher here, huh?" I took his cup and went inside. I added cream and one sugar to his refill, and nothing to mine, took both back outside, and sat. This case was one of many that we had going on, and I leaned over with my elbows on my knees and stared down the street as I went over it all in my head.

And then I saw her.

She crossed the street in the middle of the block, the crosswalk not ten feet from her. Her salmon colored skirt twirled around her legs as she moved, and I could hear the heels of her shoes click against the asphalt as she ran to beat out a car. She was all woman. Nothing had changed in that regard. The way she walked, the way she carried herself— even when in a colossal hurry—screamed sexy female. And that she was.

That she was.

She had lost weight, and I didn't like it. She possessed curves and a feminine *non so che* that had me reaching for her, touching her, holding her, at every opportunity when I had carte blanche access, and aching for her now that I no longer did. Her golden hair, wavy and a little longer than the last time I saw her, was held off her face by a pair of sunglasses that came toppling off her head as she hurried across the street. I spent many an hour with my hands buried in that hair. I knew just how it felt, how it smelled, how that cowlick on the right along her hairline drove her nuts, and how much I loved it. She stopped and bent down to retrieve her shades and was rewarded with an obnoxious honk from the Mercedes SUV that almost cleaned her clock. She straightened and stared at the driver for a moment, then she lifted her hand in apology and trotted the rest of the way across and up onto the curb.

"Look at that," I said.

"Huh. That Karen?"

"Let's see." I got up and went to the curb, intent on

crossing the street, and as I did, she disappeared through a door at the end of the block.

"Uh, dumbass. Really?"

"Oh, yeah. Maybe you're right." I returned to the table, finished my coffee, and grabbed my jacket off the table. No sense in scaring the citizenry with an exposed gun while in pursuit of a sexy female.

"You are a fucking idiot," my partner stated as I looked both ways and crossed in the middle of the block. He was right of course; nothing I'd done so far where this woman was concerned was in any way smart.

Doctor Karen Gennaro and I met under ordinary circumstances, but what happened after that was extraordinary, at least for me. I loved her then, as I love her now, but at the time I couldn't make the kind of life-long commitment to her that most women here in L.A. are pleased *not* to have. But she did. We'd not known each other long. I'd been married before, and she had come off a long partnership of her own that had gone nowhere. I wasn't looking for anything serious at the time, nor was she. We fell into each other hard, and just about the time things were getting good, I remembered where I'd come from, and where I could take her if she stuck around. I'd seen what being a cop did to the people who loved them. I saw what it did to my own mother, widowed after seventeen years of marriage. I saw, and felt, what it did to me, the only son of an only son of an only son. This was my legacy—being the son of a cop who got killed on the streets. I vowed I'd never involve someone I loved in all that. I took a rough moment in our relationship, added one big error in judgment, and let that be my excuse to end it. It was the dumbest thing I'd ever done.

I crossed the street and walked to the end of the block.

The fancy boutique had scantily dressed mannequins in the window and a doubled-sided chalkboard near the entrance boasting a 50% off sale. She stood over a round table in the middle of the store and sorted through some garments. Her hair, honey blond and wind-tousled, covered half her face. A cluster of beads and silver slapped against her jaw.

I opened the door. A woman behind a round glass counter smiled at me.

"Can I help you?"

"How much is this?" the woman at the table asked at the same time. I knew then, by the timbre of her voice, the tilt of her head, and that she'd asked 'how much', that the woman was not Karen. The sales woman kept her eyes on me, which caused the other woman to turn around.

"No...sorry," I said. "I was looking for my wife."

"Shame," said the woman, giving me the once-over.

Alex had a fresh cup of coffee for himself and one for me when I returned.

"I'm guessing it wasn't her," he said.

Looking for my wife. What the hell? All I could do was laugh.

Karen said to me once that it wasn't fair to deny yourself what was good and true, especially when it was staring you right in the face.

BUT TRY TELLING that to someone who's got all the answers.

I sat at my desk, one amongst four large ones that took up space the room didn't have. Some faced a window where you could see people passing by in the hallway. Others faced a blank wall or a white board where you could see what the day had in store for you. Positioning was everything in the detective division.

The desk sitting under the whiteboard had been detective Mark Gonzales's, back when he was with us. Gonzo was killed in the line of duty last October. His death was still under investigation, and a certain patrol cop was at the center of it. Bad cops were coming out of the department's pores lately, and Mason Laborteaux was as bad as they came. I felt sucked in by it all. I had my own legacy, of course. I wore it like a shirt you hated but put it on because your grandma made it for you.

It was in the late summer of my tenth year when I learned all cops weren't good. I woke up in the middle of a muggy night as my father shook me and fumbled around my bed for something to cover me up with.

"We gotta take a ride," he said, as he stuffed my dead-weight arms into the sleeves of the thin flannel robe my mother would replace that Christmas. He half carried me down the stairs and out to the car, and I woke up again to screaming and crying, and my father coming toward the car carrying a woman. Her face was bloody, and her clothes were torn. Her white breast, smeared with blood, bobbed free of her blouse with every step my father took. He set the woman down in the backseat. She was hardly moving. He held something in his hand.

"Johnny, take this and try to get the blood out of her eyes...see, like this." My father dabbed gently around her eyes, and the white towel came away dark. I leaned over the front seat and tried to clean her face. I could not see where injuries began or where they ended. Her face was a mess. As I took care of the woman, I saw my father restraining a man as he yelled curses at the car, and in between curses the man cried. He was sorry; he didn't mean it. And then he would curse her again. I knew the man. His name was Lou Acevedo, and he had been my father's old partner back when he was in uniform. I was afraid of Lou, always had been. He was huge, and he wasn't nice. He'd order me around in my own home—"Get me a beer, kid and be quick."—and once, when he got drunk, he backed my sister up against the wall of our dining room and cupped her boob. She was fourteen at the time. The woman in the back seat of our car, bloodied and beaten, was his wife. I remembered her being smaller than my mother with half the guts. I knew the meaning of a fair fight, even at nine, and this wasn't it.

My father drove her to the hospital and stayed until someone came to be with her. I sat close to him in the front seat as he drove away from the hospital. He went past our street and drove down the long boulevard that bisected Brooklyn until he came to Lou Acevedo's house.

"Stay here and lock the car," he said as he got out. I saw him toss his cigarette into the weeds and disappear behind the hedge that separated the Acevedo house from the street. I locked the car, but I opened the window, and I heard glass breaking and what sounded like furniture being overturned. Then I heard the unmistakable sound of fist to flesh, and it went on for a long time. My father returned to the car with his hair hanging down over his eyes, and his shirt was torn and bloody. He got in the car, lit a cigarette, and we sat in the dark, the glow at the end of his cigarette the only light. Another car drove up, and he got out and spoke to the man inside for a minute, then got back in our car and drove away. As he drove, he grabbed me and slid me over next to him, his arm snaking around me while the other hand took control of the steering wheel, the cigarette dangling from his lips. He smoked it down, never letting go of me or the wheel, and not another word was said about that night, even after my mother and sisters got home that weekend, and my mother spent the day nursing his right hand, bruised and swollen. My father was not a violent man. He was tough, but never violent. He never talked about that night again, at least with me. He never told me what happened, or how he took care of it. I don't even know if he told my mother. Nine months later I would lose him to an incredible act of violence. For all his street smarts, I don't think he saw it coming.

Or maybe he did.

Mason Laborteaux was all bad. We'd run into him on a few cases over the years. He was an asshole who believed the badge gave him free reign over those weaker than him.

He was the bully on the playground everyone was afraid of —everyone, except Mark Gonzalez

Gonz was a rare kind of cop. He was smart as hell and honest. He loved his job. He was funny, he was tough, and he never suffered fools—or bullies. He was the kind of cop who'd rescue kittens out of trees and help old ladies across the street, if homicide detectives had the opportunity to do such things, of course. It was this kind of instinctual altruism that got him into trouble with Mason Laborteaux.

Laborteaux had been shooting his mouth off in a cop bar one night. Gonz, Alex and I happened to be there. Laborteaux thought it would be cute to back one of the cop groupies against a wall outside the ladies' room. When the asshole ignored her pleas to stop, Gonz got involved. He took Labby outside and introduced him to a round of punches to the solar plexus. Gonz was killed soon after.

Like I did every day, I promised Gonz that I would find out what happened. I'd find out how a decorated homicide detective was shot twice at a crime scene secured by two patrol officers, and he never unsnapped his weapon from the holster. I promised I would get justice. He should still be out hunting bad guys. He should still be sitting across the room from me, making me laugh while I was on the phone, trying to act like a professional. He should still be here.

I knew of loss. I knew first-hand what the death of a cop did to a family. I lost my father to the streets. Growing up, he was everything to me, and to my family—even as he brought the putrid stench of betrayal into our home, he was everything. It was tough growing up trying to be like him yet somehow knowing I would be more. I wanted to be the hero I saw walk through the door every night.

"Daddy's home!" he'd say. Every night. Even when he was dog-tired from the shit of the day, he'd say it. Sometimes it would come out in an exhausted huff, and other times he'd sound elated. My sisters would both run to him, if they were home, and kiss him lightly on the cheek. He'd grab them up, ask if they'd been good. Then he'd say, "I'm the luckiest man in the world having these *two* beautiful children. Angie! Aren't we lucky we have these two beautiful girls?" My mother would smile, knowing I was hiding somewhere, ready to leap out at him. Usually one jealous sister would give away my position, but my father would admonish her with a gentle squeeze around the waist and walk toward the kitchen, bracing himself for my assault. As he'd pass, I'd leap out and jump on his back, or tangle myself around his legs, and he'd say, "Angie, did you hear anything? Man, my back's killin' me. You see if anything hopped on my back, Angie? I feel like I'm carrying forty or so extra pounds."

"It's me!" I'd shout. "Your *other* kid!"

"You hear anything, Angie?"

"No, not a thing," she'd say.

"Huh." And he'd turn around and around with me on his back. "Where is he? I don't see him, do you, Ange?" He'd spin around until I was dizzy and screaming with laughter. And then he'd sit at the chrome-rimmed yellow Formica table in our kitchen, my mother would pour a glass of wine for him, and I'd sit in his lap and search his pockets for whatever it was he brought me that day. Sometimes it was a piece of gum, or pack of butterscotch Lifesavers. Other times it would be something substantial, like a quarter or a bullet casing.

The man I didn't want to become was the one who lived another life, a life my mother knew about, yet could not seem to walk away from. I witnessed this other life. He showed it to me, believing I was too young and naive to understand. But I did. I understood what he was doing when I saw him kissing a woman who was not my mother, when he should have been watching me at the park. I knew things weren't quite right every time he'd come home late to a crying wife. On those nights, I'd pretend to be asleep and I'd listen to my parents go to war with each other. You grow up fast keeping secrets.

And then the day came when he didn't walk through that door at all, and I knew he never would again. And that was the day I grew up all the way.

I was ten.

Mark Gonzales's death had opened an old wound. I don't know how long I'd been sitting there, but a presence behind me drew me back to the land of the real. I knew who it was by the stir in the air she created wherever she went—that, and the faint aroma of White Diamonds.

"How long you been starin' at that desk, darlin'?" Ginger asked. Hazel eyes that could penetrate a steel wall when angry and warm the hardest hearts all other times slid into me like a hot knife through butter. She knew me. And I knew her. A soft, round woman, Ginger Armstrong served us well at Pacific as our civilian clerk. We depended on her for just about everything, and the big boss, Captain Dale Blackburn, claimed her as his own from the beginning. After her husband was killed in the line of duty, she became family. Her hair was pulled back off her face today, which accentuated her high cheekbones and her almond-shaped eyes. A perfectly shaped mouth pursed in concern while her eyes demanded an answer.

"Too long. What's up?"

She cleared her throat. "Let him go now, baby."

Someone had made themselves comfortable in Gonz's old chair. The intrusion—because that's what it was—wasn't so blatant that pictures of the wife and kids, the requisite hula girl figurine, and the current SI Swimsuit calendar—Desktop Edition, sat well-placed, but someone had been there nevertheless, eventual settlement the clear intent. I did need to let him go.

"I know. I will," I said to her. "Tomorrow." I stood, coffee on my mind. There was something else on hers.

"He's working Devonshire, out in the valley," she said. She was talking about Mason Laborteaux.

This was the part where I was supposed to reassure her, tell her that in time, Laborteaux would get his. This was the time to tell her that the system worked; oh, it was flawed, sure, but it worked, and in time, the truth would come out. God knew I had been digging for it since that day last September when I cradled Gonz in my arms in the back of the ambulance. This was the time to coax Ginger Armstrong out of correlating her loss with this loss, the loss of a great cop and an even better friend, because this lady had suffered loss, too, and she never did get to see that justice I wanted to speak of now.

"FID cleared him," I said. "But they don't always get it right."

"Don't I know that," she said. She did. Her husband, a sergeant in the bomb squad, was killed several years ago. Politics and a half-assed investigation got her nothing but a dead husband and his pension. She worked for us now, because letting her slip away into grief was unacceptable.

"You do," I said. "I'll fix this, sweetheart. I promise you. Not today, not tomorrow, but I'll get it fixed."

Ginger grabbed my shirtsleeve as I started to pull away. "I know you will, darlin'," she said, her voice breaking. "I know you will."

*A*ll the smog and dust from the eastern deserts hovered over the pacific thanks to two days straight of Santa Anas. But it sure made for a nice sunset. I took the long way home, past the green glass condos where Karen lived and then I passed the free clinic where she spent time during the week. The brass plaque that bore her name, along with three other doctors, hung on the outside wall of the place and was almost hidden by a hedge of white Oleandar. Karen and the others founded Para los Niños (For the Children) three years ago, and the clinic thrived on funding from their own pockets, local donations and fundraising. It almost closed last year, due to lack of funding. Karen found a benefactor—a man by the name of Arthur McGann, who ran for Mayor in the last election, and lost. I knew Art McGann when he was a DA, and he was no friend of the department. I wanted to believe I had something to do with talking her out of that relationship. I was pleased to see the clinic was still around. I assumed she found the money somewhere.

The parking lot was empty, and the lights were off. The metal gate had been pulled across the front entrance. I did this because I needed to feel her. Believing I had today, believing I'd been close, believing I'd be able to make eye contact and at least say hello lifted me. The defeat I felt when I saw the woman in the boutique was not her still sat heavy.

I was a man. I did not chase after women. I did not drive by their homes or places of employment. I did not *pine*.

Who the fuck was I?

I pulled my yellow Xterra parallel to my garage rather than get out and move the trashcans someone placed against the doors, rendering the automatic opener useless. The getting-out-to-move-them, then the getting-back-into-the-car-to-park was not happening tonight. The sun was setting, and the gold-green light that remained shimmered off Linnie Canal. The woman who lived across the street that dead-ended next to my house raised her head in cheerful greeting. Her flaming red hair and a face that looked like it had been run through a pepper mill moved slightly with the early onset of Parkinson's. She shouted something and then ushered her Pomeranian into her yard. I returned the nod as a duck waddled across my path. A gray tabby followed the duck like they were a couple of pals up to no good. A young couple walked together across the footbridge that began where the road ended, and Tabby decided they were more interesting—probably because they had food—and abandoned the duck like yesterday's *sfogliatelle*.

My house sat on a corner, where the canal forms an 'L'. Being situated on the corner offered both front and side views of the water, and I felt that I had the prime spot on the Venice canals. A vacant lot that, last I checked, was going for a little less than a mil, sat between my house and the dead-end, and once you turned the corner, it was separated again from the next McMansion by a wide walking path that led back out to the alley. Someone from the homeowners association, which was headed up by three blue-haired ladies who have lived on the canals since Old Glory had thirteen stars, had erected a trellis over the walkway on which bright pink Bougainvillea was beginning to grow, thriving on neglect. I was looking forward to all of it growing in, so that walking through at least three spider webs, especially at night when I couldn't see, was all but guaranteed. These were the same ladies who came to me two years ago, when they learned a cop lived on the canal, and asked me to head up a Neighborhood Watch-type thing, maybe speak to the group once a month on safety, or what home security system I'd recommend. I said no. Not interested in knowing the neighbors. I start with that shit and suddenly I'm the go-to guy for every rustle in the bushes or family argument. And because I want to be left alone, Esther Horowitz and Lou Wachley visit me—probably right before the meeting at which I *should* be speaking—and bring me cookies, still oven-warm. I hear about all the bad neighbors, the good ones, too, and about what aches and where. I listen and I sympathize, and I eat my cookies. It could be worse. Not sure how.

After lifting the stripe-shirted gondolier and grabbing the mail out of my gondola-shaped mailbox with *O Sole Mio* painted on the side, I entered through the gate and climbed the few steps to the French doors that served as the main entrance to my home. I scanned the few pieces of mail before tossing it all on the side table next to the couch. I grabbed a beer and fantasized about the gourmet meal my stay-at-home wife lovingly prepared for me, while naked. She'd ask me about my day after kissing me hello, while never dreaming of burdening me with hers. And after the gourmet meal was consumed, she would offer to make love to me. Yeah. Okay. I made a tuna sandwich and put the game on.

This was a world away from the semi-detached I grew up in on E. 79th. The life I dreamed for myself while growing up too fast in a mostly-Italian neighborhood in Bensonhurst was far from this. I saw a wife, kids, a career in law enforcement—and I saw myself doing it differently than my old man. I'd hold my family close, I'd laugh more, and I'd never give my wife a reason to cry. That was the dream I dreamed while I still knew how to do it. When I got wise, long about the time I avenged my father's murder, I concluded that the life I lived as a cop was not conducive to most humans. Yet, I married anyway. I married far from my roots, far from my comfort zone, far from my dream—in a word, I thought with the wrong head. Then, after being divorced for five years and getting pretty used to casual affairs whenever I felt like it, this blond goddess with a face like an angel knocked me sideways when I wasn't looking, and when I came to for just a moment, I remembered: Cop's life...not for the faint of heart. I used an issue she was dealing with as a reason to label her no good, or at least not good enough, and I let her go. How stupid can one man be? So now, here I was—fantasizing about naked Karens making me dinner.

I changed clothes, ate, and enjoyed a Scotch while I watched two unknown colleges beat each other up on the basketball court, each jockeying for a position in the Elite Eight.

I opened my eyes just as my cell went off. I was still dressed. My neck ached. Light had not yet found its way over Linnie Canal. I managed a grunt into the mouthpiece. It was Alex. He wasn't inviting me out for coffee.

———

WILD FENNEL AND SAGE, the ocean, and the unique odor of the wetlands drifted on a light breeze as I drove down the blocked off road that bordered Ballona Creek. Floodlights had been set up to illuminate the death scene from the roadside into the marsh, creating a morbid stage-like setting for what was on display. Alex's car, two black-and-whites, and the coroner's van were parked in a neat row along the roadside. I grabbed gloves and flashlights out of my trunk as Alex approached. He was gloved up and dressed casually under a blue windbreaker with POLICE stenciled on the back. I covered up what I'd slept in with a similar jacket. In the end, it didn't really matter what you wore to a death scene. A corpse was the least judgmental person I knew.

An odd-looking black bird stood watch, balanced on the branch of a low-lying bush. It looked like a crow, but smaller. Its beak was gray, and its tail fanned out wildly as it emitted an offensive chortle. A strong sense of déjà vu slid over me like a cold bath. It wasn't quite six a.m.

I logged in with a uniform and ducked under the crime scene tape.

"Let's take a walk," Alex said. I looked down as I followed him into the crime scene, about twenty-five yards in from the road. Flags stuck out of the ground at a few spots along our route, indicating the Scientific Investigation Department folks had seen and photographed something of note. My feet sank into the mud.

"Who found the body?" I asked.

"Hiker out taking pictures of the native flora and fauna."

"Huh. A little early, no?"

"Apparently not. That's him over there." Alex pointed to a pinched and nervous-looking man in a tracksuit with a camera around his neck. A uniformed officer was talking to him.

"Saw what he thought was a dead animal, he says, came closer, puked into the purple weeds over there."

"Terrific," I said. "I don't like the camera."

"Yup."

"We look inside before we let him go. We don't need death scene photos on the front page of the *Times* tomorrow."

"Yup."

The corpse was nude and on her side, legs up and together in a fetal position. A hand and half an arm stuck up and out at an angle. The face was bloated and purple due to some sort of ligature around the neck. Ants and maggots were prevalent around the center of the body, and they congregated mostly around what looked to be scratches or cuts on the torso. Fly activity was heavy, the smell sour. Three nails were broken on the hand that waved hello to our morning naturist. The area surrounding the body was boggy, which I knew could speed up decomposition. It was not my job to figure out how long the body had been here, but I was guessing, based on the degree of rigor and critter activity, eight to twelve hours. In the end, the Coroner's Investigator made that call.

A plane flew off over the water to the south, drowning out Pete Tabor's voice behind us.

"How *you* doin'?" I asked.

"Swell. You want details?"

"Yeah, you know...if you're so inclined."

"Victim is female," the Chief Coroner Investigator replied.

"Yeah?"

"Ligature around the neck, tied tight," he went on, ignoring me so he could continue to state the obvious. I learned through my career that the obvious wasn't always so obvious. Pete looked around, like there was stuff to see. Three silver hoops hung from his left ear. His short-cropped hair was bleached white. Perspiration gleamed off his brow despite the cool temperature. He crouched next to the body.

"Shallow cuts antemortem, since there's blood. Drag marks from the road," he went on, pointing to the trail through the low marsh grass and mud. I looked back toward the road I had traveled down to get here and noticed that yellow flags marked the trail, while red ones had marked evidence. Tabor pulled a thermometer out of the victim's liver with a pop. "Time of death is more than twelve hours ago, I'd say."

"Meaning?"

"Meaning, she died more than twelve hours ago, and less than thirty-six—roughly."

"That's very confusing."

"Forensics can be that way sometimes. Based on level of decomp, it's only a guess at this point. We got ambient temp in the liver now, meaning, the temperature of the liver is the same as the air—67.3—but we still got rigor, which can start to disappear in that twenty-four to forty-eight-hour window. Put those pieces together, and then add my many years of experience doing this, and I get somewhat of a magic number, which is..."

"Twelve."

"Twelve to twenty-four. Better?"

"Sure. I mean, what are you asking me for?"

Tabor chuckled. I enjoyed fucking with him, and he was gracious enough most times to allow it. "You interested in more details, or should I keep it to myself for a while?"

"No, please. Go ahead."

He shrugged. "I don't have anything else, actually. I'll know more..."

"...once you get her on the table. I know."

"So, you're a smart ass now."

"Yeah, it's early." I pointed to areas around the body. "Got some disturbances in the mud. Looks like he stood over her here..." I pointed to a large indent in the semi-soft mud near the corpse. "...but that could be our hiker/photographer, too."

"I don't think he got farther than where he puked, *padna,*" Alex said, shining a flashlight slowly over the corpse as Tabor recited a litany of the what's-missings and the what's-theres.

"Who's here from SID?" I asked.

"Oh, hello." I knew the voice. Julie Sebastian was an efficient analyst. That was all Alex and I required. We'd worked with her before. She was petite and spunky, something she hated to be called—the spunky part, not the petite part. She carried a mouthful of teeth and a perpetual smile that made her look like Mr. Ed after one of Wilbur's jokes. I was certain she wouldn't care for that description, either. She could look and sound like Shrek for all we cared, as long as she did her job. And Julie Sebastian did just that—well.

"Hi back. You've been busy."

"Yes."

"Carry on, then."

"We'll talk later." Tabor began examining the corpse while Sebastian stood to the side.

I moved a few feet away and crouched down next to the

body, one among hundreds I'd seen in my career. It never got old, never became too familiar. I was always a little stunned approaching a corpse for the first time, as if I'd never seen one before. They all had faces, and that alone made them more to me than rotting flesh. The litany of questions ran through my head every time: Who was she? Why her? Had she left a few minutes later that day, had she gone north instead of south, had she worn blue instead of red...? None of it mattered, and all of it did.

"Hey." Alex stood over me and stared down at the body. He knew I liked to sit with a victim for a minute, alone. We never discussed it; it never came up between us. Like I knew he gagged every time we came across a corpse, whether it smelled bad or not. We all had our things, our ways of getting the job done.

"Yeah." I stood and we followed the trail that led from the body to the road. Two wide indents in the soft dirt showed tire tread pointing at a forty-five-degree angle toward the marsh. A car had pulled in, then pulled out the same way, approximately ten feet from where the pavement ended. Was the victim in that vehicle? We didn't know yet. It had come to a stop well off the road and would not have drawn much attention from passing motorists. By the direction the ruts in the dirt were facing, the perp gave himself some coverage from traffic moving west, assuming he removed the victim from the driver's side of the car. Those were my thoughts. I shared them with Alex.

"Sounds reasonable. I'll ask Sebastian if she got to these tire tracks yet. They're not marked."

As he headed back toward Julie Sebastian, I looked off in the direction of Ballona Creek, a hundred yards or so in the distance and running parallel to where we were standing. The creek ran from the edge of Beverly Hills to the ocean, right through the Ballona Wetlands, the perfect place to hide a body, or anything else you didn't want found. More of the criminally minded should consider the Wetlands when shopping for a place to conduct nefarious activity.

As my eyes adjusted to the waking sun and the various mirages the wetlands could produce, I noticed something sticking up out of the marsh grass about fifty yards ahead.

"Al?"

He turned around. "Yeah."

He left Julie Sebastian to her evidence gathering and joined me. A small rise in the marsh, which during the rainy season was mostly underwater, stood away from the crime scene like an island, surrounded by high marsh grass, native flowers and bush. And, in the middle of this island, next to a huge sage bush, was a makeshift dwelling. I knew that homeless people took temporary residence in the marsh grass during the dry season, moving on when the rains came, and the wetlands flooded. The area was remote and the homeless felt safe here in the middle of nowhere.

We walked through the weeds and mud toward the structure, careful to avoid deep holes and boggy patches. Blue plastic tarp was stretched over several poles and angled down for privacy. A shopping cart was filled with rags, bags and aluminum cans and glass bottles—mostly beer and wine. Someone snored loudly from inside.

I lifted an edge, careful not to bring the shelter crashing down—at least not yet. I shined my light inside. A lump moved with each breath under several layers of textile. The smell wasn't too great—body-not-washed-since-God's-dog-was-a-pup-mixed-with-cheap-booze-and-a-fart-or-two-for-good-measure.

"Hey," I said, giving what I thought was the stern and not

the bow a little kick. The lump snorted loudly, then the rhythmic snoring continued.

"Hey," I said again, a little louder, my kick a little harder. This time the lump blasted a snort and shot straight up to a sitting position.

"Wha' tha' fahck!" he squawked, not quite having found his indoor voice. His eyes were bleary and wild with the jolt a sudden kick to the calves will give you, especially while in a dead snore. A brown scraggly beard covered an otherwise clean face. His hair was thin and plastered to his head. His white t-shirt had seen better days, and he needed ten minutes with a toothbrush and a bottle of mouthwash—the brown kind.

"Police, sir. We need to talk to you."

"I was sleepin'! I ain't bother'n nobody!"

"Have a few questions for you, now," Alex said. "I need you to focus here, pal, huh? We're not here to hassle you. Get up and get on out here while I'm still not too pissed."

"Aw-right—Christ!" He stood, the grayish t-shirt barely covering a flaccid and none-too-clean Johnson. "Lemme get m'pants on."

"Please," Alex coaxed.

The man struggled with the whole one-leg-at-a-time concept until he finally staggered outside his makeshift dwelling and looked around. He squinted toward the illuminated area where the body was found.

"Wha' da hell, now? Did Martians land?" He was missing three teeth in front.

"I'm gonna search your tent, sir, okay?" I said.

He blinked several times. "I got a choice in the matter?"

"No sir, you don't."

"Have at it, then."

"What's your name, sir?" I heard Alex ask as I shifted through the pile of blankets.

"I'm called Delmonico. And you, sir?"

"I'm Detective Ortiz. My partner in there, Detective Testarossa."

"Well, good'a' mee'cha, then. Say, what's goin' on over there?"

I sifted through various boxes and bags, then finally through his shopping cart. I came up with a rather good-sized hunting knife, matches, a bag of marijuana and a carton of plain-wrap cigarettes. As soon as I emerged with the knife, held at the edges of the hilt, Alex hooked Mr. Delmonico up to a pair of our snazzy silver bracelets.

"Say, now. No need for that. No need," he scratched out, his voice sounding like a nest of hornets had settled in his throat.

"Tell me about this, Delmonico," I said.

"Say, now. I need that knife!" he stated.

"Why?"

"*Per-tect-shun*, for one. I can occasionally find a bird or some small fishies out here. Good eatin', sometimes...hey!" He blinked at me rapidly. "What's goin' on over there under them lights?"

"A woman was found murdered, sir." I let that sink in. "You see anything?"

"Oh...oh, no. No...no, I di'nt!" He paused. "Murdered. 'Sakes. How 'bout that."

"You sure? You been here all night?"

"Yeah. I been up t'town, there, got me a smoothie. Then I came back here, read a bit, and went to sleep."

"Read a bit."

"Sure. Why's that so suprisin'? I can read, y'know. Just 'cuz I live under a shanty doesn't mean I'm *a-lliterate*." His eyes widened. "Hey," he said, pointing behind me. "Looky there." The same black bird I'd seen when I first arrived was now perched on top of Delmonico's blue tarp.

"*Suddenly I saw the cold and rook-delighting heaven that seemed as though ice burned and was but the more ice...*" Delmonico lifted his chin, nodded once, and gazed into the rising sun. The typical rants of the homeless and crazy. I shook my head, expecting more bullshit to come flying out of his yap.

"William Butler Yeats," he finally said.

I glanced at Alex. "Yeats." He rolled his eyes. His tolerance was minute when it came to the smelly and crazy. "That's nice, Delmonico, but we're gonna take a ride anyway, you understand? We got a dead body over there, and you here. We're gonna get you some food and a cot after we talk a little, huh?"

"Aw, c'mon! What about my stuff?"

"We won't touch it."

"Yeah, but..."

"There others out here?" Alex asked, yanking on the cuffs a little.

"A few, but they move around. I don't. I've lived here for..." He shook his head and sighed, defeated. "...for a while. I don't know how long."

Delmonico seemed like he came and went. Living on the streets got to the head eventually—this I knew from just doing this job. I didn't like him just yet for the murder, but we needed to make sure ol' Del didn't see anything suspicious, or see anyone else out here, and the best way to do that was get him quiet and focused. That, and he quoted Yeats.

We saw him into a patrol car, then returned to the body and the CI, Pete Tabor.

"Three of her nails on the left hand are broken," he said.
"Yeah. Defensive?"

"Maybe. I need to get her cleaned up. We'll see defensive wounds then, if there are any." He studied the body. To the south an airplane took off over the ocean, banking right. It would come directly over us in a few minutes. I looked in the plane's direction, trying to determine if it was one of the giants, or simply a commuter to the bay area. Two uniforms were standing outside the crime scene tape. One was a veteran—him I knew. The other was his green-around-the gills boot, who was keeping the log of the various people in and out of the crime scene. I nodded to the kid, wandered back toward the road, and stared south again. Another plane, this time a 777, rose high over the hill and then out over the water as the familiar *clunk* and *whirrr* of the police – issue Polaroid cut through the quiet air behind me. I stuck my head inside the patrol car. The boot would have a pleasant ride back to Pacific Station. Delmonico was ripe.

"We're gonna talk back at the station, Delmonico."

He nodded. "Hey. That there..." He pointed behind me. That bird again.

"It's a crow, Del," I said. "What?"

"It ain't no crow. Ain't native to these parts, neither. 'Fact, it ain't native to the US-of-A at all." He chuckled. "Odd."

"What's odd?" I asked.

"You say there's a dead body? Well that there bird, that Rook..."

"Rook?"

"Yeah. That there's a Rook, Detective. Know what that feller's known for?"

"Taking out the queen?" Alex said.

I knew the answer, but I could no more put it into words than recite Shakespeare—or Yeats.

"He tells ya when death is comin'. And then..." Delmonico lowered his voice, in reverence. "And then he escorts the worthy home." His eyes were wet. "He saw that little girl there home. Yes, he surely did."

I would see that bird again. As sure as breath entered, and then left my body, I knew that to be true.

I'd seen him before—many times.

4

We interviewed Delmonico while SID did lab work on the knife we took from him—just to make sure Del wasn't up to something sinister. When asked if he'd seen any activity in the area over the last few nights, he was vague on details. Finally, he said, "I drinks a little, sad to say. But I'd sure know it if someone was killin' someone else right in m'own yard." Del *owned* the Wetlands now, apparently.

The knife came back clean of blood, at least of the human kind. Delmonico saw nothing and did nothing, except kill a squirrel, he said.

"Not too tasty," he informed, scratching his thinning pate. "Won't be doin' that again."

We got him cleaned up and bought him a burger and fries. He sat in an open cell and ate like he hadn't seen decent food in a week. Since he was reduced to squirrels, I could completely understand the appeal of a Big Mac.

"How 'bout we run you over to Gimme Shelter. You ever been there?" I said.

"I surely have. Nice folks there."

"I can arrange for you to get your things and we'll see that you get there. Sound okay?"

"Well...I guess so."

"Good. Hang tight. Enjoy your food." His eyes grew, and he managed a smile. "Thank ya kindly, Detective," he said as he took a big bite of his burger. I spent the next hour arranging transportation back to his tarp, then over to the shelter in Venice. He'd be safe there, until he decided to take off again.

THE WEEK HAD GONE by in a blur. I was still working a 4-10 shift with weekends and Mondays off—not that I took advantage of it much. If I wasn't at work, I was thinking about it. I avoided dating, I didn't take vacations, I didn't belong to a weekend softball league. In short, I had nothing better to do. This was less true six months ago. Funny how a woman can take up more time than you thought you had and make you better for it. I was on my third cup of coffee when the phone rang.

"Homicide, Detective Testarossa."

"Good afternoon, Detective. Julie Sebastian."

"Hey. You got something for me?"

"A few things. I took photographs of the tire tracks and the footprint we found near those tracks. I was able to cast the tire tracks but not the footprint."

"Okay."

"I got one good cast on a tire. Tread appears to be of the type of tire that would go on a truck or an SUV. That's the best I can do on that, but the tire had wear on the inside. Based on the position of the other tire tracks, I feel certain the tire mark I cast was of the front passenger side. The tire is worn on the inside, and there was also an interesting deviation near the area where it is worn."

"How interesting?"

"Very. It looks like a standard bolt."

"A bolt?"

"Yes. A five-sixteenth hex bolt. Something easily picked up in an alley or vacant lot. I took something similar out of my tire a few months ago. If the shank is long enough, your suspect will have a tire repair soon. If the shank is shallow, it might just be caught in the treads, and if so..."

"It'll show up again at another crime scene," I finished.

"I was going to say the suspect will probably never know about it until he needs to get new tires, but I like your angle better."

"Thanks. What else?"

"The shoe is a Nike athletic shoe, possibly a trainer or running shoe. Size ten-and-a-half. I also got epithelials from under the nails of the victim, especially around the nails that were broken. We're running DNA checks now."

"Great."

"I'll get something in writing over to you ASAP."

"Thanks, kid."

"Wanna take a ride?" Alex said as I hung up. "They're doing an autopsy on our Jane Doe."

"Nah. You can go alone." I knew how much Alex enjoyed a good autopsy. The smell alone usually sent him on a walk. I never let him forget it. He didn't even respond to my comment, just grabbed the keys and walked out. My shtick wasn't working. I needed new material.

Late March. Los Angeles was a city of grit and grime and shitty air most days, but in the spring, it was like a different place. Who needed a vacation when you lived in a place like this? I said as much to Alex.

"Yeah-huh. It's a 'stop and smell the roses' kind of day."

"Not appreciating my good mood, *padna*," I said as he exited the 5 at Mission Road. "Maybe I need a vacation."

The good vibe faded into the dull gray of the worn buildings, graffiti painted in dark relief against the perfect urban canvas. Downtown traffic congealed into chaos resembling a frayed knot, someone always going to, or coming from, lost in their own smoked-and- bad-rap-filled cocoon, not giving half a shit for the guy with his own agenda in the box with wheels stuck in the next lane. It never ended, the traffic. It was always there, like a permanent stain.

"Skip the vacation and get laid. It's cheaper."

"Yeah. Good advice, *fazool*." I filled him in on my conversation with Julie Sebastian in SID as he eased his way into the throng.

WE SAT with Pete Tabor outside the crypt, where the coroner's office stored bodies awaiting disposal. I found in my years on the job that the coffee flowed the same from cup to stomach whether you were sitting in some yuppie coffee house, or outside a room full of dead bodies. What happened once the coffee landed was where the challenge came in.

We were enjoying cup number two while the crypt keeper himself filled us in on what we had, and I longed for what we needed.

"Corpse is in good shape. Not street, that I can tell," Tabor said. "Vic's last meal was a good one, no bugs or lice, body's fairly clean in terms of general hygiene. She was sexually assaulted, vaginally and anally. Tears indicate force, maybe a foreign object. We found some shallow stab wounds on the front torso of the body, like I told you at the scene."

"Yeah."

"Because of the blood present, I'd say it happened antemortem. The cloth tied around her neck is a pair of size six panties, which is consistent with the victim's size. Cause of death is asphyxia, as I originally thought. You got it all there." He pointed to an envelope I held in my hand.

"Young," I said, finishing my coffee.

"Yeah, but she found trouble somewhere. We wait," Tabor reminded, as always. Otherwise we'd call him every day. We had a picture of the victim. We'd get that out to the various agencies and get prints out on the Automated Fingerprint Identification System. I didn't expect much from AFIS, unless Jane Doe had an arrest record, worked for the government, or was in the military.

"You get anything from SID yet about your DNA compares?" Tabor asked.

"Sebastian got some epithelials, but no compares yet."

"Good." He stood and tossed his cup into the trash. A dumpy but efficient looking guy came through with a line of teens. We stood aside and gave him room as he lectured the kids on what they were about to see, reminding them that the reason they were here was so that they could see first-hand the result of stupid behavior. He ended the lecture by voicing his hope that they wouldn't be the ones under the tarps inside the room the next time he brought a batch of kids through. Then he opened the door, and they entered the crypt.

"We'll keep her on ice until you find some family," Tabor said.

"Okay." I looked into the eyes of a young dark-headed

Latina, no more than sixteen or seventeen. She looked a lot like our victim, who was sewn up nice and tight, and lying under a sheet with a tag on her toe. She sneered at me and blew into her Starbucks cup, but the sneer soon faded as she caught sight of the bodies stacked three-high like cars in a Manhattan garage.

I hoped, too, that none of these kids ever ended up here, but I knew that at least one of them would.

5
___

I'd been at my desk for over an hour when Alex came in demanding coffee.

"Just made some," I said, not looking up from the file I had in front of me.

"You're here early and ready to rock and roll because you don't have kids," he snorted on his way to the break room.

"What's that got to do with anything?" I asked when he returned, cup in hand.

"You don't have to get them dressed, fed and out the door."

"And you do?" That stopped him. "While you were getting the kids their Fruity Pebbles, ID came back on our Jane Doe." He invited me to continue with a raised finger. "Name's Josie Schuyler, twenty-two. She had a record that started when she was fifteen—truant, small possession, runaway. Then it got into more serious drugs and alcohol, she was on the streets a while. Went through a program and lived for the last eight months in a group home."

"You get a lot done when I'm not around," he said.

"Not by choice. Let's go talk to the folks at the home, huh?"

"Yeah." Alex tossed his cup into the trash. "What the fuck are Fruity Pebbles?"

VENICE BOARDWALK ON A FRIDAY MORNING. Living here as long as I have, I'd been privileged to experience the Walk at different times of the day, but none held the kind of awe for me that the morning did. Early, say around seven a.m., people begin stirring. They drift out of their homes, or out from behind a bench where they spent the night, and they move toward a new day. The people who live down here are an odd mix of middle-aged hippies still locked in the golden age of Dogtown and Z-boys, white-collar professionals, and young idealists who live paycheck to paycheck. And then there is the staggering homeless population, who choose this area because of the sunny-and-70, and the array of support services offered—40,000 at current count in LA County.

On this day, at a little past nine, people walked their dogs, coffee in hand, while vendors raised the metal doors in front of their shops in preparation for spring break tourists and locals in need of cheap clothing and beach souvenirs. A turbaned Sikh swept the previous day's dust and trash out onto the walk, while the vendor in the next stall hosed it all away, cursing under his breath in Korean. Across the walk, others set up their stands, makeshift tables displaying incense, homemade jewelry, candle holders in the shape of hands and Marijuana leaves, and one booth boasting 'Your name on a grain of rice', all for a price. Beyond this, over rolling green grass and a concrete skate park, lay the pacific. Jasmine and some other woody scent drifted from another shop, the curl of burning incense drifting out of the doorway. A young girl stood in the middle of the boardwalk handing out brochures and pleas to visit the doctor upstairs for a diagnosis of your choice and some herbal relief. Under a majestic palm tree that must have appeared in every ad as proof of the star-lit perfection that was Los Angeles, a lump moved under a faded blue quilt, a bare foot, blackened with years on the streets, peeking out the bottom.

Alex and I walked between a tattoo parlor and a hot dog stand that sold the best chili-cheese fries in the world, in addition to a not-too-shabby Chicago dog. I wanted one now, to be honest. Beyond the shops and tourists, it got less chaotic, and that is where we found the house.

It was small and sat between a six-unit apartment building and a vacant lot. The woman who ran the home met us at the gate and walked us inside.

"Jo was doing so well," she told us. "She wanted a normal life, and she was getting there."

"How many residents in the home?" I asked.

"Eight...well, seven, now."

"Men and women?"

"Just women. Jo was the youngest."

"Did she have any trouble with anyone?"

"None. She was the one everyone admired. The women here, except Jo and one other, are over thirty, and they all said how they wish they could go back to being Jo's age. She represented a second chance."

"What are the rules?" Alex asked. "When are they allowed to leave, if at all?"

"There is a nine p.m. curfew, and all but one work at something, be it volunteer work or a paying job."

"And the one who doesn't work?"

"The woman has some social issues. Because her issues are not violent in nature, she can stay here. She helps me out, but she doesn't leave."

"Never?"

"Not in two years. She'll glance out the front door, but that's it."

"And what about Josie?"

"Josie made jewelry and sold it on the walk." We followed her into a bedroom toward the rear of the house. Two twin beds and two tall dressers occupied the room, with space to spare. On a low table at the foot of one of the beds, beaded bracelets, necklaces and rings sat on a piece of black velvet.

"Nice stuff," I said.

"Yes, and she made some money."

"Would that cause anyone here to resent her, do you think?"

"No. I never saw any of that."

"Do you have records of when Josie came here, maybe something about her background?" I asked. "People don't arrive at this without some help." I emphasized *this* with a wave of my hand.

The woman raised an eyebrow. "And Josie Schuyler was no exception."

———

AN HOUR later we were back at the station with a file on Josie Schuyler. I found the oldest dated report and started there.

"Pretty much what we have on her already. Busted at fifteen for possession...some information here about school suspensions—a couple of them—then the wheels came off at around seventeen...busted once for soliciting..."

"It happens, *padna*, especially in this city," Alex said.

"Yeah, I know. Kid grew up in Woodland Hills, went to a private school through eighth grade. Doesn't fit."

"You know how many Beverly Hills brats end up where she did, and at a much older age because no one cared enough to get them help?"

"I know that. So, who got her help? And more importantly, who killed her?"

I read through some notes that had been taken by a social worker at about the time of the solicitation bust.

"Huh," I said.

"What?"

"Says here, in two-thousand-five Josie Schuyler went missing for four days." Alex looked over my shoulder. "She was found sitting on the curb at the end of her street after going missing for four days. She claims she was picked up, taken somewhere 'far', and..." Alex and I read the details.

The girl had been kept in a remote location; she could not say where. She could not see outside, and she could not escape. In those four days she was sexually assaulted, repeatedly. And then she was let go.

"Fuck me," I muttered.

"What was she, eight?" Alex sounded like something was caught in his throat. He did the job knowing his kids grew up around this shit. I didn't know how he did it.

"Yeah."

"So, what did she get herself into fourteen years later that got her lying naked and dead in the Wetlands?"

"Whatever it was, seems those fourteen years were one big shithole."

ALEX and I walked through the front door of the Stone Cantina. He had a free night without Lisa and the kids. Every night was a free one for me. On nights like this, I wasn't sorry. You find out a young person who'd gotten life kicked right out of her was close to getting it together and she ends up dead, and that is the kind of case you want solved, if you're doing this job for the right reasons.

The Stone was a clean, decent-sized bar a half-block from the beach and three blocks from home. The heavy wood-planked floors absorbed some of the noise from people sitting around scattered tables, the juke playing vintage Doobie Brothers, and the click-clack of cue ball-meeting-eight-ball from the two tables in back. Movie posters of Serpico, Colors, Training Day, The Untouchables, and any other good-guy-saves-the-world theme that Mac, the owner, could get his hands on, covered the walls. I don't know how or when it became a favorite hangout for cops, but at some point, ten or so years ago, the bikers stopped coming and we started. The Stone served their beer cold, their Scotch cheap and their pretzels stale. A decent burger joint was next door when you lost the taste for crap.

A long bar that could seat twenty stretched along the wall to the left, almost to the back. Two women sat at the end. One was in black jeans that looked painted on, and a white blouse that needed to be buttoned up one more, the other in sensible slacks and jacket. The one showing too much cleavage I had seen too little of over the past year.

Amelia Carter was with us in homicide last year and was transferred to Special Investigations. The SIU helped in hard-to-solve cases, and their involvement centered mostly on gathering evidence by tailing suspects, and other clandestine activities. While still with us in homicide, she had been partnered with Mark Gonzales. She had yet to forgive herself for not being there when he was killed. Amelia Carter was a hundred pounds soaking wet, but she was tough. I missed seeing her day to day and was glad to see her now.

Her partner, Jackie Glaser sat next to her. Jackie was a veteran detective, most recently in vice, then to SIU about a year ago. She'd been in vice longer than any woman in the history of the department. Narco had been her first foray into the sleaze after the required amount of time spent in patrol. Her hard work and service to the citizens of L.A. had hardened her like Death Valley mud. She wore the wear and tear of a job where there were no winners, and saving lives was a rare occurrence. Her curly hair was grayer, and she didn't bother to cover it up anymore. She had gained a little weight, too. Her eyes, set close on her face, looked tired. Her smile, which was her best quality, had dimmed a bit. No matter. She was a good cop.

"Ladies," I said, taking a seat next to Amelia. She was drinking a beer. Jackie had a shot of something dark and a beer chaser. I raised a finger to Mac and pointed to what Jackie was drinking, indicating I wanted the same. He poured a shot of Ol' No. 7, broke open a Heineken, and set both in front of me. Alex took the same. I raised my shot.

"Your eyes," I said to the ladies.

"Your ass," Jackie answered. We downed our shot and I chased it with a swig from my bottle.

"This is a cop bar. What are you two doing here?" I teased.

"You might be seeing more of us, so deal," Amelia said.

"Yeah?" Alex said, taking a pull off his beer. "To what do we owe that chunk of good news?"

"We're working with two dicks from Hollywood over a murdered porn actress." Amelia took a long swallow of her beer and added, "Someone spanked her a little too hard."

"You working Hollywood, then?" I asked.

"Over here, mostly. They used warehouse space over on Culver, right down the street from Pacific, so..."

"Here, Hollywierd, the valley...we get around-round-round-round," Jackie added.

I tapped my empty shot glass on the bar, causing Mac to look up and motion for a refill. I shook my head. "Who you working with?"

"Small and Jakes."

"Our Jakes?" Randy Jakes had been a uniform just out of probation when he came out on a call involving an ex U.S. Marine who shot up a convenience store, then killed himself. The kid just kept showing up wherever we were, it seemed. When I found out he wanted to try detectives, I put the word out.

"Yes, your Jakes. Steve Small's out of Community Relations, with Hollywood now."

"So, a baby dick and Mr. Touchy-Feely, on a homicide?" I chuckled.

"You see now why we're here, drinking? No one wants to be a cop anymore," Jackie frowned into her beer.

"Gosh. Wonder why," Alex said. "No autonomy, assholes who've never stepped foot outside their glass offices telling us how to do our jobs, pay sucks, can't fart without someone catching it on their iPhone and loading it onto You Tube... seriously, what's not to love."

"Tough day, honey?" Amelia asked.

"Not really," I said. A sergeant from Culver City PD shared a few stories, and when I got bored with him, I turned back to my crew.

"Laborteaux's back, officially," I said, downing my fourth shot and chasing it with beer.

Alex tensed next to me. "When did you find this out?"

"Ginger told me." Everyone was quiet for a moment. "He's responsible for Gonz," I said.

"Yeah. Keep beating that dead horse, *pendejo*," Alex said.

"He's bad news," Jackie said, looking at each of us. "He's a guy on the edge, regardless of what anyone says." She knocked a shot back. "His rep's moved out of Pacific and is currently heading east, preceding him at an alarming rate."

"Not good news if you're trying to transfer his fat ass," Amelia said. "Just watch out, John." Despite her counsel, I saw the rage in her eyes. She knew.

"He's at Devonshire now, and I'm not worried about him. He's the one who should watch out. He's on my radar."

"Yeah. Dirty-fuckin'-Harry," Alex tried again.

"Am I wrong?" I growled at him.

"Probably not, but considering he's been cleared by FID, you might want to lay low on the vigilante shit. Maybe let others handle it."

I got the hint. Still... "I want him. He killed Gonz."

"FID doesn't agree. And you saying that can get you in a world of hurt."

"Guys, huh?" Jackie said, not yet used to me and Alex.

I held up my hand. "Sorry." I took a long pull on my beer. "Not lettin' it go."

"Obvious, jackass," Alex muttered.

"He's bad news," Jackie said again. "And don't be sorry. FID's been wrong before."

"Don't encourage him, Glaser, please," Alex said.

"Bubba, let me tell you something," I said as I swayed on the barstool. "The guy's a fuckin' disgrace to the badge, and he's not long for this world. 'Scuse me, ladies."

They raised their glasses in a here-here and Alex dropped it, because he's generally smarter than me. And after a few minutes of awkward silence, we moved on to other things, and I moved on to a brunette sitting at the end of the bar. Jackie and Amelia came over to say goodnight, and my bar date excused herself to the ladies room. Alex sat down, half a beer still in his hand.

"Don't let this Laborteaux stuff make you dumb, Johnny," he said. "You hear me?"

"Yeah. Sorry about that." I felt close to sober again, now that I'd calmed down.

"I won't watch you go down because you lost your head over this."

"He's good for it, Al."

"I know that, jackass, and I'm telling you to keep your mouth shut and make like a fuckin' church mouse, *especially* in here, or he will come after you, and I mean personally. He'll have the Police Protective League, lawyers, and anyone else he can find, up your ass like a WeHo hustler. He's that fucking arrogant. You hear me?"

"Yeah. Yeah, I do." I looked at my partner. "Don't worry about me, okay?"

He drained his beer. "That's all I do, bubba. It's all I fuckin' do."

I CARRIED a glass of Scotch to my living room. It was after midnight, and the lights from the homes on Linnie Canal reflected off the slow current of water outside my door. I loved this time of night on the canals. It was quiet, and depending on the way the wind blew, the smell of the ocean and the night-blooming Jasmine growing in various yards could make you love life again.

The new issue of *LA Magazine* lay on the coffee table. A beautiful woman took up almost the entire cover, from the waist up. Her light hair framed her face and fell in just the right places to show off her best features. She wore a sleeveless dress in a shade of teal that matched the masthead. Her hands were together as if she were clapping—or praying. I knew by the half-smile and the vacant eyes that she was not comfortable. This shit was not her style.

I'd read the article about eight times. Dr. Karen Gennaro made the short-list of L.A. game changers, movers and shakers who don't stand still and wait for shit to pass them by. The bit on Karen focused on a ten-car pileup on the 110 freeway late last year. She had been in traffic going in the opposite direction when the accident occurred. So was a USC med school intern and a triage nurse. Under Karen's direction, they stabilized twelve people and got them to the hospital. Everyone, including a four-day-old infant, recovered. I knew about the accident. It had been big news. I didn't know about her involvement.

I took a sip of my drink and picked up the phone. The single piece of ice clinked in the heavy crystal glass I loved to drink Scotch out of, the peaty odor of the single-malt filling the glass as I drank. I sat in the dark—better to see what was going on outside. The phone rang on the other end. It was late. Out, maybe asleep. Maybe she was up and staring at the caller ID, wondering what she should do—answer, or let it go to voicemail, content to remember sweeter times.

If she were in bed when she answered, she'd lie on her side while we talked. I'd lain next to her enough nights to burn her habits into my subconscious. On nights she was on call, and the hospital or her exchange called, she'd sit up. If she happened to be nude when either called, she'd slip on a t-shirt or the teal silk robe she kept over the white chaise that sat between her side of the bed and the picture window that looked out over Santa Monica Bay and the marina—as if her nudity somehow lessened the importance of the call. She'd move to the chaise and speak low so as not to disturb me. When the call was finished, she'd slide that robe off her shoulders and climb back into bed. If the call went on too long, she'd leave the room. I was always sorry. I loved to watch her work, loved the intense look on her face as she listened to the caller. She'd sometimes slip on a pair of glasses to read notes from a file, as big doctor-words rolled off her tongue, her voice always soothing, her demeanor always kind. And in those quiet moments, lying next to her, waiting for her to finish up and come back to bed, I'd wonder what I did, and when I did it, to deserve her.

But that was then, when I shared her bed, when there was a 'my side' and a 'her side'; when the nightstand on 'my side' held my gun, extra ammo and a flashlight, and a bottle of Advil and massage oil in the drawer.

The ice moved again in my drink. The moon had come around and it reflected bright and shining on the water. A duck sat on the deck outside my French doors with his head tucked under a wing. I was chilly, wishing I'd thrown on a shirt instead of just the sweatpants.

Click. "Hello..."

I started to speak.

"You've reached Karen. Leave a message."

Beep.

"Uh...hi...hey..." Shit. I tapped the rolled-up magazine on the table. "Hey... it's late, you're out...sleeping, maybe. Wanted to call and tell you I saw, uh...I saw the article." I paused. What else? I could take an hour and say it all, or I could end it here before a fool took over. It was stupid to call now, so late, when I wasn't ready to talk. Hearing her voice on a machine was enough.

A shadow crossed in my peripheral. A hand covered my bare shoulder. Calling another woman when you were already with one wasn't too smart. I tossed the magazine on the table and stood. The first few pages curled back on itself so that only half of Karen was visible. It was enough.

"Well done, Gennaro. Well done." I clicked off and put the phone down. Someone stood across the canal. All I could see was the glow of a cigarette. Seemed interested in what was going on in here. Interest might have been the brunette from the bar, who stood naked behind me, wondering why I was on the phone and not with her. I stood tall and stared back. The cigarette dropped to the ground, a dark foot found it, and the person disappeared around the corner.

I turned to the woman standing in the dark of my living room. It was time for her to leave. Her smile told me she had no intention of doing that any time soon. I took her and my drink back to bed.

I think her name was Brenda.

6

"We got a hit in CODIS," I said to Alex on a Saturday, a day when we were usually somewhere besides here. "Ready for this?"

We'd spent the better part of the week waiting on results from the Combined DNA Index System, or CODIS, for a DNA match to our victim. An offender would only be in the system if he or she had been arrested and DNA samples taken. Since our victim had been sexually assaulted, we were hoping for a hit. It was one thing to find skin under a victim's fingernails: it was grand slam walk-off in the bottom of the ninth if we got a match to an assailant.

"What?" he asked.

"Get coffee. It'll keep." When he came back with his cup, I slid the SID report over to him. He looked down at me.

"Please recap. It's early."

"Josie Schuyler had three broken nails," I began.

"Right."

"We got a hit in CODIS."

"You said that."

"Matches Henry McLaren."

"Huh?

"That's right."

"Okay. How the fuck?"

"I don't know. McLaren had a record, spent some time in County a few years back. He's in the system, and his fucking skin is under her nails—what was left of them."

Alex sat down. "Let me get this straight: a homeless guy gets dead next to a dumpster in some alley in Venice, his head bashed in. A few days later we have a dead girl who's carrying his skin on her."

"Yeah."

"So, what...Henry McLaren killed her?"

"No. Henry died first."

"Then what...he attacks her, then someone kills him, then someone—maybe the same someone—kills her?"

"You're reading this the same as I am." I got on the phone to SID and asked them to cross analyze everything on the two victims, Josie Schuyler and Henry McLaren.

"How the hell does she know a guy like Henry McLaren?" Alex asked after I got off the phone.

"Who knows who or what she ran into between the group home and working the Walk selling jewelry?"

"We figure that out, Johnny, maybe we find McLaren's killer, and we put two cases to bed in a week."

"Wouldn't that be nice?"

HENRY MCLAREN SPENT a good part of his days in and out of shelters. He frequented Gimme Shelter most often. It was located in a gray stucco building on the Venice Boardwalk. It served the chronically homeless with mental and substance abuse issues. The shelter held a distinctive reputation as a safe environment for those willing to come inside on a trial basis. No pressure, no commitments. While no shelter or program that I've seen will cure the tragedy of homelessness, Gimme Shelter did an admirable job of caring for those who sought it out. It was where we dropped Delmonico a few weeks ago

The day was bright, and all the fruits and nuts were out in abundance. Barely dressed girls and dreadlocked boys cycled or skateboarded down the main walk, zig-zagging between the casual walkers and gawkers. The World's Sexiest Wino sat in a chair offering passers-by a kiss for fifty cents. Oddly, he had no takers. A Middle Eastern shop merchant argued with a tourist in too-tight shorts showing off too-white legs over five-dollar t-shirts.

The entrance to the shelter was non-descript, the words GIMME SHELTER etched across the front of the double glass doors. Above the doors, painted on the stucco, a hand reaches out to those who enter. A young, eager-faced guy in a ponytail sat behind a desk built into a low counter. A computer sat in front of him, and behind him, a wall was covered in pictures and Polaroids of success stories, or maybe they were of the regulars who came through the door looking for a night's respite from the decay and loneliness of the streets. Maybe seeing your face on the wall, like you somehow belonged, was all that was needed to bring you back night after night. A bearded man, eyes red and worn, came out into the lobby and stopped at a large coffee urn that sat on a table along the wall. I saw right away that the man was Delmonico.

"Hey, Del," I said.

He turned and focused bleary eyes on first Alex, then me. "Say! Oh, hey, now..." He thrust a seemingly clean hand out at me, forgetting that hand was holding onto a cup of hot coffee. It fell at his feet, which were bare, and he danced and hopped, ooohing and ahhhhing as coffee splashed across the floor, only a small portion hitting his feet.

"Oh...oh, damn, Jeff," he said to the kid behind the counter. "I'm sorry..."

Jeff mopped up the spill with a handful of paper towels, taking care to dab at Del's feet while he was at it.

"You okay, Del?" he asked.

"Oh, sure...sure," he winced. Then he focused on us again. "Well, say now. What brings you fellas here? Coffee?" He poured himself another cup, concentrating on not making the same mistake twice.

"No, thanks," I said for both of us. "How you doin', Del?"

"Oh, I'm good...good. Good place, here. I'm stayin' here for a while, till I, you know..." He creamed and sugared his coffee. "I'm feeling...you know, better. I am, I surely am."

"Good. That's great," I said.

He came closer and eyed me as if we had secrets to share. "Say, you find that fella that killt that poor girl?" He slid a finger up to his lips. "Shhhh."

"Investigation's still ongoing," Alex said, spouting proper police speak. To Jeff, he said, "Who's in charge?"

"Oh, uh, the director is Bev Shay. She's out right now, but she'll be back in a minute. Wanna hang? Hey, You okay, Del? Your feet hurt? They look kinda red." I looked down, and sure enough, Del was sporting a burn on the top of his right foot that looked on the cusp of sore. "C'mon," said Jeff, getting out of his seat. "I'll get you an icepack." To us he said, "Have a seat if you want. She didn't go far."

I nodded and we sat, while Jeff took Delmonico by the arm and escorted him to the back, and hopefully some relief. The door opened and a woman covered in layers of clothing backed in pulling a shopping cart filled with plastic shopping bags and cans.

"Through the back, Mary. You know you can't bring that in here," Jeff said, reappearing from the back. The woman's expression never changed as she exited as quickly as she entered. Jeff shook his head and sat down behind the counter.

"You know a guy named Henry McLaren, used to stay here?" I asked Jeff.

"Yeah. Shame, you know. I mean, I'm assuming that's why you're here, 'tho I talked to the cops a few weeks ago already."

"Was actually wondering if you also knew this girl." I showed him a picture of Josie Schuyler.

"Looks familiar, but so does everyone around here."

"You ever see her in here?" I asked.

"Maybe. Can't be sure. What's her name?" I told him. Jeff shook his head. "Doesn't mean anything to me. Excuse me a minute." Jeff disappeared through the door he escorted Del through. We sat and waited.

"Takes a special kind of person to do this," Alex said, waving his hand in the general direction of the space we were in.

"Yeah." I sighed. "You toss your job and all your cares in the middle of the room, along with everyone else's, you choose yours every time."

"Without a doubt." Alex looked up at the ceiling, then squinted at some of the pictures on the wall. "You all set for Sunday?" he said. "You didn't forget..."

"My godson's first communion? Eleven a.m., right?"

"Yeah."

"Little man nervous?"

"Dunno. Ask Lisa." I laughed as a woman came in through the door just as Jeff reappeared.

"Sorry about that," he said, sitting down. About what he was sorry, I couldn't begin to guess, nor did I care. "Oh," he went on. "Bev. Hey, these detectives are waiting to see you."

"HENRY WAS SUCH A SWEETIE," Beverly Shay said from behind a modest desk in a cramped office at the back of the shelter. "We were all so sad to hear what happened to him."

"You know he had a record?" I asked.

"I'd have no idea on that."

I asked if she knew Josie Schuyler and showed her a picture. "I think I've seen her on the Walk. She's a vendor or something."

"Well, she's dead, and we think she was connected to Henry McLaren in some way."

"I would have no idea. Connected how?" she asked.

"His DNA was found on her body. She'd scratched him. You notice any scratches to his face or body last time you saw him?"

Beverly Shay shook her head. "Henry came in on occasion, but he was in no way a regular." She paused and studied the picture of Josie Schuyler. Her face changed, a frown appeared, her brow wrinkled, and it all vanished as quickly as it appeared. She was on to something.

"Miss Shay?"

She shook her head. "The world is getting crazier, I kid you not."

Whatever passed through Beverly Shay's mind while looking at that picture was a hell of a lot more than 'The world is getting crazier." I'd come back to her another time.

7

I pulled down the alley toward my house before I remembered I had nothing in the fridge to eat. I had Scotch, and I debated whether to let that be enough for me tonight. It started to mist as I turned around and headed toward Ralph's on Lincoln.

The parking lot was full—folks grabbing a ready-made on their way home from work. I got out of the car and looked up at the green glass building where Karen lived. This was not the closest market to my house, but it was to hers—downstairs, literally. I hoped if I shopped here enough, I'd run into her. So far, it'd never happened. I went through the same ritual every time I shopped here: I got out of the car, looked up and remembered the good moments. And then I'd go back and forth about maybe going inside the lobby of the building, asking security to ring me up, believing this time she'd say yes. And every time, I stood next to my car like an ass, and did exactly nothing.

I took a cart and entered, going left, toward the produce. I bagged a few apples and looked over the cantaloupe, finally deciding on the already-cut-up ones. I was looking at plums, deciding where they could have possibly come from, it being March, when I heard a voice I recognized.

"Hello."

I smiled while my heart did a momentary yammer inside my chest. *Calm down, asshole. One doesn't mean the other.* I turned toward the voice. "Jada, hey," I said. "How's it going?"

Jada Camden was the right hand, right-brain manager of all things Gennaro. She kept the private practice of a renowned trauma surgeon going when Karen was elsewhere, and in all other aspects of the lady-doctor's life, Jada played a large and important part. She was a six-foot tall Brit by way of Kingston, Jamaica. It was good to see her.

"Fine, love," she said in the raspy British accent that was uniquely Jada. "You?"

"Good. How is Elizabeth?" Elizabeth Sorenson was a blond version of Jada—all legs, and a personality to match. Meeting them was one of the many benefits of knowing Karen—for the short time we'd *known* each other.

"She's fine, love. Just picking up a few things for dinner on my way home."

"How's Karen?"

"She's fine, John, certainly something you can ask her yourself."

"Yeah, well...you okay?"

"Of course. The slave driver is keeping me in expensive shoes, and Elizabeth and I are going to England in a month. My mum's never met her."

"Ah."

"Ah, indeed. Thank you." She bagged some organic apples. "Did you see Herself on the cover of *LA Magazine* this month?"

"Yes."

"Lovely, no?" Jada plopped a couple of apples into a bag.

"Lovely, yes. I called her."

"Did you?"

"Yeah. Got her voicemail."

"Well, John, it's a start. I'm pulling for you."

"Thanks, but I make it a point not to date famous people, and if Karen's all over the newsstands, well, I can't get back together with her now."

"Yeah, John. That's why."

"You could have rode that with me just a little," I said.

"Indeed." Jada fooled with some prickly-looking exotic fruit then rolled her eyes and shoved those in a bag. "He's been calling, sending flowers."

I knew that 'he' was Adam Shapiro, Karen's former whatever, before she met me. He'd pulled some shit I didn't appreciate while she and I were together, like running her off the road, then buying her a new car to replace the one he wrecked. Clearly, he was still in her life. She was a free woman, and that was a faucet she could turn off all on her own.

"Okay."

"Don't 'okay' me," Jada scolded. "I don't like this."

"Same, but it's not up to us, is it?"

"No, except she seems unnerved."

"How?"

"Is there some sort of restraining order she can get?"

"Is she being threatened?"

"I don't know. I don't think so."

"Okay, so? Karen's hot shit right now, so he's come around to get a piece of her action. Typical. Karen's also a big girl."

"But I don't bloody like it. He was a bastard when they were together, and he's a bastard now."

I shrugged and waited for more. "Yeah? Like I said, she's a big girl."

"Well, she got back in town a couple of weeks ago..."

"Where was she?" I asked.

"South America." Karen was part of a group of doctors who provided medical care and procedures free to impoverished areas, especially those devastated by war or extraordinary acts of God. "Karen has felt for a while that someone has been following her," Jada went on.

"He's still in her life, Jay," I shrugged, not getting why this was so hard.

"Not by choice," she said.

Okay. That was different. "So, someone's following her, she thinks," I said, getting us back on subject. "Who does she think it is?"

"It's *whom*, love."

"Is it Shapiro?" I snapped, not appreciating being corrected.

"I think it is. She won't say, of course."

My jaw clenched. "She can tell him to stop."

"Yes, and if she hasn't, I'm sure it's because she's trying not to encourage him by making contact. It's what I would do."

"Well," I said, picking up a piece of obscenely expensive imported fruit and squeezing it into a fine bruise. "That's a good idea in theory, but it won't get her a restraining order. She has to somehow communicate to him, *if* it's him, that his attentions are unwelcome. It also helps if she feels like she's in danger, or better yet, if he's threatened her in any way."

"I see your point." She bit her bottom lip.

"What else?"

"I cannot bloody imagine being married to you. I'd get away with half of nothing."

"Do you some good."

"Never mind. I have my own mother hen waiting for me at home, thank you very much." She worried her lip some more. "Last night she was working late at County, and when she went to her car, she said she felt like someone was watching her."

Jesus Christ. "But she doesn't know who."

"She told me about it very casually this morning, but I could see it bothered her. I know her, John. She was afraid."

"She doesn't get security to walk her to the car at night?"

Jada arched a brow instead of confirming or denying. "Please tell me what to do." I shrugged, trying for casual. Inside I was fuming. It would take massive restraint for me not to leave the store and go right up to her place, find out why she turned stupid overnight. "Call me if you need me. She can do likewise. And tell her to get security to escort her to her car after dark. She's smarter than that."

"Yes, she is. I was a bit surprised, too. She's been working her ass off. She's been under a lot of strain, and this is not helping. She's not herself. She's just not thinking."

"Tell her to get her shit together, or you'll call me. That'll amuse her."

"It amuses *me*." Jada placed two fingers against her lips, kissed them and waved them in my direction. "Bye, love.

"Be good, kiddo."

I stood next to my car and shot daggers up at her place, perched on the corner of the building, top floor, views in every direction

"Lady Blue, you're killing me," I muttered. It started to mist. It was a fitting end to my day.

*a*fter arguing with someone's houseguest about which property was actually mine, followed by a longer-than-necessary explanation as to why he couldn't park in front of *my* garage, then indicating with my badge that I knew best, I came around to the front of my house to get the mail, and was practically knocked down by my two neighbors, Lou Wachley and Esther Horowitz.

"Hi, there, ladies," I said, going into my mailbox and finding nothing.

"Oh, John, hello," Lou Wachley gushed. "We took a chance that you'd be home." Her gunmetal gray hair was covered in a plastic doily to ward off the mist, while the oversized lenses of her glasses collected every pinprick of moisture, causing rhythmic squinting and random pursing of thin, rouged lips. Her unbuttoned lavender sweater, which reminded me of something my parents kept on their bed, was pulled tightly around her, and probably could have made a second pass around if push came to shove. She was under a hundred pounds, even in the rain.

Esther Horowitz stood next to Lou, their arms linked

together in octogenarian unity. The smell of freshly baked ginger cookies hit me from the plate in her hand, covered in a pink-tinted shower cap thing. Made me happy.

"Would you like to come in?" I asked, throwing one arm toward the door and another behind Esther's back so she wouldn't topple into the canal.

"Oh, no. We don't want to intrude. We baked some ginger cookies, and thought you might like some," Esther said as they both took the steps up to my door. Her hair, an interesting shade of honey-pink, was perfectly coifed, her makeup had been applied with purpose, nails expertly manicured, and her velour tracksuit was a fetching shade of burgundy, to go with her hair.

"I would." I waved toward the door with my arm.

"Well," she simpered. "If you don't mind."

I settled them on my couch and the cookies on my counter, taking one, just to make sure the old gals still had game. They did.

"Can I offer you ladies a glass of wine?"

"Oh, no thank..." Lou said.

"We'd love one," Esther said.

I opened a bottle of red, poured each of us a glass, and joined them.

"I don't know if you were aware, dear, of the couple who moved in three doors down, Grand Canal way," Lou began after taking a long drag of her Merlot. I lived on a corner of the canals where Linnie and Grand met. Three doors down could mean a few different things here on the canals.

"You mean someone finally bought that house? It must have been for sale for eighteen months," I said.

"Twenty-three, to be exact. Anyway, nice young couple and they have the cutest baby. I think he's Arab."

"You think everyone who's not blond is Arab," Esther snipped.

"I do not, and anyway, I thought I saw him looking in the window of that mature couple with the gaudy art work in their yard," Lou went on.

"You didn't!" Esther said. "You are mad at him because he snubbed you at the get-to-know-ya."

"I most certainly *did* see him. He was right up in their yard, looking in their window. And I am not mad at him for snubbing me, you old fool," Lou said, turning to me and raising a finger for emphasis. "But I did not like the way he leered at the Willits girl that night. She was serving coffee for us at the get-to-know-ya—you know the girl, John. She babysits for a lot of young families around here. She is fifteen, and with her mother standing right there, too. And furthermore, I don't like how I never see that pretty wife of his. All the other young mothers walk their babies around in strollers, or meet for coffee at Linnie Park, but not this woman. Maybe we should take her some cookies. You learn a lot when you take someone cookies."

"Uh, ladies..." I began.

"That might be a good idea," Esther agreed, patting Lou's hand, which she hadn't let go of since they came in—despite the sniping.

"Hold on a second," I tried again. "You saw him looking into someone's window?"

"Yes, that lovely couple with the awful art. I was right outside my door..."

"Spying on him," Esther added helpfully.

"Oh, poo. I even sneezed—twice—and he finally decided two and two was not going to equal five and got the blazes out of there."

"You said they just moved in to the yellow house, right? The one that was for sale forever?"

"Twenty-two months."

"You just told him twenty-three," Esther snipped again.

"Oh, shut up."

"Honey, think now," Esther said, patting Lou's hand. "Did you really see *him*? Did you really see anyone in that awful, *awful* yard?"

Lou looked down at their intertwined hands and grew quiet. Then she looked up at Esther, then over at me. "I did. I'm sure of it."

"Okay. Okay, dear." *Pat pat.*

"Listen, ladies, I really don't want you taking cookies to people in order to spy on them. Bring the cookies to me and tell me all about it if you want."

"Oh, well..." Esther said. "If you think that's best."

"I do."

"What I'd like to know," Lou interjected, raising a finger and pursing her lips, "is why that producer...you know the one, darling...he does that..."

"That horrible reality show where all the young people sleep in the same house," Esther finished with a grimace. "What about him?"

"Well, you know he goes over to visit Sara Willits quite often. I think they may be having l'affaire de Coeur."

"Louella Jean Wachley, that is just gossip, plain and simple. My goodness, I am surprised..."

"Oh, poo." Louella Jean Wachley stood, and so did her sidekick. "We will leave you, John, with the following: Our eyes are peeled." Lou winked, and it made me laugh.

"Thanks for the cookies, ladies," I said, my ringing phone moving them along. I let the machine pick up. "And behave yourselves."

Esther turned and batted her eyes. "Now, what fun would that be?"

I WALKED the banks of the canals until I reached 24th street. I was ready to put both cases—Josie Schuyler and Henry McLaren to bed, but I couldn't let their connection go. Homeless guy with no history of violence, and a young girl who'd trudged through a life of shit only to have it cut short just when things were looking up. She'd fended him off for some reason, scratched him. Why? What was the connection?

The Stone was quiet for a Friday, and I took the north end of the bar for myself. I'd taken up space here before, in gloomier times—most notably the day we buried Gonz. I'd lost Karen and I'd lost Mark Gonzalez, and it all felt like way more than I could handle—at least at the time. I look back now, and I chalk that time up to the old fall-down-and-get-back-up life trial bullshit that either makes or breaks a man. I'd been through worse than that, and I was still here. I wanted 'still here' to mean something now, and to me, it meant working to get Karen back into my life in some way and find the person responsible for Gonz's death. I knew who that person was; I just couldn't prove it—yet.

I finished my beer, paid up, and instead of heading home, I headed toward the beach. The parking lot at the end of Washington was dimly lit with help from the yellow lights scattered in random rows, and the shred of light the sun, now below the horizon, still offered. I'd taken Karen here, to this beach for night walks, holding her hand, talking low about life and love and us. I introduced her to dolphins and luminescence and violence on this beach, and that was just one night, before she was sure about me. If that night didn't change her mind about loving me, nothing would, or so I thought. I had it in my mind that a woman shouldn't have to endure what my mother did, being married to a cop. I had half a year to sit on the idea and saw what a bunch of crap that line of thinking was. A cop had a right, and an obligation, to fall in love, have a life, maybe a kid or two. Alex did it, and he did it well. Just because I'd lost my old man to the streets didn't mean normal was off the table to a cop, or the people who loved them. My mother was a smart lady—still is. She knew what she was getting when she married my dad. Karen wasn't stupid, either.

I crossed the parking lot and onto Venice pier. He sat alone on a bench made from a tree log. He did some air-fishing while he stared out at the water. I hadn't seen him in months. Prior to a life on the streets, I saw him once a week, taking up the south end of the bar at the Stone. He used to be a cop, and a fairly decent one—until the drink and the drugs did him in a year from retirement. In those better times, he was Joe Treach—Tree Top to his partners and friends, because he stood six-six and weighed about a buck-sixty. Catching him on the street one night, after I'd consumed a shitty burger and too much Scotch, and he'd just come out of rehab, back before the badge and the dignity were a distant memory and not just a still-fresh loss, I'd offered an explanation for myself, and for the life of me now, I can't remember why. I said to him, "I'm just a simple man, Toppy. A simple kinda man." It stuck. I was neither friend, nor foe. I was neither his future, nor was I his past. I was Simple Man, with a keen eye for what was bad in the world, and a roll of fives in my pocket.

"It's not about the stones," he said as I approached. "It's about winter." He reared back and threw out an imaginary line, tightened it on an invisible reel in his hand, then sat back and waited for a phantom tug on the line.

"Yep," I said, taking a seat. "Winter is one tough customer."

Toppy pulled an imaginary coat around his body, forgetting the imaginary rod and reel. He wasn't in great shape, rehab a distant customer, survival, now, his bitch. The smell coming off him was ripe with decay, months of accumulated filth and his insides percolating in the cheap booze and trash food guys too many to count ingested. Tree Top was nothing new, nothing original, nothing of note. He was a homeless man. What he used to be didn't matter. To him, that life never existed. To me, it was a harsh reminder of that line, and how faded it looked after years of *this* job, and how damn easy that line was to cross because you lacked a life, friends, or the love of a good woman. His flannel shirt was thin and caked with grime, his hair pulled back in a knotted mass that he held bound at his neck with something he'd tied into a bow. His chinos were a dull gray, but his sneakers were bright white, and looked to be a size too big. The yellow lights that illuminated the parking lot crept along the pier and, aided by a bright, full moon, allowed me to see the age and the hard times etched on Tree Top's face. A gull snagged a plastic bag containing a half-eaten sandwich off the sand below us and flew out over the water.

"How you doin', Toppy?" I said. He didn't answer, so I sat and waited. I did it for five minutes.

"I saw the candle go out."

The bag came loose and raced toward the churning waves. Another gull swooped down and caught the bag before it hit the water. Gull number one, not to be outdone, dive-bombed the other in an attempt to get the sandwich back. Strength, I found, was in the holding-on, not the letting-go. I watched the gulls swoop and circle around each other, deciding that in this instance, silence would get me further than 'yepping' Tree Top to death.

"I saw it in his eyes first," he continued. "The way the eyes pled for more time. The way they told of days spent on the lean-to, not the how-to." Then he turned to me. His eyes became soft, and his lip quivered.

"No fish ever smelled like ol' Henry Mac, Simp." He laughed—a phlegmy laugh that caught in his throat and wouldn't leave. When you spent so much time living on the streets you tended to stay in one place, not drift too far. Most of the guys out here, and a couple of the women, knew each other well—slept together, foraged together, sometimes got arrested together. It was no surprise to me that Tree Top knew about Henry McLaren. I didn't expect much else.

Top looked out at the horizon, the sun now gone behind the water, the dull gray of night clouding his face. He scratched the back of his neck and his fingers came away bloody.

"I was not a comfort to him. No. I was clams-on-a-half-shell when I should have been pinecones. He begged me to cross the guard, b-b-but I tol' him I need'a go bowling."

Nighttime was the worst for the homeless, and Tree Top was no exception to this. The daylight held comfort; the night held demons. Toppy saw Henry McLaren die, or maybe he saw Henry before he died. He certainly saw him after, but many did, before we got to him. It was best, for now, to let him talk.

"You see now? You see how color-coded it all is? How easy it would have been to say no to Aragon, knowing what he knew, what we *all* knew?" In an odd way, Tree Top made sense.

"Did you see something, Top?"

He was silent again, and I thought I'd lost him for good. As I stood to go, he said, "I see too damn much out here, Simple Man. None of it good, none of it makes sense." Then he looked up at me. "Maybe we can talk tomorrow."

"Yeah, Top. We can talk again tomorrow." I walked a few feet away, and Tree Top resumed his fishing. Maybe we'd come around tomorrow, talk to Toppy again, see if coherence improved with the daylight.

I dug around my pocket and came up with four fives. I tucked them into his shirt pocket, and without looking up, he patted his chest, then raised his hand in a wave.

I sat with Alex at a concrete table with questionable stains on top, eating greasy tacos wrapped in yellow waxed paper. It was straight-up noon, and the place was packed ten deep at the walk-up window, with more waiting inside to order. Alex grabbed a squirt bottle shaped like a bear that used to contain honey, and now contained a bright orange concoction. He gave his taco a solid dousing.

"I'm glad I'm not your asshole, *amico*," I said in between bites.

"You should be so lucky," he said, mouth full.

"We're on all weekend," I informed.

"Huh. No shit?" he said, with mock surprise.

"Just making conversation," I said, raising my hands in surrender.

"You got any idea what I'm missing this weekend, and how angry my wife is about it? As you know, the less negativity I hear from my wife, the happier I am all around." He wiped his chin and kept eating. "Gonna end up doin' this whole first-communion thing herself, then I can look forward to getting my grapes squeezed about it until it's Nena's turn, and I can let her down all over again," he grumbled, "like it's up to me..." Nena was Celeste, Alex's six-year-old.

"I get it." I finished my second taco and decided to wrap up the third. In two hours I'd want it, no matter that it would be as soft and pliable as an old shoe. "Hey, how is my godson's big day shaping up?"

"Did you just hear me? I have no fuckin' idea...unless Lisa decides to keep me up 'til three in the morning telling me about it."

I gathered my taco, finished my bottle of water, and stood. Alex downed his drink, grabbed his jacket and what trash there was, and walked the few steps to the can.

"So..." he said as we started our walk back to the station, three blocks away. I waited for more of his tirade, but I got silence instead.

"What?" I asked.

He shrugged. "Okay, then."

I scraped at the gray matter hoping something would float to the top. *Nada*. I gave up. "What?"

"Nothing. You don't want to talk about it."

"I might if I knew what the fuck *you* were talking about."

"Jada," he answered simply.

"Jada?" How the hell did he know? "I can't see an old friend in the store without you getting excited?"

"Sure you can. I don't give a shit. Besides," he said, "she's not an old friend, she's your ex-lady's whatever...workerbee." He paused. "You *saw* her?"

"Huh?"

"You *saw* her? In a store?"

"Yeah. What did you think?"

"I don't know. Maybe she called. How should I know, *pinche mono*?"

"Wait...*what*?" I'm a fuckin' monkey now?

"You don't tell me a fuckin' thing. I gotta figure it out on my own."

"Why don't you fill me in on what you figured out—*all on your own*."

"You doodle."

We stopped to wait for the light to change so we could cross the street. "I *what-le*?"

"Doodle. Make drawings and such. Cases can be made from doodles, bubba. Proven fact."

"Uh huh. And you noticed something about my doodle?"

"Yup." We started to cross, then stopped for a black and white that was pulling into the parking lot. "J-A-D-A in three-D with an arrow, also three-D, leading to K-A-R-E-N. Obvious, really."

"What's obvious, *really*?"

"That you spoke to—or *saw*—Jada. Seriously, is this so hard?"

"No, it's not. I'm just stunned. Not sure I'm comfortable with you looking at my doodles."

"Yeah? Like that's your biggest problem, *güey*." Pronounced *way*, it meant buddy, loosely translated. It was better than some of the other names he called me.

"Why?"

"Why what?"

"Why are you looking at my doodles?"

"They're interesting. I was thinking of having them framed for your birthday, or something."

"There's never a dull moment with you, *seccatura*."

"I suppose I should know what that means."

"Look it up." It meant your garden-variety annoyance, loosely translated.

"So, Jada..." he said after some time went by. I wasn't going to win this one. "She's worried about Karen." And then I told him why.

"Still, with this fuckin' guy?" he snorted, shaking his head.

"I guess. She's on the cover of *LA Magazine*."

"I saw."

"You saw? And you didn't say anything to me?"

"What's there to say? You have eyes, and I think you know your way to the store."

"There's something one-sided about our relationship, Ortiz."

"Yeah? Let's go to counseling, jackass," he returned.

"She looks beautiful."

"That she does. So, what are you going to do?"

"About?"

"Karen."

"Nothing."

"Nothing?"

"She can take care of herself, Alex. She doesn't need me."

He stared at me for a long time. "Uh huh."

"You wanna know what I'd *like* to do?"

"Better not. I don't want to have to testify against you."

"Someone's following her, she *thinks*. Oh, and two nights ago she's going to her car late at night, *alone*, at County, and she thought she was 'being watched', according to Jada."

He looked at me for the first time since this colon-cleansing conversation started. "She went to her car, alone, at night? At *County*?"

"Okay?"

"That's not good." He was silent for a while. Then, "You're asking for it if you step in, bubba."

"No kidding."

"What do you want?"

"What do I want?" I laughed, not meaning it. "Nothing. Not anymore."

"You're forgetting who you're talking to," he mumbled.

"It's *whom*, asshole."

"Fuck off."

———

THREE-INCH PLATFORM WEDGE heel Converse sneakers; red, glittery. That was it. That's all she wore. The body lay at odd angles, like a doll that had been tossed out after too many summers in the closet. No one spoke. No one had to. No one wanted to. Two homicide dicks and a few uniforms from Hollenbeck were loitering, lost, mumbling that they had one that age, and so on. This was out of our neighborhood, but we had a case going, and word gets around.

She was younger than Josie Schuyler, but the condition of the body was the same. Heavy makeup said she was street. Deep red painted lips, lots of eyeliner and shadow, too young to want to look this old, yet she did. Deep purple bruising under the ligature tied around her neck hinted at how she died. The hum and click of the police-issue camera echoed against the grimy walls of the L.A. River while Pete Tabor worked the body.

The phone and a splitting headache woke me at two, and despite the shower and a strong cup of coffee, I was still bleary. It had rained. The unexpected, but highly-welcome-to-all-but-us deluge came and went like a fresh-baked Challah on a Friday at 6. It left slick roads and more than a few puddles and loosened the slime and crud that had spent the better part of two months baking to the bottom of the river in the hot, dry sun. The triple arches of the Olympic Boulevard Bridge loomed over us, the dim lights of the nine sets of four-clustered street lamps spanning the bridge cast an eerie glow over the scene. Otherwise, it was quiet, the street people and late-night workers heading home the only signs of life at three a.m. in this industrial section east of downtown L.A.

She was on her back. Shallow stab wounds covered the upper torso, like Josie Schuyler. Eyes open, stunned into a quick silence, then dumped like trash. Limbs lay at odd angles, the drop from the bridge a long one. Dead before she was dumped, or did the fall kill her? Tabor would get on that. For now, she was young, and she was dead. The lights from the skyscrapers downtown came together to form one huge galaxy of color. It looked worlds away. A runoff tunnel large enough to drive a car through was illuminated from the other side by the train yard set parallel to the river. A tent and lots of junk sat in shadowed relief inside. Some uniforms were ushering the living out of the tunnel while questioning them about the dead below. This was no river. Rivers had dirt bottoms and plant life; a spot for fishing if a boy had an idea to—like I knew of rivers. The Hudson and the East were my reference points.

Normal humans, the ones who smile at strangers, the ones who shake hands with meaning, the ones who pray—even if it's the desperate kind—the ones who call their mothers once a week because they want to, not because they have to—those people should never have to see *this*. When you believe, after close to a quarter-century on the force that you've seen it, smelled it, done it all, something always comes out swinging to shatter the fluffy-clouds-and delicate-ribbon half-truths you tell yourself in order to survive.

That was all.

Josie Schuyler wasn't a one-off. The underwear tied around the neck, the shallow stab wounds, the sexual assault, perhaps with objects, was the MO of a killer and, for now, we were going with the same killer for both girls.

10

We learned the identity of our current Jane Doe within a day. Cops and DCFS knew Kandy Kane, and because of her age—sixteen—organizations like Children of the Night tried to get her off the streets. They would succeed, for a time. Her given name was Clarissa Sparks.

We sat on a low wall on a construction site in Temple City while Gary Sparks got hold of himself.

"God...I'm sorry." He was a big man with a ruddy complexion and an open demeanor, until we gave him the bad news. He collapsed against the low wall, which brought several of his coworkers over to see what was up.

"Wife left right after Clary took off for the last time. Figured now all the kids were out of the house, why stick around, you know? That poor kid...what kind of a father am I that I can't help my own kid? She's my youngest. Got two out living their lives—one's married, kid on the way. When I found out about my first grandkid, I told my son there's no pain greater, and nothing sweeter, than your own child."

I asked when all the trouble with Clarissa started.

"Well, things got bad once she started middle school. The grades started falling, she was in trouble socially. Things never clicked for her. But of course, with what happened to her, it wasn't a surprise."

"What do you mean, sir?" I asked.

"Huh...thought you knew. In oh-seven she disappeared. Just vanished. We were frantic. No one seemed to know anything."

"Where was this?"

"Where? Valley. Woodland Hills. Anyway, it was the longest four days of our lives."

I looked over at Alex. "Four days?"

A cement truck that had been expelling goo into a hole had retracted its trough and was leaving the site while rhythmic hammering continued to echo from within the condo project behind us. Clouds moved across the sun at odd intervals, causing shadows to dance across the bare wood stacked to our left. Sawdust and sweat and gasoline fumes merged on a breeze that couldn't decide on a direction. Sweat trickled down the side of Gary Spark's face as he rubbed a small silver cross between callused fingers.

"Yeah," he said. "Four days after she disappeared, I found her sitting on the swings in the backyard when I got home from work." He cried as he described what had been done to his ten-year-old daughter. "It's no wonder," he concluded. "That sonofabitch killed her. It just took her six years to die."

———

"TWO KIDS GRABBED and kept for four days, fuck-all done to them. Then, years later they're murdered."

"Both from the same part of town when they were

taken," Alex said. He scratched something onto a legal pad. "We got Josie Schuyler, who disappeared in oh-five, and Clarissa Sparks who goes missing for four days in thirteen. That's eight years apart." He looked up at me. "It might have made the news, Johnny, but I wonder if anyone put two and two together."

"So, there might be others." I got on the computer and searched *missing for 4 days*. The first six pages were blogs and articles about missing cats. On page nine an *LA Times* headline from 2010 stood out: *Child Missing for Four Days Is Found*.

"Here we go." I read to Alex. The child, Emily Knox, went missing on October 24, 2010, and was found outside her school four days later. The child was unable to identify who took her, but she had been sexually assaulted. No DNA evidence was found on the child. "She was ten," I finished. I continued the search.

"We'll be at this all night," Alex said.

"Preston!" I shouted.

Ginger, on her way to the copy room, stuck her head through the doorway. One shaped brow rose high on her forehead. "Really, with the shouting?"

"Sorry. *Preston!*"

The kid skidded to a halt in the doorway, almost knocking Ginger over.

"Child, you do not have to come charging down the hall every time this man bellows," she scolded.

"Yes, he does. Preston, I need you, buddy."

"Sure, Detective Testarossa," he said, shoving his black glasses back up his nose. "Sorry, Ms. Armstrong."

"That's all right, baby." Ginger scowled at me and went on her way.

On occasion the department took on interns, many

unpaid. Most were useless—groupies who crushed on cops. They took up space and spent most of their time flirting with the uniform or playing on the computer. Not this kid. Preston McConnell was seventeen and taking a gap year before he went off to MIT. He loved cops, loved computers, and would probably rule the world one day. Until September, he was ours, and I appreciated him. I filled him in.

"I need to know if other kids were taken and returned or showed up four days later. That's the key—abducted and returned four days later. So far, we go back to ninety-nine, and they all seem to be from the same area."

"Okay. I got it."

"You need more info, you come see me or Alex."

"Sure...yeah, okay." Preston McConnell became jittery, like he did all the other times we gave him something to research. He was eager to get started, and the only problem we'd have with Preston now, and until he gave us what we were looking for, was getting him out of here on time at the end of his day.

"You can start tomorrow. It's almost five, and Mrs. Armstrong will have your skinny ass if you're here working past five."

"Yeah, I know. I have a way of getting around that."

"Do you know, Preston, that we catch more criminals because of a certain flaw humans have?" I said.

"Yeah?" he said, his face lighting up at the anticipation of learning something new.

"Uh huh. It seems that most people, when they've done something wrong, or are about to do something wrong, have the insatiable need to share that fact with others." I let him sit with that a moment.

"Oh."

"Follow the rules, and we can keep you around." His face fell, but he nodded. "You have a computer at home?"

"Yes," he said.

I shrugged. His face lit up again. "Got it. Thanks, Detective Testarossa." A strand of dark hair flopped over one eye as an ink stain spread in his shirt pocket. Of all the clichés that was Preston McConnell, a pocket protector was nowhere to be seen, and it appeared to be the thing he needed most.

"You just gave him his first woody, *padna*," Alex said.

"Yeah. I'm like a Dutch Uncle."

$\mathcal{I}$ couldn't sleep. A chilly breeze blew off the water as I drove east on Rose Avenue with no destination in mind. The streetlights gave an eerie pink illumination to everything as hip young couples walked together with their coffees. Homeless men and women pushed carts down the street and babbled to themselves. Immigrants exited city busses with small children in tow, having come from a day of hard labor on the other side of town.

The clinic was dark, and as I passed by, I noticed that Karen's car was the only one in the lot. I was able to see it as I looked up the driveway that ran along the east side of the clinic—a red Lexus convertible, with vanity plates that read TRMA QWN. The car was new; the plates weren't. It sat in a corner, illuminated by the streetlight on the next block. The rest of the parking lot was cloaked in darkness. And then I remembered Shapiro, and that she was being followed, harassed, pestered—pick one. I felt this was as good a time as any to stop, have a chat with the woman. What the hell she was doing here alone on a Friday night was a mystery—one I was determined to solve. I made a U-turn in the middle of the block and made a right into the lot. Maybe the guard was patrolling the grounds.

I pulled around to the rear of the clinic and parked under an overhang. I exited my car and just closed the door when I saw the rear door to the clinic open. I was expecting to see a heavy-set guy in uniform patrolling the grounds—or just standing still. I didn't care. Instead, I saw two figures step out the door and look around. I ducked and unhooked my gun from its holster. I approached from the side, realizing they had a perfect escape route down the driveway and out onto the street.

"Police, motherfuckers," I said calmly. "Do *not* move." I held my Glock at eye level and pointed at their heads. This was not going to go well for me. Police Procedure 101—always position yourself *between* your suspect and their escape route, not on the other side. All they had to do was start running down the driveway and out onto the street, and they'd be gone. I didn't chase bad guys much anymore, and I certainly wasn't in the mood to do it tonight. Miraculously, they turned to me, their eyes got as big as saucers, and they slowly raised their hands in the air. They were kids. Just kids.

"On your knees. Let's go. Get the fuck down on your knees." They both fell to their knees and put their hands on top of their heads. "On your faces. Now!" And they dutifully stretched themselves face-down on the asphalt. I got on the radio and called for backup, and in less than three minutes, a 14-L patrol unit rolled up—a one-man unit out of Pacific. I brought him up to date, and then told him I was going inside.

"The car belongs to one of the docs," I said. "I'm going in for a look."

"Let me call a backup for you before you go in."

"Go ahead. I'll be fine in the meantime." As always where Karen Gennaro was concerned, know-better went right out the window.

I entered the back door of the clinic and eased my way down the long hallway, my gun still drawn. I opened each door that I passed, searching the exam rooms for more intruders. I didn't allow myself to think of all the bad things I could find—Karen's body, for example. I turned left and walked down another hallway. I didn't hear anything. I passed a room at the end of the hall, next to a small conference room. Glass lay on the counter and the floor. Vials and bottles of narcotics littered the room. They had been after drugs.

I retraced my steps, turned right, and continued down the hall toward the front of the clinic and the reception/waiting area.

"Karen?"

I heard conversation coming from an office to my left—hers. Her voice was raised, and her tone was not happy.

"Karen?"

"You're not hearing me!" she said from behind the door. She wasn't hearing a whole lot herself.

I reached the door and opened it a crack. A light was on. I pushed the door open with some force, and it banged against the wall. I leveled my Glock into the middle of the room. She screeched and flew to her feet, pulling the phone that was attached to her ear to the floor. It fell with a resounding crash, taking a few items on her desk with it.

"What are you doing?" she yelled.

I looked around the room, saw she was alone, and slipped my gun back in the holster. Someone on the other end of the line was speaking—a man.

"Karen...? Karen...? Are you all right?"

Her eyes narrowed and those angry lines around her mouth became more pronounced.

"I need to call you back," she said into the receiver. Then to me, "Are you *insane?* What are you doing?"

I took a deep breath and glared right back at her. "Don't move." I made one more round of the clinic, searching more thoroughly, now that I knew she was safe. I came back out and pushed on the front door to the clinic. It was unlocked, and there was no sign of forced entry.

"Goddammit," I said, loud enough to bring her out of her office. She stood in the reception area now. I turned and faced her.

"What happened?" she repeated. "What's going on?"

"I caught two people coming out the back door, Karen. I'm guessing they came in through the front door. You didn't hear anything?"

"No, I didn't, and you appear agitated."

Okay. "I caught two people coming out the back door."

She blinked several times, trying to put sense to my words.

"Karen?"

"What do you mean...?"

"B and E. Burglary in progress." I was raising my voice now, patience all but gone with this woman. "I caught them coming out the back door. They're taking it easy right now in the back of a patrol car. You didn't hear anything?"

Without answering, she headed down the hall toward the rear of the clinic and the drug room.

"Stop. Gennaro, stop." She ignored me, so I followed her.

"Shit," she muttered. "Well, they knew what they wanted —Vicodin, Codeine..."

I stood in the doorway. "Come out of there, please, before you hurt yourself." I reached out and took her hand,

and as she started to falter stepping over the glass, I swooped her up in my arms. She yelped and gave a couple of feeble kicks before I set her down in the middle of the hallway. She didn't know what to do next, nor did I. The awkward moments after the intimate one in which I held her in my arms wasn't lost on either of us. I had no right to be mad at her, no right to scold, no right to kill her where she stood—much as I wanted to.

"I don't understand, John," she said, finding herself again. "What happened here? What are *you* doing here?"

"I drove by, saw that all the lights in front were out, looked like no one was inside, the gate's not across the door like it should be. So, I pull in back, see your car, just as these two jackasses are coming out the back door. Here I'm expecting maybe the security guy..."

She held a hand up. "All right..."

"... I come in, I'm looking around, trying not to picture your dead carcass behind every door..."

"Clearly I'm no worse for the wear."

"The night's still young."

"Charming."

I closed my eyes and took a breath. "It could have been anyone coming through that door, Karen. That's all I'm saying."

"Okay," she said calmly. "I'm fine, no one's dead. So, what else?" Then she blinked a few times, as if some sort of light bulb went on. "It's you."

"What's me?"

"You're following me, aren't you?"

So, she *was* worried. Jada was right to be concerned. I needed to handle this right. Before I could say anything, she went on.

"What do you want from me, John?"

"Want from you?"

"Why are you...are you following me, checking up on me?"

"As much as I think you need a good dose of checking up on, I haven't got that kind of time. You worried about something, Gennaro?"

"What are you doing here?"

"I explained that already. Just passing by."

"Uh huh." She started to walk away.

I snatched her by the arm before she got too far. "I'm going to blame shock for your lack of clear thought, so I'll speak slow: looking for you and thinking the worst wasn't fun, and I'm in no mood for a battle. This is a crime scene and you're in my territory now." I stared at her a while. "Okay?"

She looked down at my hand wrapped around her forearm. "Let go."

An electric charge raced through me. More than my anger was on the rise now. What I should have done, of course, was let her go. Instead, I pulled her close until her face was inches from mine. I brought my hand up to her throat, just under her chin, and tipped her face up. Our eyes locked. I knew the chance I was taking, handling her like I had a right. Her high cheekbones pinked at the intrusion, and her full lips parted slightly. I thought about kissing her; I thought about throttling her. Instead, I brushed my thumb over the corner of her mouth. The pissed look gave way to resignation. She sighed and closed her eyes.

"Let's start over," I said. Her eyes opened, the underlying meaning not lost of either of us.

"May I have a minute?" she said and swallowed hard. "Let go and give me a minute."

"Take two." I released her and walked over to a long

couch in the waiting room. She spun on her heel and returned to her office. I looked over at the unlocked door again.

No expense was spared in the free clinic. The reception area was filled with large, comfortable chairs, with heavy square cubes in between, on which magazines sat. The floors were a light shade of wood, the walls painted a soothing sea-green color. A large aquarium sat on a platform behind the reception desk, water undulating with the serene movement of colorful fish. Framed pictures of x-rayed seashells and fish served as the artwork. The large window looked out on to Rose Avenue, now covered partially by light colored wood vertical blinds. The smell was rubbing alcohol and Karen. She was very proud of what she had created. I was proud of her, as well.

"Time's up." I got up and found her in her office. She was standing at the window, looking at the kids in the patrol car. "Get away from there."

"Why?"

"Because I said so," I said with some force. I closed my eyes and counted to ten. "I don't know anything about these guys, Karen. I'd rather they not see you. Is that explanation enough?"

She shook her head, unmoving. "They're just kids."

"Right." I closed the blinds and she blinked, then turned and looked at me. "Opie and The Beaver. Do you know how lucky you are?"

"No, but I'm sure you'll tell me."

"Who knows what these yahoos are up to? They're addicts or they're stealing for addicts. If they're in a gang, they don't give a shit who they hurt to get what they want. Do you understand what I'm saying to you?" She stared at the blind-covered window. "Karen."

Arms crossed, a hip jutting defiantly to one side, she met my eyes. No woman in my experience could infuriate and bring me to my knees all at once, quite like she could. I tried again. "How did you not hear anything?"

"I was on the phone." She pressed the bridge of her nose then shook her head. "They came in...and I didn't even hear them."

"Where's your security guy?"

She sat in her chair.

"Karen?"

"I sent him home."

"Why, for Christ sake?"

She glared at me for a while before she said, "We had a long day, he'd been here since 6:30 this morning, and I was on my way out, too, when I got a call. Okay? Is that satisfactory? Is the third degree over now?"

She stood and walked out of her office. She sat down hard at the reception desk, crossed her legs, and then crossed her arms over her chest. I followed. She looked up at me. "Who taught you to be this way? To think it was all right to...to *be* this way?"

"What *way*? I pass by, I don't like what I see, so I investigate. I'm a cop. It's what I do."

"So I recall."

"How 'bout I change all that, just for you, huh? Instead of a cop, I'll play the passive...oh I don't know...architect. That way you can get stupid and no one will call you on it."

"That's a...what's that supposed to mean?"

"Never mind. I'll be right back." I started walking toward the back of the clinic. "Will you be okay for a minute?"

"I've been okay for the past six months," she mumbled. "What's another minute?"

I turned around and walked back to her, invading what little space she had left.

"In the beginning, that was my doing. But me standing here, and you sitting there, and me not holding you? That's *your* doing. You really want to put all this aside and have that conversation, Gennaro? Do you?" *How about all the other shit that's going on in your life, keeping you up nights*, I wanted to say. *Wanna talk about that, too?*

She rested her chin in her hand. "What happened to 'let's start over'?"

"Stop pissing me off."

I headed for the rear exit of the clinic. The patrolman was holding a bag. Another car pulled in—a two-man unit this time.

"Found all this in their pockets," the uniform said.

"Yeah, they hit the drug cabinets. Place is smashed up pretty good."

"Want me to get 'em outta here?" He looked behind him as the two backups exited their car.

"No. Not yet." To the backups I said, "We're good here. All safe inside." I addressed the two boys in the back. "You with the Third Street Boyz?"

"Nah," said one. "We don' mess w'da gangs."

"Yeah? Then what the hell were you doing?"

The one who spoke stared out the window.

"Hey! I'm talkin' to you. How old are you?"

He turned back around. "Fourteen." He looked big for fourteen.

"So what the hell were you doin', Fourteen?"

"Wha'choo care?" he sputtered.

"I don't." I turned to the patrolman behind the wheel. "Get 'em outta here." Then the other one spoke.

"His mama got cancer. She in pain. We's gettin' the drugs fa' her."

"Foo', shut up," said Fourteen.

"That true, Fourteen?"

He looked at me with eyes of steel, and then they melted into liquid pain, leaving a trail down his dark cheeks.

"Yeah," he said, wiping his face on his sleeve. "It true."

"Your mama at home now?"

"Yes, sir."

"Someone with her?"

"No, sir. She alone."

"Where do you live?"

"Oakwood."

I straightened and paced in front of the car. Jesus. So many of these kids didn't stand a chance, yet here were these two, breaking the law with a purpose.

"Wait here," I said to the officer behind the wheel. I went inside and walked down the hall to the reception area. Karen was pacing in front of the reception desk now, a thumbnail caught between her teeth. She turned and we stared at each other down the long hallway. She saw something on my face.

"What's up?"

I was pretty good at switching gears. I was about to find out if she was. "Uh...I need your help. Can you get some pain meds together and take a ride with me?"

"I believe the newest residents of juvenile hall have them all. What's going on?" I told her. "Let me throw a bag together," she said as she passed me and walked down the hall.

"Just like that?"

She turned and smiled. "Yeah, just like that."

*N*ow that I had her in the car with me, on a mission to save the world, or maybe just a kid's mother, I felt awkward as hell. Going from zero to sixty and then back down below the speed limit in twenty minutes would bring awkward on nicely. I handled this one the only way I knew how. Didn't make it ideal.

"We okay?" I said as I drove out of the clinic lot with the Adam car in front. The other car stayed behind. Karen would need a formal police report for insurance.

"I didn't appreciate you storming in my clinic like a lunatic and taking over like you own the place—and me... and I'm not stupid."

"No, you're not. I'm sorry. I didn't know what I was going to find after catching those two coming out the back door. All I could imagine was finding you in a bad way. I'm sorry I came off strong. I have no right to do that—act like I care, pretend you're accountable to me, shit like that." That coaxed a smile out of her.

"Was I accountable to you?"

"As much as I was to you. That's how it works."

"Well, under the circumstances, I'm glad you stopped by tonight."

"You might change your mind in a minute."

"I doubt it."

"Just like that?"

"Just like that."

We pulled up in front of a housing project, each building looking the same as the next—beige and devoid of charm. The two patrolmen, and Karen and I followed the two boys across the mostly dirt courtyard and up a flight of stone stairs. Two young men sat half way up, barely moving aside as we passed.

Fourteen let us in to a small apartment. The odor was overwhelming. A combination of sick and garbage hung in the air like a smog. Cockroaches scurried for cover across the living room carpet, which was thin in places, and torn in others, revealing cheap Formica beneath. The counters in the kitchen were covered with dirty plates and food left out to spoil. It was only after I'd taken in the scenery that I heard the moaning.

Karen took over, following the sounds until she came to a bedroom. Two twin beds and a four-drawer chest competed for space in the tiny room. The walls were black with the grime from the streets and years of cigarette smoke. Phone numbers and other notes were written on the wall near a small nightstand where I assumed a telephone used to be. Bed sheets that were once white with small yellow rosebuds, now filled the role of draperies, and hung limply, barely covering the window. I couldn't imagine they kept out much light during the day or hid private goings-on at night.

It was clear that Fourteen shared this bedroom with his dying mother, having to smell her decay and her cigarettes, and lie helpless while she moaned in her sleep. She was delirious, but not so much that she didn't notice strangers in her room—white strangers, two of them in police uniforms.

"Tariq, what's happening?" Her voice, small and soft, carried a dignified tone, despite her condition.

"It's okay, Mama. The lady's a doctor."

"I don't *need* no doctor. I tol' you...!"

"Hi, there," Karen soothed. "I'm Karen. Tariq tells us that you've been sick..."

"Tariq..." Her voice was filled with fear.

"He's right here, and he's safe," Karen said.

"What are they doing here?" Her dark eyes were wide with fear, the whites bloodshot and yellow. She stared at the two uniforms in a panic.

"They're here to help me, all right? What's your name?" Karen brushed the woman's wild hair out of her face. I could see the greasy film of sweat the woman carried, but Karen didn't seem to care.

"Tania. Tania Harris."

"Tania, are you under the care of a doctor?"

"No, I...I can't get...I go to the hospital when it gets bad, but..."

"Do you know what stage you're in?"

"Four."

"Where is the cancer, Tania?"

She opened her blouse, revealing one breast already gone.

"Looks like you lost your breast a while ago. How long were you in remission?"

"Two years."

"That's a good fight." Karen smiled then, her voice low and soothing. And Tania Harris began to relax. "I'm going to get you over to the hospital now, so you can be more comfortable. Is there someone Tariq can stay with?"

"Uh…" I heard one of the uniforms say. I knew what he *wanted* to say—that the only place Tariq was going was to jail. I tapped him on the arm and motioned him out of the room.

"We can't take him in," I said. "Not now."

"Are you kiddin' me, Detective?" Officer Rangoon asked. I bet he got all kinds of shit with a name like that.

"I won't press charges," Karen said, walking out of the room and holding a cell phone to her ear. "You hear me, officer? Yes, hello, this is Doctor Karen Gennaro, and I'm at…" She snapped her fingers and the cop gave her the address. She repeated it into the phone, and Officer Rangoon resumed giving me the hairy eyeball.

"Stage four breast cancer, she's dehydrated…temp one-oh-four…" She paused. "I have no IV here, and I'm five minutes from my clinic. I don't want to move her. How quickly can you get here?… all right…I'll have a uniformed police officer wait out front and escort you in." She hung up.

"You heard the lady, Raccoon," I said.

"It's Ran*goon*," he corrected.

"And she's not pressing charges. Did you hear that, too?"

He shook his head and raised his hands in surrender. "Whatever, Detective." To Karen, he said, "I'll go out front, Doctor."

"Thank you, Officer Rangoon." After he left Karen turned to me. "Did you call him *Raccoon*?"

"What is it…*Ragu*?" I walked over to Tariq. "Who can you stay with tonight, kid?"

"He can stay wit' me," said the other boy.

"What's your name, Jesse James?" I asked him.

"Marcus."

"You got a parent at home now, Marcus?"

"Yeah."

"Introduce me. We'll have a little talk."

Ten minutes later, I was back, with Tariq, Marcus, and Marcus' father in tow. Marcus' father was not the least bit happy with the news that his son had broken into a clinic. But he put that aside once he saw Tania Harris.

"Mercy, Tania. Why di'nt you tell nobody?" he said, standing over her as she lay on the ambulance gurney.

"Watch Tariq for me, George. I won't be long...day or two," she moaned. I looked over at Karen and her mouth twitched slightly.

"'Course. You just take care now." To the EMT, he asked, "Where you takin' her?"

"County, sir."

"It'll be all right, Tania. Damn, girl, you know how to get my attention."

They took Tania out, and Karen gave instructions to her and to the EMT. She'd arranged for an Oncologist to see Tania, and he would be there waiting when she arrived.

"Mama?" Tariq called out.

"It'll be all right, baby."

"We gon' take you to see her tomorrow, boy, a'ight? Meantime, you wit' us." George slipped an arm around Tariq's shoulder protectively. "And we gon' have a little talk 'bout this evenin'." I was guessing George was the closest man in Tariq's life at this point. It was a start.

Karen walked over to Tariq and handed him her card. "You call me anytime, okay? You get worried about her, you have any questions, you call, day or night. My home and cell numbers are on the back. Do you understand, Tariq?"

"I'm sorry about..."

"I know, honey. We'll fix it, don't you worry.

When we got back into the car, I turned to her. "What do you think?"

"She won't last the week." She nodded toward Tariq. "What happens to him?"

"Don't know. We may still have to pick him up."

"I won't press charges. I meant what I said."

"I know you did, but it may not be up to you. We'll just have to see."

She turned in her seat to face me. "You fix this, John. I will not have him going to jail. I'll hire a lawyer for him, I'll testify…"

I chuckled. "Okay." I reached out and squeezed her hand.

"Tania said she wouldn't let him call anyone. They're uninsured and an ambulance ride cost money."

"Yeah. I got that."

Karen sat back in her seat and shook her head. "It's all backwards, Johnny."

"Yeah."

"That kid needs to be with his mom. She's in bad shape. She doesn't have long. You get my point here?"

"Yup." I squeezed again. "I'll see what I can do. If he has a record, he's toast. And frankly, if he does have a record, especially for a B and E, I'll come get him personally."

"Please speak English."

"Breaking and Entering. I can't help him if he's done this before."

She paused for a long while and then she nodded. "Fair enough."

"Okay, where to?"

"My car—and you don't need to follow me home."

"What makes you think I want to follow you home? First I'm stalking you and now I got time to babysit you?" She smiled and stared out the window.

I headed back to the clinic, and while I drove, she made

a couple of phone calls to arrange hospice care for Tania Harris, a woman she didn't even know. Karen's compassion always stunned me, but never more than at this moment. I pulled up next to her car.

"Will you keep in touch with me about Tariq, John?"

"Sure."

"Thank you...I don't know what else to say."

"My pleasure, babe."

She smiled, unmoving.

"What's on your mind, lady blue?"

She shook her head. "Nothing." She turned to open the car door. My hand on her arm stopped her.

"What do you need to tell me?"

She shook her head and stared out the window. Finally, she said, "Nothing. I'm fine."

"Yeah?" I stared at her, trying my best to affect a smile that eased her anxiety, not make her want to run for the hills.

"I got your call." She faced me and smiled. "Thanks. That was sweet."

"You're welcome, and that's not what you want to tell me."

She gave a little laugh and went back to staring out the window. Finally, she said, "I'm dealing with...a personal issue right now, and..." She shook her head. "I'm trying to figure out the best way to handle it." She faced me. "That's all."

"That's all, huh? Is this personal issue following you around, worrying you?"

No answer.

"Were you on the phone with this personal issue earlier? No? Nothing? What's this personal issue's name? Shapiro?"

She stared at me and shook her head. "The 'architect' comment was very subtle. Jada called you, didn't she?"

"No."

"John..."

"No, Karen. She did not call me."

She stared at me a moment, then sighed, not wishing to get caught up in semantics. "God *damn* her."

"Don't. She loves you."

"She has no right to get into my business."

"She loves you. And I'm here to help if you need me."

She shook her head and stared out into the night.

"Does he want you back?"

"It's more complicated than that, John."

"What do you want?"

"Not him."

"Who?"

She stared out the window and didn't answer for a long time. Finally, she said, "You're too much for me, Johnny."

"Yeah? Well, maybe that's what you need. From what I've seen, you've had a life full of not enough."

She turned and looked at me. "I'd settle now for just right." She smiled then. "Goodnight."

"Goodnight, sweetheart," I whispered.

I drove away. It was either that or nail myself to a cross while a mage etched Dr. Gennaro's name across my chest with a rusty knife.

───────────

INSTEAD OF HEADING home to the canals and a cold bed, I headed north and east toward Westwood. This visit was overdue.

I parked on the street in front of the high-rise apartment

building on Wilshire. I nodded to the doorman and walked to the elevator. He didn't stop me. The gun and the badge tended to freeze people in their tracks.

I pressed 15 and waited. I'd been here before. I knew where the guy worked, where he ate, where he slept. It was after eleven o'clock. I figured I'd find him home. I rang the bell. I heard footsteps, then I saw an eye appear grotesquely through the peephole.

"Yeah?" he said after a long hesitation.

"C'mon," I answered. "Be brave."

"You here on business?"

"Yeah. Sure."

I heard a click, then the door opened. "You were video-taped coming up."

"Hope they caught my good side."

I hadn't seen Adam Shapiro since the car incident. He hadn't changed. He was dark and handsome—the usual. He wore his hair short and styled just so. His eyes showed intelligence and gave the illusion of humor. He wore baggy sweats and an Abercrombie & Fitch t-shirt. I smelled brownies.

His mouth curled at one corner. He looked me up and down, and his eyes came to rest at my hip. I'd opened my jacket casually/on purpose. He jerked a thumb over his shoulder.

"C'mon in."

I did.

"I'm not alone."

"Congratulations."

"Drink?"

"No. I won't be long."

"Shame."

I stared at him. "You asking for trouble?"

He chuckled. "Depends who's dishing it out."

"You following Karen around?"

"Why would I do that? If I want to talk to her, I just call."

"Uh huh. And email, and send flowers...sent any cars lately?"

"Not lately. Why, does she need one?" He suddenly looked bored. "Is there a reason for your visit, John?"

"Leave her alone."

"She ask you to come here?"

"No. She wouldn't do that."

"Right. She'd get on the phone and tell me herself, wouldn't she? Odd, she hasn't made that call yet." He paused, backed up a little. "I made a big mistake letting her go. You did, too, by the way. Wait, *you* didn't let *her* go, did you?" He smirked. There would come a day when I'd find out how he knew anything about my relationship with Karen. For now, this conversation would be about him.

"Stay away from her," I said, grabbing for the door handle.

"And if I don't?"

I shrugged. "We'll see."

"Yeah, John. You bet."

I walked toward the elevators and he stuck his head out.

"Hey."

I turned.

"Back in the day, we'd be choosing dueling pistols about now. You know, we *could* shoot a game of pool, winner gets to kick the other's ass *and* get the girl. Or, we can just flip a coin."

I turned and walked back to him. I almost grabbed him, but decided I'd get another chance someday soon. I wanted it to mean something when I finally cleaned his clock.

"The reason you're not with her anymore is because it was always just a game to you." I came right up to his face.

"Yeah? Karen and I are joined at the hip in more ways than you can imagine. I'll be in her gravy for a good long time." He paused. "How about you? What's your excuse?"

I had no answer. "Contact her again, and I'll kick your ass just for fun."

"Yeah. Sure, John," he said with a smirk, then turned and went back inside.

I stepped outside onto Wilshire Blvd. I'd never fought for anything in my life—not my first marriage, not for a return to the dignity my mother lost at my father's indiscretions, and certainly not for Karen. I let her go once. I wasn't going to do it again. Not for anyone.

13

"I don't know what it means, Detective. But I think it's good."

Preston McConnell was aquiver again, and it could only mean good news. The kid hadn't let us down yet. This time it had taken less than twenty-four hours.

"I kept it simple at first," he said. "I searched the Internet for similar stories and kept it broad, you know—like, all over the country. I didn't get much, so I narrowed it down. I got one hit, an article in the *LA Times* about a child who had gone missing in 2010..."

"Yeah, I told you about that one."

"No, not Emily Knox. This one disappeared a month later, in November. They never found her."

I grabbed his notes, realizing I had no way of deciphering his chicken scratch. "Disappeared from the same area?" I scanned the page, wanting to answer my own question. It was impossible.

"Yes. And because it was a month after Emily Knox, it made the news.'

"Yeah, it did. So, details about the case?"

"A follow-up article a week or so later, saying that police had no new leads. Interesting, though."

"What's that?"

"This last article spent a lot of time talking about jurisdiction, and how the family of this girl..."

"Name?"

"Sorry. Kristen Holmes. The family of Kristen Holmes wasn't too happy, because apparently no one could decide who was in charge. Look." Preston set out a satellite map of an area bisected by the 118 freeway. "Kristen Holmes went to school here, according to the *Times* article." He pointed to a barren area south of the freeway. "The authorities think she disappeared from here, because she went to school and never made it home. But you see this area up here?" He pointed to a slightly mountainous area above Santa Susanna Pass, a mountainous road that cut through the hills above Topanga Canyon Boulevard. Like most of the canyon communities in Los Angeles, the area was home to hippies, artists and old vets who laced their strawberry tea with marijuana and told war stories. "This is under Ventura County Sheriff's jurisdiction, not LAPD."

"Right." I tapped my finger on the photo.

"So, anyway, this one made news. The child never returned."

"Okay," Alex said. "We now have three who disappeared for four days, and one was never found. What else?"

"Wait," Preston said. "I'm not done." He passed a neatly typed list across the table. "I had to go back a ways, and I had to look into the archives of newspapers that no longer exist, like *The Herald Examiner* and *The LA Free Press*. Between *The Times*, *The Daily News*, even *La Opinión*, I found stories about all the girls on this list."

There were eleven names, with two dates next to each, four days apart. The oldest one was in 1988. The latest, 2017.

"I'm assuming the first date is when they disappeared, and the second date is when they came home?"

"Yes. Now, this is where things get interesting. I was surprised to find something as far back as 1988, especially in *The Free Press*, because it was a pretty liberal rag in the sixties and seventies, then became a porn magazine, basically, before it was shut down. But in March of 1988, *The Press* did a two-part article on a girl who had gone missing—this one here."

"Grace Dashiell."

"Right. It made news, apparently, because her father was a hot-shot under Tom Bradley, the Mayor of Los Angeles at the time. And *The Press* made the point that it was only because of the father's influence that every cop in the city was on the case. As with the others, she showed up four days later."

"Okay, that's good, but…"

"That's not the interesting part."

"Kid, that was pretty interesting."

"I know, right? So, *The Press* closes down after Larry Flint tries to make a go of it and fails. It opens again in two-thousand-eleven, and the first issue is another two-part article, and it was about this girl, here."

"Tiffany Funk."

"She goes missing in twenty-eleven, shows four days later. And the 1988 case was referenced in the article, so I was able to cross check. This almost-underground newspaper is the only source that picked up on the idea that these abductions happened before. I got most of the names and dates from the oh-eleven article in *The Press*. They did all the work for you, Detective."

"I love when that happens."

"Yes, sir."

"Where did you get the rest of the names?"

"Well, this one, in 2017, I got from a blog and then found an article in *The Times*. The others I got from other news sources."

"Wow," I said. "This is really great work, Preston."

He beamed. "Thank you. I'm wondering if this one—Kristen Holmes..."

"Yes?"

"Well, I'm wondering if, you know, because she was never found, if..."

"*If?* Come on, Preston. Don't stand on ceremony. Spit it out."

"Well, I'm wondering if maybe this is one of your cold-cases, you know, those cases where..."

"I know what a cold-case is, Preston. We'll look into that."

"Kid did a good job," I said to Alex after Preston left.

"Yes, he did. You know, we have cold-cases going back years. What do we say to those guys when we call and ask them to open up the Kristen Holmes case again?"

The LAPD, along with most larger police departments, has a separate unit that handled just cold cases. "We don't, Alex. Not until we have more to give them."

"And the parents who've sat around waiting for their little girl to come home wait a little longer."

"Yes, unfortunately." I studied the list of names Preston gave us. "Look, all of these girls, including the two that we're investigating now—Josie Schuyler and Clarissa Sparks—have one thing in common: as children they were taken by someone and kept for four days. Bad things were done to them and then they were returned. Some, like Grace

Dashiell here, are in their forties. It looks like one, Jade Warren, could be between ten and twelve now, if the ages of the girls at the time of their disappearances remains consistent. That's what we know. Nothing more. Two are dead. Why? What do these two girls—Schuyler and Sparks—have in common? Is it age? Josie Schuyler is six years older than Clarissa Sparks. Is it the profession? Clarissa Sparks was a prostitute. Josie Schuyler was a troubled girl who was getting her act together, it seemed. You could even speculate that both these girls got into some bad shit later in life because of what happened to them when they were young.

"What about these others, the ones on the list? I'm guessing that some of the younger ones, like Jade Warren, are not taking the Clarissa Sparks path, but the kid is a mess and probably getting some help. How about this Grace Dashiell? Is she a functioning human being?"

"I don't know Johnny. What you're saying makes sense. I think maybe we go down the list and talk to these people, or the families. And, what is the connection with Henry McLaren and Josie Schuyler? He died first. He ain't our killer."

"No, but something's up with that." I shared with Alex my confused conversation with Tree Top.

"Not that I enjoy spinning my wheels in any way," he said, "but maybe talking to him is worth another try."

TAKING a guess that Tree Top was better in the daylight, we took a ride down to the Venice Walk. It was crowded because it was a beautiful day. Finding Tree Top in this mess, at this hour made the whole needle-haystack thing a breeze.

"You really think we're gonna get something outta Tree Top," Alex said.

"I don't know. He wanted to tell me something the other night, but he was all over the place. Maybe we get nothing."

"No maybe, bubba." He watched a bald guy with tribal tats covering his head like a beanie as he pulled up the steel security door to a shop called Tats, the name spray painted graffiti-style along the top of the wide doorway. Other signs advertised tattoos, piercings, and 'smoking pipes.' Alex moved toward the guy, so I followed.

Both arms were covered from shoulder to elbow in half-sleeve tats. The left arm was so busy it would take me the day to decipher it all. The right was clear and simple, yet very intricate: Jesus wrestling with Satan. Rays of light shone down on the adversaries from above, fire threatened to engulf them both from below. A man conflicted. I could dig it. His white wife-beater was tight around a barrel chest, his baggy brown Dickies showing just enough tats on his calves to tell me he was pretty much decorated from head to toe.

"Hey, Dusty," Alex said. "How's it going?" Dusty gave Alex a look that said, 'Going to shit, thanks to you', but said instead, "Okay, man." He caught my eye. "You guys?"

"Good. Lookin' for a transient name of Tree Top," Alex said as I walked through the wide opening and admired the tattoo drawings on the wall.

"You the artist?" I interrupted, forcing the tatted dude to look up from the photograph Alex handed him.

"I am." A black spike pierced each eyebrow—which were shaved—and a half-hoop, also black, was pulled through the right side of his upper lip.

"You're good." I meant it.

"So...Tree Top?" Alex prodded.

"Yeah. Bagger hangs out around here sometimes. Usually sleeps across the way there, between those palm trees."

I squinted across the boardwalk toward the water as two tall, skinny palm trees swayed in the breeze. Something lay spread on the ground between them, but I couldn't see details.

"Where the hell does this go?" Alex asked, tapping the glass top. It was filled with various objects that got stuck into a lip, or an ear, or an eyebrow, after this guy made a hole in said location with a big, long needle.

"Your dick," Dusty answered.

Alex flinched and tapped against the glass at what looked like a nail with a ball attached to the side three-quarters of the way up. "Your dick," he whispered. He looked pale.

"Called a Prince Albert Wand," said Dusty, his mouth curled into a grin. He opened the glass and removed the silver object. "This part goes through the urethra..."

"Stop," Alex begged. Dusty chuckled and returned the jewelry to its rightful place—thus far.

I handed him my card wrapped in a $20. Guy was running a business and he didn't need us hanging around. "Thanks for your time."

"No problem, guys."

"How do you know him?" I asked Alex as we headed across the grass toward the swaying trees.

"Coaches basketball at PAL, believe it or not. Bryan went to camp for a week last summer. Good guy."

"Yeah, real altar boy." The Police Activities League is a crime prevention program aimed at kids. They figure if they can get hold of a kid early enough and create some positives between the kid and cops, it's a good thing. That an NYPD copper created the program back when was a good thing, too.

The ground between the trees was flat, but was covered with blankets, newspapers and a couple of sleeping bags. We walked across the almost-empty concrete skate park and onto the sand. The waves were high, the water choppy. I scanned up and down the beach, saw a few joggers, a couple of walkers. I did not want to scrape the beach looking for Tree Top; that was for damn sure.

"Hey, assholes," came the hoarse greeting. Behind us, and fifty feet away, Toppy leaned against the waist-high wall that separated the park from the beach. He wore light pants that looked clean, and faded flannel with a black t-shirt underneath with 'I only drink on days ending in Y' printed in red on the front. He offered a lopsided grin that exposed a gap where an incisor used to be.

"Lookin' good, Top," I said.

"Yeah," he said. "Today's a good day." He eyed my partner. "Alex," and stuck out his hand. Alex took it without hesitation.

"You been on m'mind, Simple Man," he said.

"It's cuz I saw you a few days ago."

"That right?" He thought a minute. "Yeah. I dunno."

"You weren't in good shape."

"Could use more days like today, Simp."

"You talked about Henry McLaren, remember?" I said.

"Yeah? What the hell did I say?"

"A lot of stuff that didn't make sense, Top. But I felt like you still had something to say."

"He your big case?"

"Might be part of a big case. What do you know?"

"Not much. One day he's around, next day he's not. Per usual 'round here."

"I hear that." I leaned against the wall next to Tree Top, and Alex stood away and at an angle, enough distance to give me the show, yet near enough to pick up a nuance I might miss. I knew Toppy best.

"You know, you're a cop..." I began. Tree Top interrupted me with a hearty laugh.

"Oh, boy...oh-fucking-boy..."

"...puzzle pieces all over the table, Toppy," I continued, "and it always seems like there's too many for the puzzle."

"I remember those days," he said.

"See, reason Henry's part of a bigger case is that his skin was found under the fingernails of another victim. In other words, they had contact."

Tree Top's eyes narrowed and he twisted his neck to look at me. "Who's your victim?"

"Young girl named Josie Schuyler." I let it rest on that.

"Chick works a table along here somewhere," he said after a few moments.

"Yeah. Sold jewelry."

"That's right. What the hell did she have to do with Hen...?" Tree Top paused for a moment, then said, "Huh."

"Huh what?" I asked as casually as I could.

"Shit, I don't know. Hey, that fuckwad captain still at Venice with you guys?"

"Not called Venice anymore, Top. We're Pacific Station now," Alex said.

"Remember him, Simp? Goddamn city'd be burning to the ground and he's bitching about a missing button on your uniform."

Tree Top was talking about Captain Jeff Riggs, and the man was an asshole. Top had that right. Riggs retired five years ago, I informed him.

"Good. Save a copper a week away from snagging his pension from killing the sonofabitch."

Tree Top jabbered on about not much, and I could see Alex growing impatient. These things took time, and even after a lot of it we might come away with nothing from this guy, but I was willing to hold out.

"Hey, remember that kid went missing over in Wilshire?" Toppy said, snapping his fingers. "Hell was her name? Little kid ...fuck, big-ass deal. Ol' man was some exec at Capitol Records."

I remembered. Long time ago—ten years or more. Lots of people went nuts over the manpower devoted to finding a rich white kid. This was familiar, yet the area where the girl was taken was different. I remembered the case Toppy was talking about. One of the girls on the list had a similar story...except she came home. I looked over at Alex and he nodded. He was thinking the same.

"Damn," he went on. "Henry, why he..."

When nothing more happened, I spoke. "He what, Toppy?"

"Hell if I can remember what that kid's name was."

"Were you on the case?" Tree Top was with Wilshire for a while.

"Talk of the city, that case—remember?"

"I do."

"Anyway, 'ol Henry, why..." Tree Top scratched the stubble of hair under his chin.

"What's bothering you, Top?"

"Henry couldn't a known that kid, could he, Simp?" Alex stood straighter.

"I don't know how, Toppy. That was a lotta years ago."

"Ha, more than a lot," he went on, interrupting himself

with a raspy cough. "She wasn't the only one, you know... that kid. Henry knew it, too."

"Did he talk about it, about anything like that case?"

Tree Top pressed the heels of his hand into his eyes and growled. "Ugh, God, no. Fuck, I got it all wrong. How *could* Henry have known? But..." He looked up at me, and his eyes were bloodshot. Alex moved in closer to us.

"Toppy, it's important. If Henry said anything to you..."

Tree Top shook his head.

"We're gonna let you go, now, Toppy." Alex's eyes went wide. Usually wanting to end these free-for-all conversations with the fruits and nuts after about three minutes, I could see that the last thing he wanted to do now was let this go. I felt him. We were close to something, but I didn't think we'd get any more out of Tree Top today. I pulled out my card and another twenty—my last. "Call me if something comes to you."

He stared at the bill, then met my eyes. "You ever seen Jesus standin' under a streetlamp, Simple Man?"

"Can't say I have, Top."

"Well, you see it, someone always dies. I'll tell you that fo' sho'." He pushed away from the wall. "I had it right there! Right-fucking-there!" He slammed two fingers against his temple as he walked away.

"Dammit," Alex muttered as he paced in a circle. "I wanted that, T. I fucking wanted that."

"So did I, pal. I remember that case out of Wilshire. And while the location is different, it sounded like the one on the list, the kid in 1988, whose father worked in the Mayor's office."

"Yeah. I picked up on that, too."

"So, what the fuck did Henry see, or hear, and then repeat to shit-knows-who-all?"

"I don't know, but he saw something, or heard something, and put hands on Josie Schuyler, who winds up dead."

"Yeah." I pondered the rumbling and mumblings of the homeless, how their brains seemed better at certain times, and at other times they were catatonic. Tree Top was a mess last time I saw him, but he was pretty clear just now—up until the end. Something he said niggled at me, and a strong sense of déjà vu poked at me, too. What the hell was it?

"You think it's worth it to look into the case?" I asked.

"Yeah. Let's dig a little, see what pops."

I nodded. "Yeah." Then it hit me. "Jesus."

"What?" He followed my eyes, which were focused on nothing.

"Jesus. Tree Top said something about Jesus."

"Yeah?"

"So did Cletus Dietz." Cletus was the homeless man Alex and I talked to weeks ago. "He said he saw something, remember?"

"Yeah...Jesus." Alex paused. "Huh."

"What are these guys seeing?"

"I don't know, *güey*, but we file it, along with the dozens of other bits of shit, and pull it out when we need to. We do what we can with what we've got. So," he said, jerking a thumb behind us. "You still interested in that Prince Albert? I'll hold your hand."

"You've got problems, Alex. Serious fucking problems."

14

*A*lex and I sat in a room, files and photos strewn across a worn wood table. Case number 2597354, Rebecca Daly, age eleven, missing April 3, 2008.

"Out riding her bike, says here. Seen getting into a late model pick-up." I looked up at Alex. "The tire tracks SID cast at the Schuyler crime scene. Julie Sebastian said they were larger tires, like for a truck.

"You're kidding." He leaned over my shoulder. "That's too easy, man."

"Seeley Marks, the friend she was riding with says, 'Becky rode down an alley and I went straight. I turned around and went down the alley, and I saw her getting into a blue truck. It was dirty. Her bike was laying down in the grass, not on the kickstand'. So, like, she was coming back for the bike in just a minute, right? I mean, I would lay my bike down for a second if I was coming right back to it, but I'd set up on the kickstand if I was going to be a while." Alex stared at me. "You know, just thinking what a kid would do."

"Yeah, I could see that," Alex said. "And this Seeley Marks saw her getting in *willingly*?"

"Let's find her. This might turn into something we can actually pass on to the cold case dicks."

———

"I T' S S O hard to think about that day," Seeley Marks said, running a hand through a mass of tight curls that no beauty salon could replicate. "I've blocked so much of it out." The now-twenty-one-year old woman sat in a back office at Tom Ford in Beverly Hills. She wore a tight multicolored green skirt that fit snug on her slim body, and a leaf green sleeveless blouse that she wore tucked in. She was a buyer for the company.

"I can understand that," Alex said. "You know what a cold case is?"

"Sure," she said. "I watch TV."

"Well, something's come up that made us look into the case again. You made a statement to police at the time that Rebecca got into a blue truck." He pulled out a dozen pictures of blue trucks of various model years. "If you can try to remember, did the truck you saw Rebecca get into look like any of these?"

She looked over the half-dozen photos. She tapped her finger on one. "Not like this...or this," she said, tapping a second. "Too clean. The one she got into was more..." She glided one photo toward Alex. "...Like this...dirty, old looking. Except, the top was white, and there was white here..." Seeley Marks slid her finger along the side of the truck in the picture. "Part of the design, you know, vintage. I mean... not a stripe..."

"So, the white was like a panel, or indented?" I clarified.

"Yeah, and the top was white, but rusted, you know, dirty. The whole truck was...not new."

"You have a computer?" I asked. I knew what she was talking about. Ford came out with the two-tone trucks in the seventies. I found a website listing all models of Ford trucks since 1965.

"Yeah, there you go. This one—except rust up and dirty the paint, fade the white to weathered..." She put her face in her hands. "Ugh! God, I thought I'd put it all away." She lifted her head and looked at me. "I still see her parents once in a while, but I've compartmentalized, you know. Like, they're not her parents; Becky's not their dead daughter. Fuck. Sorry," she finished.

"That's fine, Seeley. You're entitled. Sorry we've had to bring it all back to you, but it's important."

"I know. I understand. I want to help any way I can."

"What do you think would get Becky to get into a car like that—like the one you described?" I asked.

"I don't know. I mean, we got lectured all the time, at home, at school, about getting into cars with strangers."

"You think Becky knew this person?" Alex said.

"I don't know how."

"Did you see the person in the truck?"

"No. A man, that's all."

"Was he alone?"

Seeley Marks cocked her head, then shook it. "I...maybe a child, but it could have been Becky I was seeing. I mean, it happened so fast."

"Okay. What if the person in the truck offered her candy, or a toy?"

"That was the big warning, you know? 'Don't take candy from strangers'. I don't think so. Shit, maybe."

"What if the person needed help finding a lost puppy, or kitten?"

She sat back in her seat and crossed her long, thin legs.

She was a gorgeous girl, and I admired her grace at twenty-one. "I don't know about that," she said, "but I can tell you one thing for sure."

"What's that?"

"Back then, if someone had come along and said they lost their puppy, I'd be in that car in a heartbeat."

"Come on," I said, maybe a little too sharply, but *come on!* "After the warnings, the lectures, the visiting policeman to your school?"

"I know. It's terrible—I admit it. I loved animals —still do."

"How about Becky?"

Seeley chuckled. "You know, she and I talked about becoming vets and owning our own vet hospital. We were going to build it ourselves, out in Hidden Hills, or some other 'horse-country' area." She looked up at me, and I watched her eyes change color. "Yes," she said. "I think she would have."

———

"CHRIST," I said to Alex as I looked through the file on Rebecca Daly again. "You're a father, right? I know you are up your kids' asses about safety, getting into cars, going off with strangers and all that. How the fuck do you make the impression on them? These two girls knew better, yet one gets in the fucking truck and the other says she would have."

"Good question. We beat it into their heads, but I'll tell you this: Bryan would not only run screaming the other way once candy or kitten was offered up, but he'd barge in to the nearest house and call the police. Stevie? He'd get in the car."

"Not my godson," I argued.

"Your godson. He's friendly, he talks to everyone, he's curious, and he's easily distracted. He's the perfect victim. We're hardest on him. He goes wandering off and he gets it. Jury's still out on Nena."

"Thanks, pal. Thanks for that. I get to worry about my godson now. I'm talking to him."

"Good. The more the merrier."

I stared at Alex in admiration. "How do you do it?"

He looked at me. "How do I do what?"

"Not lock 'em in a cage—all of them, including the ol' lady. No one gets to 'em then..."

He chuckled. "I think about it—a lot."

"It's not easy, is it?"

"No, but don't let it discourage you, *güey*. Keep your goddamn head in that game, and it'll end up being the greatest thing you've ever done. Creating a life with someone you love? The beauty of it will fucking break your heart."

15

*P*arking was fierce at St. Marks on the day of my godson's first communion. I felt better when I saw Alex circling the block as well. It had been a long time since I'd been inside a church with an open heart. On this day, I would open it wide and stand with Steven Antonio Ortiz as his godfather.

I watched my partner and his family file out of their SUV. Alex's wife, Lisa, one of the finest women I'd ever met, looked beautiful in green, and Alex, in his dark blue suit, looked anything but like a cop. Bryan, eleven, and Steven looked like miniature versions of their father. And little Celeste, six, wore a flower print dress and white shoes, her hair braided down her back. Theirs was a family I envied—I always had. Alex had it good; good woman, good kids.

I kissed Lisa and picked Celeste up, carrying her across the street to the church.

"Good practice," Lisa said, nodding toward the little girl in my arms.

"Yeah," I laughed. I lifted her like a basketball I was about to shoot as I boxed out her brother, Bryan.

"Please don't get them wild, John" the mother scolded. "I've got exactly one half a nerve left."

We walked through the door of the church. Kids were crowded in the vestibule, a woman wearing simple shoes and a scowl trying to herd them into a bunch. Alex took Lisa and the two kids into the church, and I stayed behind. I motioned my godson over to a corner of the room, giving Simple Shoes the hairy eyeball when she tried to snatch him back. I took his chin and tilted it up. Steven sported bright hazel eyes that danced, even when he was upset, which was rare. He was the happiest kid I'd ever seen. His light brown hair was freshly cut, his round cheeks slightly flushed. He could have passed for a suburban kid, circa 1960. All he needed was the striped shirt and cuffed jeans with a slingshot hanging out of the back pocket. I was sorry now a silver cross was all I could come up with for the communion gift. He would have liked the slingshot more.

"You ready?" I said.

"Yeah."

"You remember what to do?"

He nodded.

"Show me how you hold your hands." He clasped them, one on top of the other, in front of him.

"When Father says 'body of Christ', what do you say?"

"Amen."

"When he puts the wafer in your mouth, don't chew. Let it dissolve, right? You don't want Jesus to think you're in a hurry to gobble him down."

He gave me an earnest nod.

"And when Father offers the wine, take a small sip. Don't gulp. Save some for the others. You're too young to drink anyway."

"Okay."

"Okay." I straightened his tie, adjusted the silver cross so it rested just right below the knot, and swiped some chocolate from the corner of his mouth. "Glad to see your father sprung for a real tie and not a clip-on."

"What's a clip-on?"

"The tie comes already knotted up here, see? And it has little clips on the sides, and you just attach it to your collar."

"Sounds easier than this. Dad said lots of swears when he was trying to tie it."

"Yeah?" I laughed. "What did he say?" I caught Simple Shoes giving me the eye again. "Never mind." I adjusted the shoulders on his jacket. "I wore a clip-on tie every day to school. We didn't wear the pants and the collared shirt you get to wear now. I wore a shirt like this..." I pointed to the shirt I wore. "...except white, and thin. And I wore a jacket with the emblem of my school right here..." Above the heart, in case the beatings didn't make you appreciate where you were enough.

"You went to Catholic school?"

"Uh huh."

"Did you go to church when you were a kid?"

"Every Sunday, plus during the week for school."

"Do you go now?"

I thought for a moment how to answer. "No," I said, opting for honesty.

"So, you'll come to church with us from now on. You have to. You're my godfather."

"Yeah? I'll go with your dad."

For some reason, that got the kid going, and he laughed and laughed. This brought a more pronounced scowl from Simple Shoes. She waddled over and informed us it was time.

"Okay. Get it together now. You start yuckin' it up in line and your mom'll have both our butts."

"She'll have your butt first—it's bigger."

"Your butt's the biggest butt I've ever seen. The Queen Mary is smaller than your butt." He giggled as I dusted lint off his shoulder. "I'm proud of you, buddy. This is a big day for you." He smiled and shrugged, and I reluctantly turned him over to Sister Scowl.

I entered the church and walked down front to join Alex and the rest of the family in the front pew. Celeste crawled into my lap and held her hand up. Five cloth people covered four fingers and a thumb. The people were all brightly clothed and represented every ethnicity. She wiggled in my lap until she found a spot she liked.

"I understand church attendance is mandatory," I whispered to Alex. "I told the kid we'd go together, you and me. Mark out our own special pew, maybe get our names carved on the back."

"Yeah? Good luck with that, *pendejo*." That brought a scowl from Lisa.

"The kid asked me the other day who *INRI* was." I pointed to the Jesus hanging on the cross on the wall above the altar, the letters *INRI* above.

"Yeah? Thank God he asked you and not Sister Delfina. He'd be taking his first communion when he's twenty-one. What did you tell him?"

"I told him it stood for 'I'm Nailed Right In'." We both turned to Lisa for a reaction. She made the sign of the cross and vowed to kill us both.

"I think he's ready for this now," Alex finished. "I really do."

The priest stood and began the mass. A youngster carrying a large cross came up the aisle, followed by the future brides and grooms of Christ. Steven led the pack, and his hands were placed perfectly in front of him, eyes straight ahead—until he passed me. He smiled and let a little laugh escape.

When he came and sat down, I leaned in. "Nice work. You looked good—except for the booger hanging out of your nose." He laughed and covered is mouth after his mother shot him a look.

"Stop it," she hissed at me.

Each child, when called, went up with two designates and took on the body and blood of Christ. I remembered my first communion. I remembered the fear, the anxiety, the repercussions the next day if a mistake was made. I remembered my father, standing up with me while I took on blood and body. He squeezed my shoulder. *It'll be okay. This is nothing compared to life without.*

Steven's name was called, and he walked up, flanked by his father and me. We placed a hand on his shoulder while he took the wafer, mumbled an amen at the appropriate time, then sipped the wine. He didn't gulp. When he sat in the pew again, he looked different. He smiled his big, goofy smile, but it was different—older somehow. For some reason, I wished he'd gulped.

I called Nick Bevins and Charlie Kool the next day, two veteran coppers who headed up our cold-case unit. I wanted to make sure we weren't stepping into an active case if we pursued this. I filled them in on what we knew so far, and the direction we were planning to go to solve this case.

"So, you're saying this bastard is coming back for more years later?" Charlie asked. They were on speakerphone.

"I don't know about that, Charlie," I said. "The MO years ago didn't seem to be killing, like it is now."

"Except for the two that never came back," put in Nick.

"True."

"You have a list of names?" Nick asked.

"Yeah." I bragged a little about Preston McConnell.

"Nice. Send the list over. I'll check the names against our cold cases. Maybe we can scratch a few off for you."

I did that, and then Alex and I sat with the list. "The younger victims will remember more about what happened," I said, "but the older ones will be easier to talk to."

It took us all day and into the evening to locate everyone on the list, complete with addresses. One had passed away: Breanna Delacroix—taken October 19, 1998—died in a car accident in 2010. That left seven on the list to locate and talk to. One, possibly two, were still minors, so we would talk to the investigating officers first before we asked to speak to the children and their families. That left five adults, still living, still surviving. According to police reports on all the victims, they identified the same man, but could not say where they were taken. We started with the oldest.

It took Grace Dashiell three phone conversations before she would agree to see us. Her office on Wilshire Boulevard looked out over the Hollywood Hills. She stood looking out of a floor-to-ceiling glass window when we arrived. She spoke without turning around.

"I hold a Ph.D in Clinical Psychology from St. Johns, and a Master's degree in Forensic Psychology from Marymount University. I am well-read, well-educated, and I am a strong, confident woman. At least that is what others think of me." She turned around and addressed us directly. "There are portions of my life that I can't remember—like graduating high school or marrying my ex-husband." She swallowed past a visible lump in her throat. "You can understand why I don't want to talk about this again."

Dr. Grace Dashiell was an attractive woman who possessed all the sophistication she said others saw in her. It was not an illusion. Her caramel skin was flawless, and her eyes were bright. They hid pain well.

"We're sorry, Doctor," I said. "This can't be easy, but we could use your help."

"It's not, and you can have it—as much as I can give. Please sit. You shared a little about your case over the phone, Detective. Can you elaborate?"

"Sure," I answered. "We have two victims, and the one thing they seem to have in common is that when they were children they disappeared and returned four days later. They had been molested..."

"Oh, yes," she nodded.

"We're trying to figure out if that is their only connection to each other, because we don't have much evidence to go on."

"What evidence do you have?"

"We have tire tracks at the scene of one of the crimes, and the size is consistent with tires that would go on a truck."

"Mmm hmm," she nodded.

"It is believed that both victims were sexually assaulted, perhaps with objects. Both were killed somewhere else and dumped where they were found." As always, I left something out. "You seem to know about the truck."

Grace Dashiell stood and walked across the office, her rust skirt and long jacket floated across a curvy body as she moved. She stopped in front of a wall of bookshelves and wrapped her arms around herself as if to ward off a chill.

"I would know that truck anywhere." She described it as Seeley Marks had. "He drove me...somewhere. The road was bumpy. I was crying, but he didn't seem to hear me. I was a week shy of eleven."

"You were older at the time you were taken than the other girls, and you're the oldest survivor. I'm not sure what that means yet."

"What happened to the others—the ones who are gone?" she asked.

"Two were murdered—the cases we're working on now —and two died of other causes."

"How many of us are there left?"

"Seven that we're aware of. Two, we think, are still minors."

"He's still out there."

"As of 2017, it appears so."

"Is she one of your victims?"

"No. Our latest victim went missing for four days in 2013."

"Dear God."

"You saw him. Can you describe what he looked like?" Alex asked after a long silence. He stood but didn't move from his chair. "I know it's been a long time."

Grace Dashiell turned as if she'd forgotten we were in the room. "Huh? Sorry." She blinked rapidly as if shaking herself free of something. "I felt and heard everything, but my vision was blurry, I remember that much. I know I wasn't much help to the police back then." She shook her head, a pained confusion set in her eyes, after all these years. "He... forced himself into my vagina, my rectum and my mouth. I bit him; I remember that. He didn't get angry. He made me do it until I got it right. His voice was soft, and he was patient. He would...he would wait until I calmed down before he'd continue. It was the voice that confused me the most. It was kind and pitched on the high end. He also used objects." Dr. Dashiell was quiet for some time. "I spent three days in the hospital. The press was all over the story because my father was a Deputy Mayor. My disappearance got a lot of attention, and the more attention I got, the less I said.

"I worked the prisons at the start of my career, hoping I'd find him. For some reason, all the child abusers and molesters found me, and for years they were all I counseled. I wanted to kill them, make them hurt like I did. I finally had to get out of that. When I opened my own practice, I realized I couldn't counsel sexual abuse victims, either. I was too close." She turned to face us. "You expect someone like that to be angry, violent...but he wasn't. I cannot reconcile that at all. He hurt me, and he did horrific things to me..." She shook her head. "With all of my training, I cannot reconcile that. The abuse was methodical, and almost...ritualistic. Like a...like a parent who sprays a cut and bandages it. The parent knows it stings but it...it has to be done. It's hard to remember being afraid." She said this at a barely audible whisper. "There was only one time, one moment, where I believed I was going to die."

It was Alex who moved from between the white leather chair and the oversized glass desk and approached her. "When was that?" he said.

The hum of a sleek white air purifier to the right of the desk was the only sound. The desk held essentials and nothing more. No photographs sat at an angle, no wind-up toys for her, or guests, to fiddle with during idle chat. The chairs were comfortable, and the office was bright—stark, actually. White carpeting, white leather furniture, black and white photographs on the walls, white roses in white or clear glass vases scattered around the room. White bookcases line one wall, filled with clinical how-tos, poetry, biographies. A red crystal heart sat on a metal stand on a credenza behind the desk. Eight or ten inches tall and almost as wide, it was the only color in the monochromatic office. Soft curls framed a face that looked shattered with the memories we forced her to dig up. An ex-husband was mentioned. I wondered about children; I wondered about patients, troubled people who came to her for counsel and guidance, having no idea that she was more fucked up than they. Shiny copper earrings moved as her head swiveled from side to side, as if the very motion would bring the memories up to where they belonged—or maybe they would disappear, this time forever. A black feather floated through the air and landed on the white carpet like a stain. I had no idea where it came from.

"He took my panties," she said, "and he tied them around my neck. I saw him then—smooth face, light eyes. Beanie cap--black. He said, 'Don't tell. Don't tell on me, now, Grace. Don't tell on me now'. And then he pulled tight." Tears ran down her cheeks. "I thought I was going to die. I couldn't breathe. And then, he let go." She stared at Alex, and then brushed her cheeks with her hands. "The next thing I remembered was being home."

Alex took a step closer to her. He was not one to become emotional or show personal opinion much in any case, but I watched him, now, handle this one differently.

"Why now?" Grace said. "Why now, after all these years, can I suddenly see his face?" She focused on my partner and then gave a knowing chuckle, raised her face to the ceiling and shook her head. Of course she knew why, *suddenly*. It was her life's work to know *that* answer, if no other.

"If we asked you to sit with a sketch artist, could you?" Alex asked.

One corner of her mouth curled, and for the first time since we walked in her office, her eyes brightened. "I think I could."

———

I STARED at the sketch of the man she says took her thirty-one years ago. She became uncomfortable as she described who she saw that day, the day she thought she would die, after four days of abuse. I wondered if she was seeking help, or if she ever sought help.

The blue, rusted-up truck played into the picture now,

so I put out a BOLO. I had nothing but blue, rusted, dirty, blue two-toned, probably a Ford F-150, late model. Now, maybe I had someone to put in the driver's seat.

"C'MON, *NINO*! WETS GO!" It was Friday night, and Alex and I had been told the weekend, and future ones until we were told differently, belonged to the LAPD. Alex was taking advantage of that edict tonight by taking his wife out, while I stood on my deck watching my own date standing in the Johnboat, yelling for me. *Nino* was a bastardization of *Padrino*, which meant Godfather. I was that to Steven only as far as God, a lawyer, and the Ortiz's were concerned, but all three kids called me *nino*.

Alex and Lisa had managed to rid themselves of the two boys for the night, and that left Celeste. That I was available to help out said a lot about my life. I didn't know whether to be proud of that or disgusted. As steady as the boat usually was with its wide shape and flat bottom, it stood little chance of keeping still under a six-year-old's influence. Celeste hopped over the seats and did a crazy dance-and-sing while I conjured up plausible explanations to her folks as to why I allowed the child to fall into the drink.

"Sit down, sweetheart. I'm coming," I said from the deck. I turned my back for a second to lock the door and imagined how that particular explanation would go over in the unfortunate instance that the kid went ass-over. *Yeah, you know, she was standing in the boat...yes, I said standing. What?*

"*Nino*, I want to fowow the ducks. Pwease hurwy."

"I'm coming, babe," I said, bounding down the steps. I stood on the five-by-five-foot dock in front of my house and waited for her to settle down. She knew from experience with me that we couldn't take off until her butt was in the seat. Her apricot dress and pink socks would not have been what I'd have chosen for her to wear on this expedition we were going on, but what the hell did I know about little girls? This one was a character. I let her get away with much more than her parents did. I wasn't her father. I didn't have to be tough. I just had to give her back without breaking her. I had to watch her every second, which was why I amazed myself sometimes at the level of stupidity I could tumble to when I'd do something moronic like turn my back on her while she was standing in a John.

"Sweetheart, keep the majority of your body inside the boat, or you're going to fall in," I said as she leaned way out to pet a duck. I paddled along at a pace that would bore an ant, but I expected her to tumble into the brackish canal water at any moment, and I needed to be able to grab her up before she drowned.

"Wook at the babies!" she said as a mama paddled away from the boat toward shore with ducklings in tow.

"How many do you see?" I said. As she counted them aloud, I surveyed the houses we passed along Grand Canal. A few were for sale, and a few others were under renovation. Every time I thought about moving, I'd go to an open house, and my throat would close. The amount of money these houses were going for made me happy for my place, which was just perfect for me, and the mortgage was close to paid off. I had my eye on the vacant lot next to my house and had a hundred plans for what I'd do if I ever got serious about buying it.

"E-weven! E-weven babies!" She stood, placed her hands on the seat she was sitting on, and hopped over the seat and back again like it was a pommel horse. She sang a song about trains and dinosaurs as her white sandals slapped loudly on the aluminum boat bottom.

"Eleven babies!" I said, grabbing her around the waist and setting her on my lap. "Imagine all the peanut butter and jelly sandwiches their mama has to make every day."

"A wot, huh?"

"Yup." I set her next to me and resumed paddling. We explored three canals before she got bored and asked to return home.

I ordered a pizza and we watched Shark Week until she couldn't keep her eyes open any longer. As she slept next to me on the couch, I thought about this case. Two were missing from the list that we could confirm were dead. We weren't sure about Kristen Holmes or Rebecca Daly. We weren't. All we knew about Kristen Holmes was that she disappeared a month after Emily Knox, from the same area of Los Angeles, roughly. But unlike Emily Knox, Kristen Holmes never made it back home. Rebecca Daly was kidnapped, with a witness present, eleven years prior near Beverly Hills, 40 miles from the other kidnappings. She also never made it back home. They could be related, but they might not be. Things happen. Kids disappear.

I looked down at Celeste Audra Ortiz, who was the light of her parent's life. She breathed in and relaxed into a deeper sleep, the kind of sleep a safe, secure child enjoys. I brushed the hair off her forehead. How does a parent survive the loss of a child? What was done to their child, how many times, and where...there was no relief for that in a parent's heart. I knew of rage, and I knew revenge. It sat in my soul like an old but weary friend. I would hunt down any motherfucker who harmed a child of mine, yet all the girls on that list had been harmed. Some were dying years after surviving what I could assume was the most horrific ordeal of their lives. The reward for surviving such an ordeal was life and trying to live it to the fullest. At least that's the way I saw it. When trying to find the cause of the dying, I found it best to first deal with the living. There were eleven on the list. Two were dead. The youngest was a pre-teen; the oldest was my age. And we had everything in between. Tomorrow, Alex and I would find these people, and then find this asshole, before he struck again.

Like with everything, it was the not-knowing that sucked you dry.

17

*I*t was late in the day when Jackie Glaser called and asked Alex and I to meet her and some others for dinner. We pulled up to Lucy's El Adobe, located across the street from Paramount Studios in Hollywood. Jackie lived in the neighborhood and worked out of Hollywood, so the location made sense—to her. It was a ride for us. Lucy's served adequate Mexican and decent margaritas. Randy Jakes and Steve Small arrived at the same time. Both worked out of Hollywood station now, and they were collaborating with Glaser and Carter on their case. I saw Glaser's car in the lot, taking up two spots. She was the single worst driver I've ever encountered, and that was the truth.

We became acquainted with Randy Jakes while he was still working patrol, and he kept showing up at our crime scenes. He was young and efficient, and still unaffected by the job. He was thirty. What did he know?

Steve Short came over from a now-defunct department that specialized in solving crimes against L.A.'s rich and famous, including the many people in show business. I guess after a few police brutality lawsuits, whoeverwasincharge realized that there was simply no more room in the budget for handholding and coddling. The smaller divisions within the LAPD, short staffed usually, absorbed most of the detectives, and Hollywood got Short. He stood six feet and was reed-thin. Go figure.

We took a table in the bar area, big enough for six. I sat with Jackie at a booth against the wall. Small and Jakes sat across from us. Alex disappeared with the phone against his ear. The room was dark and it took some time for my eyes to adjust. We ordered two pitchers of margaritas; one blended, for the lightweights, and one on the rocks, for me. I needed it. We made small talk until the pitchers came. I poured Jackie a glass, then filled mine. I told Jackie we wanted Amelia back in Homicide. She told me to talk to her captain, and then wished me luck. "We love her, and she is by far the best partner I've ever had."

"Don't care, Glaser. She's ours."

"Caveman much?"

"How's she doing, seriously? We don't see her nearly enough socially. Not like we used to, anyway."

"Working things out with Dan. She confides in me sometimes, when it suits her." Dan Rios, who worked in the DA's office, had moved out a few months ago. Between that and the loss of Mark Gonzales, Amelia was dealing with some shit.

"Yeah. That works out fine when she's partnered with a bunch of guys who don't want to hear it, but I can see it doesn't fit with your way...being a girl and all."

"It's fine," she said. "We're partners, not friends. And she is a great partner. She's smart, thorough, gutsy. I've had a few partners in my career, but none as good as Amelia."

"I'll agree with that," Short said, and then turned his

attention to Jakes, who had turned his attention to a woman sitting at the bar. They both got up.

"Subtle, guys," I said.

"They're young," Jackie reminded. I stretched my arm out over the back of the booth while she sat forward.

"I was done, John...seriously," she said. She spoke softly, and I leaned in to hear her. "I was done. I couldn't do it anymore. I'd seen too much, too soon in my career, and I was burnt out, completely. What I see *live* people do to each other is killing me inside, and it's killing me slow."

"I know." I gave her shoulder a squeeze.

"The move to SIU was a good one for me, and let me tell you, a good partner makes all the difference."

"I said I want Amelia back. Save your sob story for Short. He's still all sensitive from helping J Lo find her dog."

She smirked at me and leaned back against my arm. I took a long drink of my margarita, the salt around the rim complimenting the too-sweet mix perfectly. "Amelia Carter in Special Investigations is not for the long haul, Jackie. Let's be clear." I leaned across her to get a chip, then she spoke something into my ear, and as I leaned back, I answered her, speaking close to her face. And then I saw Jackie look up, and I figured Alex came back, or maybe it was Short and Jakes, rejected once again by a woman. Instead, I looked into the heated eyes of Karen Gennaro. No sound. Maybe it was me, locked up in my head, heart pounding, mouth open but no words. My gut folded in. I wanted nothing more than an extra few seconds to take it in, that she was standing here and I should be doing something about that.

"Hello, John," she said, her tone clipped.

"Hey...hi..." I stammered. Like seeing your third-grade teacher at the supermarket, Karen's presence was so out of context I felt at once glued to my seat and an uncontrollable urge to flee. "Uh." I started to stand.

"Oh, don't bother," and she shoved her hand in Jackie's direction. "Karen Gennaro. Nice to meet you."

"Hi, Karen. Jackie Glaser." The two seconds of silence that followed seemed like an hour, and then Karen turned to me.

"A moment?"

"Sure, uh...yeah." I followed her out the back door. A warm fire lighted the covered patio, empty for the moment. The pit, located in the center, was filled with colored glass that sparkled and flickered with the flames that rose out of the center. Red rounded candles sat in the middle of wood tables surrounded by benches, and off to one side a bar stood empty and lost without a bartender.

I was master of my game, in control of my ship, the *decider*; yet, at the moment I could not breathe. I felt like I'd been caught with my hand down my cousin's pants, or something.

One delicate hand rested on her hip as she paced in a small circle. She wore a dark dress—olive green, it looked like in the light—that came to her calves. It was sleeveless and hung straight down over her curvy body. Long earrings glittered in the dim light.

"Karen, Jackie's my..."

"I don't *care* who Jackie is, John. I couldn't care less who you're fucking."

I jerked as if she'd slapped me. "Hey," I said. "What is wrong with you?"

"Did you know that Tania Harris passed away?"

Tania Harris. Tania Harris. "Who?"

"The woman with cancer...her son broke into my clinic?"

Right. "Well, unless you called and told me that Tania Harris passed away, how would I know?"

"They covered her with a sheet, then two uniformed officers came and took her son away in handcuffs. He's just a kid. You said you'd handle this. How did this happen?"

"I don't know, Karen. I'm up to my ass on another case here."

"Yeah, you look up to your ass."

"I told you that this might happen, didn't I?" I said, ignoring the jab. "That 'kid' broke into your clinic—smashed the place up pretty good, as I recall."

"How do you do that? How do you just...*do that*?"

"I didn't *do* anything. And, you know what? I'm sorry about that kid's mama, but at the end of the day, he broke the law." I seemed to be breathing fine now.

"I've hired a lawyer for him, and I will testify in his defense."

I laughed. It wasn't appreciated. "Okay."

"I've already done it, John. It's done."

"Good. Fine. Maybe it'll do some good. I doubt it. And you're just going to get hurt."

"Yeah, right...I forgot. You don't get involved, do you?" She paced around the patio now in widening circles. "How do you not...help? When it's within your capacity to help, how can you *not*?" A busboy started out through the door, and a glare sent him back inside.

"What the hell do you think I do every day? I can't get personally involved with this kid. I don't have that luxury. If you do, that's great; have at it. He broke the law, and it wasn't just the two of us there that night. Cops came, reports were written. It's done." I was back now, game face on, standing firmly at the helm.

"Yes, and what about you? What will you say?"

"No one's asked, and when they do, what would you like me to say, Karen? Tell me what you want."

"I can't imagine what that kid is going through. I mean... where is he, do you even know?"

"No, I don't. You just hit me with this. And it isn't my responsibility to know where he is. I'm a cop, Karen, and the kid broke the law. Given the choice, I'd probably let him ride —give him another opportunity to land in the slam, or in the morgue. But it isn't up to me."

"You are unbelievable, John. Clearly, you have no intention of dealing with this. I'll figure it out." She spun on her heel and walked away.

I had no idea where this shit storm had come from, but now I was pissed. "Hey." She kept walking. "*Hey!*" She turned around and I walked over to her. We stood in the middle of the parking lot while cars navigated around us so we could stare each other down.

"You are way, *way* out of line here." A woman came over to us, and I saw then that she was the woman Karen was with inside the restaurant.

"Karen, is everything all right?" she asked.

"We're going to need a minute," I said to her. The woman looked from me to Karen, and it was clear that she was appointing herself Karen's chief protector. I was in no mood to battle two of them.

"I'll be there in a second, Shelly." Shelly wisely headed for her car. Karen turned to me.

"You said you'd handle this."

"I *never* said I'd handle this, but we're beyond that now. I warned you that this might happen. You're smart enough to know that this cannot work out the way you want it to, and you're also smart enough to know this isn't my fault. But let's put all that aside for the moment. Right now you are eighteen different kinds of pissed, and it isn't about Tania Harris."

"*Really?* Then what is it about, do you think?"

"I don't know, and frankly I don't care. Get your shit straight, and if you want my help, call me when you can act like a human."

"Fuck you, John," she hissed.

I advanced on her, putting us nose to nose. "Yeah?" I whispered. "Well, fuck you, too, sweetheart." And there you had it. I'd never spoken that way to her before. I always tried to avoid getting in the gutter, especially to join an angry woman who had already made herself at home there. Another rule of mine, broken.

Yup. The *decider* was back and in fucking control.

I walked back inside the restaurant and stood near the staging area where they refill waters and saltshakers. I stepped into the head when I realized I was just in the way. I pissed, washed my hands, and splashed water on my face. The man in the mirror looked older; he was someone else; he was someone I was just getting to know. Didn't care for him at the moment.

Jackie stared at me as I came back to the table, waiting for me to break into song, or an explanation. I did neither. Alex had returned, and Amelia Carter was just walking in. Jakes and Short had returned to the table.

"That was a chilly encounter," Jackie smirked, breaking the ice as only she can. "Current or former?"

"Former." I sat.

"Why the dramatics?"

"Glaser, please..."

"Sorry, I didn't mean to pry." She took a sip of her frosty margarita. "Was I the subject of the fight?"

"Not sure. Not sure of anything."

"Mmmm." She sipped her drink and looked at me over the rim. "We're a confusing bunch."

"Was that...?" Alex began, his thumb jerking in the direction of the back door. I stopped him with a raised hand. "Oooookeeey. This for me?" He picked up the pitcher of blended.

"Not for you, my man. Order yourself a Tecate and quit fucking around. We ain't sharin"

Alex looked from me to Jackie, then back to me again. "Okay...yeah. I can see how this could be miscon*screwed*."

"You're a fuckin' comedian now?"

Jackie dabbed at her eyes with a napkin, then started laughing all over again. They were having a great time over this, and all I wanted to do was run after her, shake her up, straighten her out about doomed kids who don't come up right, from the start; apologize for words I didn't mean that came out of nowhere; beg her back into my life.

"Fill us in," said Jakes, now sitting next to me on my right.

"I think I just saw Karen in the parking lot," Amelia said. She looked around the table. "What did I miss?"

"Oh, my goodness," Jackie laughed, taking a pull on Alex's beer as soon as the waiter set it down.

"Hey! Dammit, Glaser," he barked.

"Sorry, I needed something. We have drama." She cleared her throat and started giggling again.

"We don't have drama," I said.

"Yes, we do," said Alex and Jackie in unison.

"What's going on?" Amelia said.

"We never have any drama in Hollywood," said Short.

"Please," argued Jakes. "Remember the time we were out celebrating Kizansky's promotion, and you happened to have your arm around that civilian PA out of Wilshire when your wife arrived...unexpectedly? I remember. Whatever happened, Steveo?"

"That was not drama, young sir. *That* was a misunderstanding. You kids like to take one event and have it end years of love and commitment."

"Yeah? When was your divorce final?" laughed Jakes.

"No divorce," he informed the rest of us. "I'm still very happily married."

"How long?" I asked.

"Ten years this September."

I reached across the table and shook his hand. "Well played, Short. This business is tough on a marriage. Nice to meet someone who can keep it together...besides Alex, I mean."

"It's work," Short said. "I won't lie about that. You ever married, John?"

"Yes, once."

"Didn't work out?"

"It worked out fine till I caught her in bed with someone else."

"Ouch."

"Yeah...it's all good now."

"Except for the lady who just peeled out of the parking lot with her hair on fire," offered Jackie helpfully.

"That's enough," I said.

"C'mon, what did I miss? Will someone please tell me what's going on?" Amelia tried again.

"I'd like to know, too," Short said, raising a brow. "Goddamn, I love a fiery woman."

"Forget it." I raised the empty pitcher that contained margarita on the rocks only moments ago. The waiter saw me and nodded.

"Then allow me," offered Alex.

"Finally," said Amelia.

"Hey, *cagherone,*" I hissed.

"Doctor Karen Gennaro is a trauma surgeon," Alex began, oblivious. "A very beautiful trauma surgeon, over at County. Don Juan over here met her last year after a patrolman we know was shot in the line of duty. They dated, they fell in love, and then Don managed to fuck it up—royally." He looked at me. "How'm I doin'?"

I shook my head.

"No? Time for a *cerveza.* Want a shot of Patron, *Juan?* Looks like you could use it."

Jackie wiped away a tear. She couldn't stop laughing.

"You're buyin' shots for everyone, *testacazza,*" I shot back.

"She was pretty," Jakes offered. "At least from the rear."

"Hey!" Now, that I did not like.

"She is lovely, from every angle...and she's jealous," Jackie added, then cleared her throat again in a feeble attempt to stop laughing.

"The green monster ain't just a wall in Boston," Alex added.

"God, I love you for that," Jackie cooed, a Bostonian by birth.

"Okay, can we stop, now?" I dipped my finger in my margarita and flicked Jackie. That sent her off into peals of laughter again.

"They fought over me," she informed the group, then guffawed again.

"Glaser, I am warning you...." I hissed at her.

"Let me finish," Alex went on.

"Would you please," Amelia pleaded.

"All right, let me be clear," I said, looking at each one of them. "We're done with this conversation." Alex sighed and rolled his eyes.

"Just when I was getting to the good part." He saw my face and raised his hands. "Okay, fine...fine. I'm all done."

"Good."

"Darn it," Jackie said, and then giggled again. She asked Alex what I said to him in Italian.

"I have no idea," he said.

"The first word, *cagherone*, means big mouth, blowhard," Amelia said. "The second, *testacazza*...well, it's quite rude..." She blinked several times at me. "And I'm a lady."

"Here-here," Alex said, swigging his beer.

"Jackie's a different story," I said.

"I beg your pardon," she retorted, laughing again.

"It means 'dickhead', Glaser," I said.

"Oh, that *is* rude," she agreed.

Only good friends would treat you this shitty.

"CAN YOU DRIVE?" I asked Alex while he waited for his car.

"Yeah. Hey, thanks for last night. Nena had a good time." Nena, I learned over the years, was a typical nickname for little girls. It meant, literally, 'little girl'.

"So did I. I found out last night she can count to eleven... no, I'm sorry, *e-weven*."

"She can count to a hundred, *cabron*, and her speech impediment is adorable."

"It is. A hundred, huh? Can she swim yet?"

"No."

"Okay, good." A valet pulled up with Alex's car. Before he got in, I said, "She asked me last night if there is such a thing as *ghot-stes*."

A furrow appeared between Alex's forehead, then his

eyes got wide. "Ghosts! See, I can understand my daughter perfectly."

"So can I, apparently."

"And what did you tell her?"

"I said only at her house."

"Great. Thank you." He got in his car. "Asshole."

"We all have our crosses to bear. Drive safe, jackass. You've had too much to drink."

"I'm fine. Figure this shit out, *padna*."

I watched his taillights disappear down the street, and I knew he was speaking of Karen.

My cross.

$\mathcal{I}$ got home at 11:45 and poured myself a Scotch. I took it out to the patio and watched the lights from the houses on Linnie Canal dance on the water. The night was cool, and it was quiet. Both could not have been more welcome at the moment.

I finished my drink quick and got another. I thought about Gennaro, and what the hell sprung loose in her tonight. I wasn't happy about it. Whatever bad she had going in her life these days I got a taste of tonight, and it wasn't about Tania Harris. A man walked along the path across the canal, past dimly lit houses, a cigarette glowing in his hand. This man, this cig smoker, had no idea about dead girls who got the shit knocked out of them early in life, and no happily-ever-after. He didn't know about angry women who had no idea what the hell they were angry at. He didn't know about kids who break the law so they can give their mama a moment's relief. I resented the vanilla bubble so many lived in. Not often, but after a rough day or two, I'd let that unreasonable part of me come on out and wave a tiny flag around for a while, until I'd get disgusted with myself and put it away again.

I sat back on the chaise and put a foot up on the cushion. A dog barked in the distance, and a noise made me turn to my front gate. Karen stood on the other side.

"And the hits just keep on comin'," I said. Before I could advise her that coming by for round two was a mistake, she sighed and said, "Maybe I should have called first."

She wore a brown leather jacket over the same dress. Her hair was tossed around. A soft breeze blew in from the west, charged with negative ions and pheromones, and as dark as it was, her eyes shone like beacons. The sad fact that I noticed all of this, when all I wanted to do was shake her till her teeth rattled, went to my complete inability to let her go.

"Good to know you still have my number."

SHE SAT on a chaise across from me with a glass of Chianti in her hand. I was still wound up over the scene at Lucy's, and her presence, while welcome, was out of context, again. I was livid. I was terrified. I wanted to toss her in the canal. I wanted to tie her to my bed. I wanted to fuck her up against a wall. Instead, I took all of it in. I didn't know how long I'd have her.

"I was out of line, and I'm sorry," she said.

I leaned toward her with my Scotch between my hands. "Yeah."

"Seeing you tonight caught me sideways, Johnny."

"The woman is a colleague—Amelia's partner, that's all."

She shook her head. "You don't need to explain."

"You're right, I don't."

There were tears in her eyes. "You're angry, and you have every right to be."

"Yeah."

She looked down into her wine. "Maybe I should have called first."

I covered her hands with mine and leaned my forehead against hers. "You don't ever need to call."

"This is dangerous," she whispered.

"Only if you want it to be." I kissed her lightly on the mouth. "Drink your wine."

After a few moments she said, "This Tania Harris thing...it got to me. I came at you because you were there and I had no one else to attack."

"Let's pretend for the moment that I believe you. Why didn't you call and tell me she died?"

"It just happened this morning. You don't believe me?"

"No. Shocked?"

"Yeah." She set her glass down on the teak side table. "So...Amelia's partner."

"There it is."

"I suppose I have no right to..."

"To?"

"To feel...this way."

"What way?"

"A gentleman would allow a lady to wallow in self-pity to preserve her dignity."

"And I'm nothing if not a gentleman."

She sighed and stood. "I should go." She started to move past me to leave. I grabbed her wrist, stood and pulled her against me. A smile played on her lips.

"Green ain't your color, lady blue," I whispered, lifting her chin until her eyes met mine. "This is out of character."

"Yeah, that's me. Rigid, devoid of emotion—cool as a cucumber."

"That you are. Come here." I kissed her, softly at first, to test the waters. When she responded, I took her mouth hard. I laced my hand in her hair, then moved down, tracing the lines of her face, the contours of her cheeks, her chin, her neck, the shell of her ear, the nerves in my fingertips hot and firing against her skin. I released her bottom lip from between my teeth and rested my forehead against hers.

"You can feel any way you want. I'd react the same if I saw another man's arm around you. I might even overreact before I knew what the real situation was. I might even make something up to confuse you as to why I'm insane with rage."

"I wasn't insane with rage."

"Yes, you were." I kissed her again. The smell of her, the way her eyes glistened, the lies she kept telling herself. I wanted her in my bed. "You need your ass spanked." She gasped, and her eyes grew hooded.

"Maybe I do," she whispered.

"Stay."

She sighed. "How did we get from practically killing each other in the parking lot of Lucy's El Adobe, to 'stay'?"

"That was foreplay, sweetheart."

"God."

I ran my nose along the soft part behind her ear, my hands barely touching the angles of her jaw, the curve of her cheek, the fine hairs at her temple. Her smell told me everything. My terms, now.

"Sit down, finish your wine," I whispered. Her hands came up and rested on my shoulders, and her eyes met mine. I saw longing, and vulnerability. It would be so easy now. So easy.

"Drink your wine," I repeated.

Karen sat, a bit resigned, and took a long swallow. We were quiet for a while, and then she said, "I'm a little out of my league here with this kid. Tell me what to do."

I leaned back and shrugged. "Well, I think you have to play it out now."

"If I don't testify against him, what can they do?"

"Nothing."

"What do you think?"

"You already know what I think. I think there's not a lot of hope for this kid, and I say that from experience, not because I don't care."

"I know. I know you care, and I know you can't know everything that's going on. Obviously one of those situations where it's not about the toothpaste cap, right?"

"We both like it on, as I recall."

"Yes, that's true."

"Look, I can make a few calls tomorrow...find out where Tariq is, what his status is, okay?"

She nodded. "Thank you."

"I loved the article, and the cover shot," I said, referring to the *LA Magazine* spread.

"It's been a little...overwhelming. Thank you again for your call. It was...it was nice to hear your voice."

"I didn't know you were at the scene, Karen. It's incredible."

"Yeah. Right place, right time, I guess."

"Don't do that. Don't downplay what you did out there. You saved a baby, for God's sake."

"Well, maybe we'll get that trauma wing sooner than we thought." She sighed, and she gave me a half-smile. It was still the greatest, even at half. "You must think I'm pretty foolish, getting involved, taking this Tariq thing on."

"You know what I think?" I took her hand in both of mine and kissed the back. Five minutes ago, I was angry enough to toss her ass in the canal, and now I was filled with warmth and love for her—a feeling that never ended for me, or even died down. Not for a second.

"You...*overwhelm* me." She tsked, and then I noticed her eyes fill and her bottom lip start to quiver. "You stun me with your brilliance and your compassion. You blow me away with your heart, and your courage, and your tenacity. You are, without a doubt, the most stubborn woman I have ever met. You are hot-tempered and petulant and passionate and spoiled and sexy and tender, and you are by far the most beautiful woman I have ever touched, kissed or loved. And I love you now. And I loved you then, and all the moments in between. I love how you smile, I love how you cry, I love how you smell and taste and feel..."

"Stop..."

"No." I massaged her fingers between my own and continued. "I asked you to get involved in this thing with Tania Harris, and you did it, without question. You got into my car, not knowing where we were going, or what we were doing, because I asked you to, and you did it pissed as hell at me. I expected nothing less than this, right now. None of this surprises me. Do I want to see you hurt or disappointed? Of course not. Will you be? Probably. But am I surprised by any of this? No."

She turned away.

"Karen...." She faced me again, tears sliding down already moist cheeks. I wiped one away. "Foolish? You are many things, baby, but foolish isn't one of them."

She did one of those laugh/cry things that most women can pull off successfully, but that she was particularly good at. "You really know how to make a girl feel bad."

"That's some kind of female-reverse-logic thing we aren't supposed to understand, right?"

"Right." She looked at me a long moment, wiped her face with the back of her hand, and then she chuckled and shook her finger at me. "This is how I fell in love with you the first time. This...this...*thing* you do."

"Can't be helped." I kissed the back of her hand. "Now, about that spanking."

She laughed and stared into her drink. She took her time, sipped slow. And when her glass was empty, she stood. "I have to go."

"You sure? How about another glass of wine?"

"I should go," she whispered.

"Okay." I stood, too. She didn't move. I kissed her, and I made this one last a while. I steadied her after I broke the kiss. That made my night.

"Walk me to my car."

"You sure?" I asked.

"No. Do it anyway."

I did it holding her hand. Her car was parked on one of the residential streets outside the canals. She got in and I leaned in and kissed her lightly on the mouth.

"I breathe you in and it makes me stronger. You're everything that's good in my life. Marry me, baby. Right now. Tonight. Because I won't ask again."

She looked me dead in the eye, and said, "Yes, you will." The engine rolled over, and she slid the car into gear.

"*Dimmi che mi ami.*" Tell me you love me.

She put her hand over mine, and I saw the tears glisten in her eyes. "Relax, Johnny," she whispered. "You'll get the girl." And then she sped away. I watched until her taillights disappeared down the block.

"Yeah," I said to nobody. "When?"

I followed the sidewalk to the alley and intended to enter through the back gate. The dark figure across the canal stopped me. I didn't know how visible I was to him, but I could see him, the glow of his cigarette against the dark background of a tall hedge fronting a Craftsman. Whoever this was had taken an interest in me, and I was going to find out why.

I crossed the alley and stepped onto the footbridge at a good clip, and I was halfway across before my intentions registered. I could see that the smoker was a man—a decent sized one. He dropped the cigarette to the ground as I got to the downslope of the bridge and took off around the corner.

I ran the sidewalk that fronted the homes on the canals and turned the corner. Houselights shimmered off the water. A dog barked in the distance. A television blared a sitcom from the house I stood in front of. What I did not see, or hear, was the guy with the cigarette, who always seemed to be looking in on me when I had a woman around.

I decided then that I would attend that bitch-and-stich for nosey neighbors. It was time I met mine.

19

*I*t was tough for cops to come together when you didn't work side by side, and a lot of the time we got in each other's way to the point where cases were compromised, sometimes irretrievably. Today the stars were aligned.

When we arrived at the scene, west of Chatsworth Park in the San Fernando Valley, L.A. County Sheriffs and members from L.A. Parks and Rec were already there. The area had been roped off and Chief Coroner Pete Tabor was already getting out of the meat wagon, having been called specifically at our request.

She was a meth addict, back when she was still breathing. Hair a dull, lifeless brown, cheeks sunken to almost skeletal, the telling open sores on her face and arms, teeth rotting out of her mouth, forced into a freakish grimace caused by the ligature tied tight around her neck. The victim was nude, open sores covering her body, ribs outlined under dry and too-thin skin. Her feet rested flat on the ground, knees bent and spread, the smell overwhelmingly death and meth. We'd experienced it before, Alex and I, because we worked and lived in L.A. and the drug was cheap and addictive. Her genitals were red and raw, but that could have been from what her life had become, and not part of our killer's MO. The teenage hikers who found the body were talking with an officer. Boulders as big as houses towered over us, nested against the hillside. California Live Oaks, sycamores and eucalyptus trees covered the area beyond the fire road where the body lay, half-hidden under low brush. Drag marks went from an area ten feet from where she now lay.

It looked like she'd been beaten up, unlike the purplish discoloration that occurs as livor mortis sets in. Pete Tabor noted the same, and fixed time of death at more than twenty-four hours.

"Fucker's nothing, if not consistent," I noted. I nodded to a deputy with the LACSO. "ID on the vic?"

"Annie Reynolds. Has a record—vagrancy, petty larceny, prostitution."

"Anyone ask around, see where she might live?"

"You came fast, so...not yet."

"No problem." I motioned to Alex and a patrolman to follow me a couple hundred yards down the fire road to an unkempt property with a small and equally unkempt house —shack was more like it. Various appliances, cars and electronics littered the property in different stages of repair, typical of meth addicts, who fixated on projects that never got finished.

"Annie Reynolds on our list?" I asked Alex. He opened his nine-by-twelve leather binder and flipped through a few pages. "Anne Smythe," he said, spelling the name for me. "Taken June 1991. Age at the time of abduction, nine."

"Okay, so that would make her thirty-seven now."

"That dead woman looks sixty-four, Johnny."

"Yup. Thirty-seven's the new sixty-four on a steady diet of Scooby Snacks."

We stepped over dog shit, metal pipes and trash that had been released from a plastic bag, never having made it to the trashcan—wherever that was—on our way to what I could only assume was the front door. It was open.

"Hello?" I banged on the door. "Police." I smelled it immediately, and so did my partner. Rotten eggs married with ammonia made for the toxic mix of a meth lab. We drew our guns.

"Call for backup," I said to the patrolman. I was about to take the house room by room when I saw movement, and the movement was lower to the ground than that of your average size adult.

"Shit," Alex said, seeing what I saw. We entered the house, guns drawn. The main room of the house was littered with garbage, and whatever flat surface there was served as holders for coffee cans filled with nuts, bolts and screws, or bowls with moldy food caked to the bottom and sides. A rolled up disposable diaper sat on a table next to a stack of newspapers, on top of which an animal had taken a shit. Several more diapers filled a small trashcan on the floor. The ammonia smell was strong in this area, due, I guessed to the diapers, but the smell didn't stop here.

I saw the movement again, and then a face came into view from the next room—what would have, in effect, been the dining room, had this been a normal home. The face was smooth, lips wide and swollen and pulled taut by scar tissue. She was about twelve. The eyes were dull, and it meant nothing to this kid that two strange men were standing in her house. She turned her attention back to *South Park*. I heard steps behind me, and turned to see the patrolman, back with two other officers.

"One of you get her out of here, the other walk the perimeter," I said. "And call CFS."

"I've got two searching the property already," the first uniform said. "Smell that?"

"Yeah. Get this kid out of here. You," I said to the remaining two patrolmen, "come with us." We moved through the house, Alex and I taking the route we started, the other two taking the wings—the bedrooms, bathrooms, etc. Filthy dishes sat piled in the kitchen sink and it smelled of sour milk and cat box. Trash littered the floor, which was a color and material I couldn't begin to guess at. The chemical smell got stronger as we moved through the kitchen and out a door into a side yard. More trash, car parts, bedsprings, plastic toys, an old crib mattress, a lot of weeds and one dead cat littered the mostly-dirt yard. Where there were diapers and a crib mattress, there had to be a young child.

"Another kid around," I said to Alex.

The smell got stronger the closer we got to a wood shed behind the house. The door of the shed stood open enough for me to see in without opening the door and startling whoever was inside. When I saw nothing move, I pushed the door open and stepped in, gun up. The two patrolmen moved ahead of me and scanned the room.

A workbench lined on side of the shed and was littered with all the paraphernalia used to manufacture crystal meth. The drug itself littered the workbench, the small crystals glittering in the sun that managed to make its way through the dirt-caked window. Someone left in a hurry because beakers were filled, tubes were connected and meth was being cooked. Only the cook was missing.

"Get out there and look for this fuck," I said, recalling the burned face and dull eyes of the child inside the house.

"And we need Haz Mat here." One patrolman got on a radio while Alex and I kicked over boxes and looked under workbenches and behind old half-torn-apart appliances to make sure no one was hiding. The fresh air, once we got to it, was welcome. My eyes teared and my chest ached with every breath.

"Here we go," I heard one of the sheriff's deputies say as he dragged a scrawny man across the property.

Open sores covered his buzzed head and gaunt face. Black rimmed his red eyes, and his ratty clothes hung from his body. He struggled against the cuffs and the deputy, who outweighed him by a hundred pounds.

"Get the fuck down on your knees," I said, prompting the deputy to put him there for me. He also produced two glass pipes and some crystal, which he found in Gaunt and Smelly's pocket.

"Richard Reynolds," the deputy introduced.

"We got a dead body up there, and an active lab in there. Don't know where the woman was killed but assume for now this is the crime scene and take precautions," I said.

"You got it."

"Dead body?" Reynolds said.

"Keep him tied down. I think we might be missing a small child." I turned to Richard Reynolds. "You got children, Mister Reynolds?"

"Uh, yeah...uhhuh."

"Where are they?"

"Uh...yuh, in the house...yeah. In house. No?"

"Anyone else here with you on the property?"

"No."

"Don't lie to me. You say no, I believe no, then someone comes around the corner, loved-one could lose a life. You hear me?"

"Yuh ahyuh. Uh...wife's somewhere." His jaw worked back and forth like a pendulum.

"What's her name?"

"Annie."

"When was the last time you saw Annie?"

"Yauhh, um...hour or so ago? No. Uh...hmmm." He looked up at me with his hollowed-out eyes. "I don't remember. A while, maybe."

"Okay. Stay put. I'll get back to you." I motioned for Alex to follow me, and we walked through the house again. We looked under beds, in closets, in bathtubs. More cops showed up while we searched. I led the way across the property and toward the area where the sheriff's deputy came from, dragging Reynolds behind him. Pete Tabor was caring for our dead body, and we'd hook up with him later.

"This is a fuckin' cesspool, Johnny," my partner stated, as if I'd just arrived. "What possesses a person to ingest chemicals—not talkin' pot here, but kitchen chemicals—to escape for a while?"

"You realize how quickly we'd clean up the place if we had that answer?" I looked ahead as we pushed up an incline south of the property. "Oh, shit."

He came out from behind a boulder and locked eyes with me. He was no more than three. His naked body and face were covered in open sores and scabs, and his penis, which should have been the size of my thumb, was three times that size, red and throbbing.

"Dah!" he said, and then toddled down the hill toward me. "Dah! Dah!" When he got to within twenty feet of us he lifted his arms to me. I pulled my jacket off, wrapped it around him, and picked him up. He reeked of ammonia and something sweet. He was wet, sticky, and he had something in his hand he'd been eating, which hit the floor the minute I lifted him up.

"Hey, buddy." My voice cracked. Alex swore under his breath. "What's your name, kiddo?"

"He probably doesn't even know, *padna*," Alex said.

"Dah!" the child said and pointed toward the house.

"Hey, there's Dylan," shouted Richard Reynolds when we came into his view.

"Someone from CFS here yet?" I asked the assembled.

"I'll check," said a horrified patrolman. He turned away and spoke on the radio.

"Chemical burns all over his body, also got a raging infection." I turned the kid around. A chorus of muted curses went up. A sheriff's deputy came along with a blanket. I handed the kid off and took my jacket.

"Dah!" he said, reaching for the half-human who I assumed was his father.

"Hey, Dylan. Hey, Dylly-boy!" Reynolds looked up at me. "Where they takin' him?"

"Hopefully somewhere you'll never see him again." I bent low, so only Reynolds and the deputy holding him could hear. "And if I had five minutes alone with you, I'd only be capable of inflicting half the pain you've caused that baby, and the girl." I grabbed him under his chin and shoved, realizing my mistake as a chunk of skin came off in my hand. "Motherfucker."

"Where is Lindsay? Where is that girl? She's supposed to watch her brother."

I wanted to wrap my hands around his neck—skin chunks be damned—and squeeze until life left him. This wasn't a disease; it was a choice. Choose all you want when it's just you, but don't involve your kids.

Not the kids.

20

*A*s with most situations like this, once CFS took the kids away, we'd likely hear nothing more about them. Our focus needed to be on who killed Annie Reynolds, formerly Smythe. Richard Reynolds would be our first suspect, then we'd fan out from there—but I knew. I knew who did it, and it wasn't this fuck-up, who could barely hold his head up, let alone take the time to do all the things that were done to Annie Reynolds. We'd ask him who might have come on to the property in the last twenty-four-plus hours, or where Mrs. Reynolds might have gone off to. I held out little hope of a coherent answer. We'd keep trying. But that didn't stop my mind from going back to the condition of those kids, and what their life had been like, up until today. I worried more, though, about what their lives would be like from today forward. Like with their mother, shit usually didn't turn out for the better once you got the bad start.

Annie Smythe had been abducted in June of 1991 and returned four days later. She was nine at the time. It took us a couple of days to dig up the police reports on the abduction, but everything fit. That little girl's story was the same as the others: did not remember much, description of her abductor was vague but fit with Grace Dashiell's description closely enough. All the other rotten things that had been done to the others had been done to little Annie Smythe.

Alex pulled the list of names out, stood and walked over to the whiteboard above one of the vacant desks.

"Let's start from the top." He wrote each name on the board, starting with Grace Dashiell. This is how Alex worked—lists, patterns, I's dotted, T's crossed, ducks in a row. When he was finished, it looked like this:

GRACE DASHIELL – 1988 (living)
>   Dana Torrance – 1989 (living)
>   Annie Smythe (Reynolds) – 1991 (murdered)
>   Jane Dobson – 1995 (living)
>   ~~Breanna Delacroix – 1998 (deceased)~~
>   Josie Schuyler – 2005 (murdered)
>   Emily Knox - 2011 (living)
>   Tiffany Funk – 2011 (living) pos. minor
>   Clarissa Sparks – 2013 (murdered)
>   Jade Warren – 2017 (living) minor
>   Possible victims still missing:
>   Kristen Holmes 2011
>   Rebecca Daly 2008

I LEARNED MORE from my partner every day. We had five potential victims left, two possible minors. The killer seemed to be going after the most vulnerable of his prior victims—if it was the same guy who abducted them as children. We didn't know that, and we couldn't assume it. We had no physical evidence. And without it, we were flying blind.

I'D PROMISED Karen I'd look into what was happening with Tariq Williams. I made a call and got to someone on the first try. The kid was in juvenile hall and was being arraigned in children's court later today. As soon as I hung up, I got a call from the DA on the case, a Stanley Potter. I knew him from other cases I'd been involved in.

"We'll need you at the arraignment, Detective."

"I understand Dr. Gennaro is not pressing charges. Why do you need me?"

"To talk her out of it."

"C'mon, Stan. When's the arraignment?"

"Four-thirty."

It was three already. "Let me call you back." Karen was taking this kid on faith and nothing more. I knew better. I knew how this would end. I was too set in my ways to change my attitudes about life now, but Gennaro had a way of making me see things differently. I decided to have a little faith myself. I went into my desk drawer and I pulled out two business cards. I made my first call.

"MS. GENNARO IS REFUSING to press charges," Stan Potter whined into my ear when I called him back an hour later.

"I told you. Is she there now?"

"Yes, she's here now. She has no idea…"

"I know. Let me speak to her, will you?"

"Be my guest, but know this—and I have told Ms. Gennaro already…"

"*Doctor* Gennaro. I think she's earned it."

"Yes, of course, by all means, let's be formal. I have informed *Doctor* Gennaro that Tariq Williams has an aunt—his mother's sister—and she's in town for two weeks. She goes back to New Orleans at the end of those two weeks, and she cannot take Tariq until sometime in November, which means he goes into foster care until then."

"Okay."

"*Doctor* Gennaro needs to understand that she can't go halfway here. She's involved now, and I think it's only fair that we explain what happens next."

"Let me speak to her."

"Hi," she said into the phone.

"Hey, sweetheart. You okay?"

"Sure, yes." We both sat with the silence for a minute. I wanted to rehash last night instead of talking about Tariq Williams or listening to Stanley Potter. I wanted to consider what-ifs with her—what if she'd stayed, what if we'd shared coffee this morning, what if she'd said yes to all of it.

"Mr. Potter is sputtering."

She chuckled. "You should see it from my end."

"So, do you understand what the issues are? The aunt is here for two weeks, then the kid goes into the system. Not good, for a million reasons."

"I understand. I need to figure out what to do with him after his aunt leaves," she said.

"Right, and that does not mean taking him into your home, Karen, do you understand me?"

"Yes, I understand."

"I have another option, and this will be best for both you and Tariq. Okay?"

"Okay."

"Good. First, call a friend of mine. Name's Hank Petra. He's a social worker." I gave her the number. "He's a good guy. I've worked with him before. If you can find a place for the kid to stay until November, Hank will help you. He's expecting your call. The other person you need to call is Bill Grayson. He's the Athletic Director at Campbell College. He's also a minister. I got to know him last year when we worked on the David Crane case. He might be able to help you find a place for Tariq. This is right up his alley."

Bill Grayson had taken my call immediately, and when I explained my problem, he said, "John, I deal with this a lot. I think I can help." This was sight-unseen, without even meeting Tariq Williams. I knew he was someone I could turn to who would help, without question.

"Okay, I've got it."

"You hired an attorney for Tariq?"

"I did."

"Keep his or her number handy. You'll probably need it again. Stan'll tell you that Tariq will be released into his aunt's care, but you need to keep in touch with her, too, so you don't lose him again."

"Okay. I can do that."

"Two weeks, Gennaro. That's all the time you have."

"I know." She paused and her voice got soft, like it did in those intimate times we shared when all the walls were down, and we felt nothing but the good. "It was good of you to do this. I don't know how to thank you."

"Meet me for a drink tonight."

"That's a small price to pay."

"It'll do for now."

She cleared her throat. "I see."

"Not yet, darlin'. But you will. I'll call you later, lady blue."

"I look forward to it."

21

"*W*as hopin' to make your day over there, give you some more time to sun yourselves at the beach," Charlie Kool said. Commotion in the background competed with his voice, in case I was wondering if the Cold Case cops worked in a cave. We worked the same land, inside buildings and out, so our noises were familiar.

"Yeah, Charlie," I said. "That's exactly how we spend our free time. Glad to hear some remorse about not making our day bright. Disappoint me now, please."

"Well, I thought I could knock off a few names for you here on that list you sent, but no dice. The only thing I can tell you is the Kristen Holmes case was solved in oh-eleven."

"Spill."

"Her body was found in a remote area near Chatsworth, sexually assaulted, possibly with objects, underwear tied around her neck. Carpet fibers were found on the victim. A transient was picked up in the area, and in among his rags was the kid's sweater. Kristen Holmes' hair and the same carpet fibers were all over him. Transient claims he spent a few nights in an abandoned truck, covered himself with an old piece of carpet, found the sweater in the truck, and kept it. I'm looking at the interview report now. Jesus, these cops wanted to solve this case."

"What do you mean?"

"Lots of transcription on the interview. Means they interrogated him for a long time. Transient—Samuel Cotts—ends up hanging himself awaiting arraignment."

"So, all they had was carpet fibers and the kid's sweater."

"Yeah. I'll send over the file. You might see something useful."

"You're helpful. Don't let anyone tell you different."

"I don't. Keep in touch and cross this one off your list."

"I will. Weird thing is, Charlie: in 2011, Kristen Holmes disappeared a month or so after another girl, Emily Knox, was abducted and held for four days—same thing in common with our three murder victims. It was thought back then that the two abductions were connected, but Holmes wasn't returned like Emily Knox and the others. She was, we know now, murdered. Same MO, incidentally, as the three murders we're investigating."

"Tell me again about your three."

I filled him in on the details concerning Josie Schuyler, Clarissa Sparks and Annie Reynolds (Smythe), including the DNA found under Josie Schuyler's nails that matched our homeless man, Henry McLaren.

"So, connected, then?"

"Somehow, but McLaren was murdered before Schuyler."

"So, he didn't kill her."

"No. All three of our current murder victims were abducted at around age ten, returned after four days, then their lives went to shit as they got older, and now someone's coming back for more."

"You think it's the same guy who abducted them as kids?"

"Of course that's what we think, we just can't prove it. No physical evidence, then or now."

"How the fuck can that be?"

"Locard's Theory..."

"... Something is brought to the crime scene and something is taken away. It's how we catch 'em," he said.

"It's the one thing we can count on, yet not this time. Little Kristen Holmes never made it to adulthood, never made it home, like the others. It's the same guy coming back now for more, and he's hitting the ones who are vulnerable, because I have girls—women—on that list who have managed to survive what happened to them all those years ago—at least they're surviving on the outside—and they're still alive. The oldest victim of the childhood abductions is forty-two and she's a professional woman."

"Which one is she, on the list?"

"Grace Dashiell. We have one more on the list who we're sure is of adult age, based on when she was abducted as a child. Haven't talked to her yet, and the other three are minors—one, possibly not. That'd be Tiffany Funk on your list. Might have hit eighteen by now."

"Okay. That's a lot to go on. I'll look into some of our cold cases where the circumstances are similar."

"I was hoping you'd say that, Charlie. Thanks."

"Yup. We'll be in touch."

I filled Alex in, and an hour later we had the file on Kristen Holmes. I pulled out police reports, photographs, DNA findings, and finally, a picture of the victim.

The body had been badly decomposed, which made looking at her more clinical. Still, the cloth tied around her neck, what the reports claimed were her underwear, was visible. Photos of a truck, sitting amongst weeds and rock, the large boulders of the Chatsworth hills in the background, appeared to match the truck Seeley Marks described as the one Rebecca Daly got into. The transient, Samuel Cotts, says he slept in the truck for a few days, covering himself with a carpet, the fibers from which showed up on him. The same fibers were found on the victim, Kristen Holmes.

"So, the only physical evidence they had on this transient is the carpet fibers. No hair, skin or other evidence connected the two, yet they arrested this guy, and he kills himself in jail," I said to Alex.

"Which means nothing, or it could mean everything."

"And, don't forget, no physical evidence on any of these little girls, and none on our three victims—except for Henry McLaren, who we know didn't kill Josie Schuyler."

"So, our killer understands physical evidence."

"Cop?"

"Shit, John." Alex stood and paced.

"This truck is out of circulation, now, right?" I said, moving off my suspicions for the moment, disturbing as they were.

"I'd guess. Does it say who it was registered to?"

"Hang on," I said, looking through the file. "Uh, says here vehicle was not currently registered at the time found, and last registered to B. J. Mardigan in 2008." I stared at the truck, looked at the list of names. "Not registered since 2008, but it is possible that Kristen Holmes was in that truck in 2011, because of the carpet fibers found on her body. Says here that it appeared the truck hadn't been driven in a while —tires flat, webs around tires and under truck body. This is oh-eleven now, at least six months since Kristen Holmes went missing."

Alex sat on the edge of his desk. "So, the truck's not registered, not since oh-eight. Whether Kristen Holmes was picked up in the truck or not is unknown, but how the hell does he get away with driving that thing around without getting stopped?"

"I don't know. Maybe he was stopped and ignored the tickets."

"We can find that out easily enough, but it's not important now. Suppose Kristen Holmes had been in that truck in 2011, wrapped in the carpet or came into contact with the carpet. Sometime later Samuel Cotts comes across the truck. He covers himself up with the carpet, like he says. He's going to have carpet fibers on him that match what was found on the girl, and if the girl had contact with that carpet, her hair would be on the carpet, and could transfer to Cotts easily, right?"

"Right. Locard's Theory as written."

"So, it's possible this poor Cotts had no knowledge of Kristen Holmes or anything else. He finds a kid's sweater and adds it to his rag bag. Doesn't mean he killed her."

"I'm following," I said.

"Is it also possible that 2008 was the last time that truck was registered because that was when Rebecca Daly was taken, and that abduction became too high-profile?"

"It's very possible."

"So, the tire tracks found at the Josie Schuyler death scene...new truck."

"Yeah."

"Let's work the list, Johnny. It's the best we have right now."

"Yeah." I called off the BOLO for the late model truck. Then I put Preston McConnell on finding B. J. Mardigan.

22

*W*e found the next woman on our list in the small town of Brenton, north of Santa Clarita. It was a hot town, steeped low in the valley, small and worn, dusty and slow. Jane Dobson agreed to see us after a lengthy conversation in which she denied what happened to her in 1995, when she was ten years old.

"I've left all that behind me," she said. We sat on uncomfortable stools in a dark bar off the main drag. It was two p.m. and the bar was empty, except for one aging gentleman who looked as if his ass had grown roots into the stool he sat on. A short old-fashioned glass sat in front of him with brown liquid sitting in the bottom. I knew many who went to that place and stayed. This guy looked good and comfortable.

"You okay, Gus?" she called out over the country-western tune playing on the juke. Gus raised his hand in the affirmative, and Jane Dobson turned her attention back to us. "I can't see the point in bringing all that up again. I spent a lot of years trying to forget it."

"I understand," I said. "We're not trying to bring up old

hurts, but we could use your help. Three women have been murdered, and they all experienced as children what you did."

"I don't understand." It was clear she didn't. Her eyes were dull and colorless, and she had erected walls to protect herself. What she wore, how she looked through rather than at, the way she carried herself; it all screamed, *don't look. I'm not here.*

"We have three women," I tried again, "all killed the same way. The other thing they have in common is that they were abducted as children, molested, and returned four days later."

"Am I in danger?"

"We don't think so. These women...their lives didn't turn out like yours, and some of the others..."

"There are others?"

"Yes. Some are dead; others are still alive. The ones who are still alive have jobs; some have careers. Our three victims all took a bad turn—prostitution, drugs..."

"And is it the same asshole, coming back for more?"

"We think so. The MO is the same."

"MO?"

"It means Method of Operation, and it has to do with clear habits or rituals of a person, in this case, our killer. Serial murderers tend to kill the same way, every time."

"I see. So, what do you need from me?"

"Can you tell us what happened to you when you were taken?"

Jane Dobson blew out a breath, and then looked over at Gus. "Another?"

Gus raised his hand in the affirmative. She went behind the bar and filled his glass, and I thought I heard her say, "On me." When she returned to us, she motioned us to follow her, and called over her shoulder, "I'll be over here, honey, if you need anything. I got something I need to do." Again, Gus simply lifted his hand.

We sat in a black plastic booth along a wall covered in old license plates and faded black and white photos. The veneer table was sticky. "Drink?" she asked us. I asked for water; Alex took a Coke. Jane Dobson returned with our drinks, a bottle of Bud for herself, and a damp rag, which she used to wipe the table. She tossed it on the booth seat next to her and sat.

"I was ten. I came home from school, like always. My mom worked, and usually didn't get home 'til around seven. I wandered down to the store, about a mile away, and when I was walking back, a truck pulled up and asked me if I'd seen a puppy."

"That the truck?" I said, pushing toward her a photo of the abandoned truck Sam Cotts napped in.

"Yup. Looks like it. Probably cleaner, but yes, that's close enough."

"Then what happened?"

"I said I hadn't. He asked if I would help him. He wanted me to get up into the truck. I said no. He shrugged and said fine, and I said I'd keep my eyes open. I knew better than to get into that truck."

"What do you remember about the person driving the truck?"

"He was a little strange. Looked like a kid. Smooth, all over. He was very friendly, and I didn't feel afraid of him, I remember that."

"So, then what?"

"I started looking for that puppy as I was walking back home. I walked down an alley that went behind my house, and the other houses on my block and the block over..."

"So the alley ran between two blocks of homes."

"Right. So, I'm walking, and the blue truck turns the corner ahead of me, and he drives right to me. The rest happened so fast. He opened the driver's side door, and lifted me in. That was it. I don't remember much, except I couldn't see very well."

Alex and I exchanged a look. "Do you remember him putting anything in your eyes?"

"No, but they were stinging, and everything was blurry."

"How long did it last?"

"Until he took me from the car—the truck."

"What did it smell like, do you remember?"

"Nail polish remover. I think I threw up before we got where we were going. I really can't remember. Even now, I can't walk in to a nail salon—not that I can afford that shit anyway."

"Where did you end up when the truck stopped?"

"House, maybe. We were inside."

"Okay. Can you tell us what happened?"

Jane Dobson told us what he did to her, and that it went on for four days. She said the same things Grace Dashiell said regarding the man's demeanor. She also described the last day, when he tied her underwear around her neck and pulled tight.

"I thought I was going to die. And that smell was back— that chemical smell. I threw up; I remember that. He didn't get mad. He cleaned up and told me we were going home." Jane Dobson drained her beer. "What happened to me? *It* was what I became. Not 'The girl that... fill-in-the-blank'. I became 'The-girl-who-was-kidnapped-and-raped-for-four-days'. It has defined me."

"I'm sorry," I said.

"Yeah. Me, too." She stood. "Get this motherfucker."

"We're trying." We stood, too. "Thanks for your help."

———————

WE MET in the dark bar of a boutique hotel about a mile from Karen's. My drink had just arrived when she filled the doorway and scanned the dimly lit room for me. She wore a snug fitting black dress, sleeves down to the elbows, hemline to the tops of her knees, neckline showing off that part I loved to kiss between shoulder and neck. Red shoes set it all ablaze, purse and an overgarment in the same color. I couldn't breathe. I let her stand there another thirty seconds or so before I stood and signaled to her.

"Am I late?" she asked, setting her purse and little jacket down on the third chair. "You always arrive before I do."

I set both hands on her hips and hers went automatically to my biceps, and there we stood. "I like watching you walk in."

Eyes hooded, a slight smile crossed her mouth. "Hi," she whispered.

"Hi." I kissed her--tasted her, really: cherry on her tongue, a hint of jasmine at her throat, and that fucking dress. "You should be arrested, young lady," I said in her ear after I broke the kiss.

"You have your cuffs?" she said, eyebrow arched in that pretty way of the innocently wicked.

"Say that to me again, and I'll take you right to dessert—fuck the drinks and dinner."

"Oooh, I'm getting dinner, too?" She sat.

"If you're a good girl."

She crossed her shapely legs. "Define good."

I stared at the legs. "That line is blurred at the moment."

"Belvedere martini, cold and dry, several olives," she said to the waitress. With a nod she was gone.

I sighed and stared, a combination perfected by zitty high school virgins, yet here I was. "You wear that to work?"

"Yes. Why?"

"I've got a secret for you: it isn't your considerable brilliance that cures the sick and mends the wounded: it's the dress."

She grabbed my Scotch and took a sip. "Do you plan on admiring my mind at all tonight?"

"Only if it's attached to that dress."

Karen smirked and shook her head.

"It's good to see you, sweetheart."

"It's good to see you, too, Johnny."

"You settled about today?" I asked after I'd ogled her too long.

"Yes. I know what I need to do. Thanks again for your help. I called Hank Petra and Bill Grayson. Both were amazingly helpful, and both had good things to say about you."

"They're good men."

"So are you."

"Makes me happy you think so."

Her drink arrived and I saluted her. We let the quiet set in comfortably. Karen picked up a clear pick speared through three olives and twisted it back and forth. "I need to say something before we go too far, Johnny."

"Uh oh." I said it with a smile, but it didn't feel good inside.

"I wasn't ready for...*you* last year. We fell hard and we fell fast—too fast. The way it ended..."

"Karen..."

"No, please." She met my eyes. "I purposely kept you at a distance about Adam, and I knew it would break us. It wasn't a reason to end things. I made it one. The business with Adam, your reaction to it...to *him*. It was baggage neither of us needed."

"I could have handled it for both of us."

"As I recall, neither one of us was handling anything very well. You'd lost Mark; I was fighting off Adam. Even after all that dust settled..."

"Gonzo was killed after we broke up, babe. You smacked some sense into me outside the OR, remember?"

"God." She shook her head at the memory: me insane and blaming her for not saving Gonz. I had her by the arms and I was revving up to throttle her when she slapped me. It had been a fitting end, as I recalled.

"And when you came after me, in Cambria. I was numb, John. I wasn't in a place to take it on again."

"Why are you telling me this, babe?"

"I need you to know that it wasn't because I didn't love you. When I kicked you off my beach in Cambria, after you'd come all that way to make things right, and I rejected you...I knew you believed it was because I no longer loved you. I saw it on your face, in your eyes. And that broke my heart. I wanted so many times to call you and at least tell you that."

I sat with that a good while before I offered my own confession. "I haven't stopped loving you, either. Not for a second."

"I know that," she said. "I knew it when you came busting into my clinic like the Lone Ranger. White hat on straight, silver guns at your hips, all swagger and so damn cock-sure." She shook her head again. "A woman like me has no business with a man like you, but God help me, I can't shake you." She sipped her drink. "So, there you have it."

"I can do this better. I can."

She put her hand over mine. "So can I."

I drained my drink and signaled for another. Karen's was half way down but I ordered her another anyway. "So, what the fuck are you doing with Shapiro now?"

Karen threw her head back and laughed. "Oh, my. There he is."

"I said I'd do better, not become the schmuck who holds your purse. What the fuck is going on, Gennaro?"

Karen sighed and took a fortifying sip of her drink. "My father entered into a business deal with him that turned out to be not so legitimate."

"So, you're spending time with this asshole hoping he'll get your dad out of a bind?"

"Well, that was the theory at first. Daddy's a big boy, and he's not stupid. He had to know something was up with this deal."

"Right."

"And hooking myself to Adam is not going to make it go away. And I care nothing for him, so there's that."

"So, we're done with him now?"

Karen chuckled. "As far as I'm concerned." She met my eyes with a steely glare. "You will stay away from him, too, Testarossa."

I hid a smirk with my whiskey glass.

"Did you really think he wouldn't tell me about your visit? You can't do that, John."

"Why not? He's nothing."

"He isn't nothing." She bit an olive off the pick. "He is rich and he is connected, and he has zero scruples."

"Doesn't concern me, Blue. You think I can't handle a guy like him?"

"You're a street fighter, John. He's the guy who stabs you

from behind after the fight is over. I'm not worried you're incapable of blacking his eye; I'm worried that he's capable of ruining you in ways you cannot recover from."

"Please."

"Power comes in all sizes, shapes and colors. You need to be able to see him coming."

"Okay. I get it. We'll both stay away from him, right?"

"Don't patronize me, John."

"I'm not. I promise. Don't you worry about him, or about me."

"Do you remember the conversation we had when we were first getting to know each other?" she asked. "You were put out that I had previously dated..."

"Dated? You lived with him for half a dozen years."

"Okay. You were put out that I *lived* with someone who had money. You wondered why I left him, and what I thought you could offer me after all that. Remember?"

"Yeah. It was our first fight."

"It wasn't our first fight, but it was a touchy conversation. Money has never meant anything to me. It makes life easier, sure. But I've always had my own. I certainly didn't need Adam's. What he had was power. He got things done. He'd walk into a room and people would take notice. They would adjust, for him. People fear him. I believed..." She shook her head again and stared into her drink. "Did I ever tell you I had a brother?"

"No."

"I came home from school one day, and David was face down in the swimming pool. My mother was asleep in a lounge chair. I pulled his body out of the water. I was twelve."

"How old was he?"

"Two. My mother never recovered from that. The

woman you see today is a shell of her former self. My sister and I raised ourselves—or rather assisted our father in raising us. I grew into adolescence believing that anything could happen at any time. I chose men I could control because I felt I didn't have any.

"I believed when I met Adam that his power could, somehow, save me from more dead brothers and withered mothers. I became a doctor so I could control life. I believed power would save me from that kind of pain." She looked up at me. "And then I met you, and I learned the meaning of safe." Karen tapped the point of the now empty pick against a cocktail napkin. "A woman like me has no business with a man like you. Clinging to you will be the death of me. Depending on you will lose me to me. Yet here I sit, telling you secrets and wanting nothing more than to sit in your lap."

Those words stabbed into me and set something lose. She was the one person who knew how to do that to me with such precision it blew me away.

"Christ."

And right there in the restaurant bar, with a waitress and a bartender our only witnesses, I pulled her out of her seat and into my lap.

"I'm here, baby," I said. "I'm here."

23

*A*s I went out the front door of the station for a head clearing walk around the block, Ginger was explaining to an irate gentleman that, no, she would not run a 'make' on a car belonging to the guy he believed was 'doin' his wife. When I returned ten minutes later, the irate man had been replaced by Alex and Grace Dashiell.

"Hey," I said. "How are you?"

"I'm sorry to just drop in like this," Grace said. "Do you both have a moment?"

"Sure."

She followed us back into the bowels of the station and we found an empty room.

"Coffee?" Alex offered.

"Please," she said, her eyes not leaving his. Alex left the room and came back a moment later juggling three.

"I should have called," she said, "but something's come up, and I wanted to talk to you about it. I'm assuming your case is still open."

"Yes," I said.

"Well, I don't know if talking to you about...what

happened triggered something in me, but I haven't been able to get my mind off...off that time in my life. Good lord, I'm a therapist. I should be able to say it."

"You're not a therapist right now, Grace." Alex said, resting a hand on her shoulder. A tenderness sat in Alex's eyes like I'd never seen before. "Use whatever words you want."

"Okay, well...huh. I'm not even sure this will be helpful."

"Let us decide." Alex sat next to her, and I took a seat across the table.

"This memory kept coming to me after your visit, and I don't know if it's related. It's worth mentioning, only because children have a way, an intuition. When they're uncomfortable, they're uncomfortable. There's no explaining it, but what I've learned in my practice is that most adults who end up in my office have spent their childhoods having their intuitions ignored. And, this relates to me, and perhaps to this case." She took a deep breath. "There was a man who worked for our family when I was a child. I was three or four at the time. This man did some work for us, and he lived for a time in our pool house. I remember I was afraid of him, yet fascinated. Even at that young age, my hair would stand up on the back of my neck whenever he was around. He was perfectly nice to me, but he was strange. He looked strange."

"How so?" I asked.

"Well, he was bald—completely. No eyelashes, no eyebrows, no hair on his arms. His smile was a little crooked, and his teeth were spaced—all of them. And he smelled weird, like a chemical smell, almost like ammonia —like the cat box you try to hide, but that smell gives it away." Grace paused for a moment. "He was there, and then he was gone, and I forgot about him—until after I sat with the sketch artist. I started to think back on the abduction, really think about it. And the one thing that kept coming back to me was that same feeling I had with this guy I had with the man who took me. Now, this man who took me had hair—weird hair, but hair."

"Could it have been a wig?"

"Could have been, because there were moments during that four days when he wore a beanie cap, like I described for your sketch artist. But most of all, I remember the teeth. And the smell." She looked at Alex. "I think it might have been the same guy."

"You were three, four years old, Grace. It was another five or six years before you were taken," Alex said.

"And this is what I'm talking about. Yes, I was young, and yes, a long time, in kid years, passed. But I can't forget that feeling, and for a long time—my whole childhood and adult life up until now, I've blown it off—dismissed it. I'm not going to dismiss it any longer."

"You're right. I'm sorry," Alex said. "It's just that the memories from forty-plus years ago are tough to sell."

"Who do you need to sell them to? I'm telling you this so maybe it's one more thing you've got. That's all."

Alex nodded. "How old was this guy when he worked at your house?"

"He drove, ran errands for my mother, delivered things for my father. He was younger than my parents, and older than my brother. I'd say eighteen to twenty."

I did a quick mental calculation and put this guy in his fifties now.

"What was his name, do you remember?" The hum of the air conditioner cut into the quiet of the room, and voices outside the room threatened interruption. The walls, minus posters and all other distractions, needed an update from the dull putty color someone thought would work well during hours-long interrogations, but only created nausea now. Half of one wall, the glass one where observers interpreted what the cops didn't, was dark. No reason for anyone to be behind the glass today. The cheap veneer desk held on to every scratch and moisture ring like a lifeline, and the chairs caused shifting among those unfortunate enough to sit in them for too long. The smell of coffee coming from our cups brought a sense of calm to the room, and to the face of a woman determined to bring some truth to us, and some peace to herself. I could not know what Grace the girl had gone through, except in strict terms of the law, and I had no idea of the woman sitting before me now, except that she was looking for closure. We wanted to give it to her—a tough sell, as Alex pointed out. We'd try anyway.

"Branch," she said. "His name was Branch."

"First or last name?"

"I don't know. It was just Branch. Had I thought to say his name when he had me for four days, maybe he would have let me go."

"Why do you say that?" Alex asked.

"Because if you make him human, make it about a relationship, it changes things—maybe. If it was the same guy, he had the advantage."

"How so?"

"He knew me. I didn't know him."

We both nodded at that.

"I want to help. I want to help you profile this guy." Her eyes were bright now, eager, hope shining through like a beacon. "For whatever reason, he took these girls as youngsters knowing that they couldn't, or wouldn't, identify him. How many girls?"

"Grace..."

"How did he think he'd get away with it if he let us all live?"

"Grace..." I tried again.

"How many of us did he take over the years?"

Panic rose in her eyes as Alex placed his hand on her shoulder again. "We can't have you working with us on this, Grace."

"Why?"

Alex looked up at me and I gestured for him to go on. "You're too close. You need to be objective here, and you can't be. You just can't be, no matter how much or how easily you think you see into this guy's brain, you're too close. The same reason why you don't treat sexual abuse victims, you can't help us here."

"You're right. But I still think I can help."

"You've helped a lot," I said. "Go home and let us take care of this now."

"I want him." She stood.

"So do we." I led her as far as the door before she turned back.

"I became a therapist so I could help myself. I thought that through helping others, I could help myself. Do you know how I've spent the last twenty years? Locating his other victims."

"You what?" I said.

"I never contacted them, but I knew there were others. I followed the news, I Googled stories obsessively once that avenue was available. I thought that if I found them, I'd find him."

Jesus Christ. "That stops right now, Grace," I admonished. "Okay?"

"Yes, okay. That's probably wise."

Alex walked her out. I was at my desk when he found

me again.

"We can pick her brain another time," he said.

"No, we can't," I said without looking up. "And I shouldn't have to say that to you."

"Yeah. Okay." He sat.

I looked up from my work. "Don't get involved."

"I'm not."

"I've never seen you this way."

"What way?"

"I've never seen you react like this to someone involved in one of our cases. I've known you a long time, *padna*, and this woman has your eye."

"My eye?"

"Yeah. And don't go on about how married you are. She's a victim and a witness, now, possibly. She's not your pal."

"What are you saying?"

"Probably too much, but I know you, and you're too close. Leave it at that."

"That's fucked up, Johnny. Seriously fucked up." He hunched down over some paperwork.

I looked at my partner and friend, someone I'd known a long time. I'd seen him fawn over his wife, unable to keep his hands off her. And I'd witnessed raging fights with curses and small objects flying at each other. I'd watched them go through good times and bad, and through it all, I saw the love. I'd never seen Alex look at another woman, not even accidently, if that's possible. But he was looking at Grace Dashiell. His tone of voice changed when he spoke to her, his attention was fixed. His eyes changed, got that hooded look I sometimes saw in those passion filled moments with his own wife. I was sure nothing more would come of it, but I didn't like the direction he was headed.

"Yeah," I said. "Okay." With a few minutes to myself and a few questions, I picked up the phone and made a call.

"Hi, sweetheart," I said when she answered. "How are you today?"

"I'm very good. How's your day going?"

"All right. Do you have a minute?"

"Sure. Hold on." I heard a door close. This case and my questions were a good excuse to call her, but after the night I held her in my lap in a hotel bar, I figured I didn't need an excuse. "Shoot...so to speak."

I told Karen about the case, in rough sketches, and then asked her what could be going on with a person to make him smell like a nail salon—or a cat box.

"A lot of things: medications, meth users sometimes have an odor like you describe."

"What else?"

"Give me more."

I did, going into detail about the case, and about what Grace Dashiell described.

"Well," Karen sighed. "Sometimes an insulin spike in a diabetic can produce a sweet smell, but in the same diabetic, ketoacidosis can produce that acetone smell you're describing. The person could also be Herxing..."

"Hang on," I said, writing it all down. "What, now?"

"Herxing." She spelled it. "It occurs when injured or dead bacteria releases endotoxins into the blood and tissues faster than the body can handle. This provokes an exaggerated inflammatory response. People on prolonged doses of antibiotics can experience this. Someone with a tick-borne illness such as Lyme's disease might have this problem. That help?"

"Yes. Thank you. And please make note that I am admiring your mind right now. I want credit."

"Noted."

"When can I see you again?"

"The other night didn't scare you off?"

"You know better."

"I have to go out of town tomorrow, just for a few days."

"Where?"

"D.C."

"Why?"

"I'm speaking at a symposium on trauma care in the U.S."

"Sounds very fancy."

"Yeah. I'll be wearing a new dress and someone from the White House will be there. Would you like to spend the night?"

"A little forward, aren't you? We've only kissed and done the lap thing."

"So, you'd like to build up to it, is that what you're saying?"

"I don't know what I'm saying. The thought of spending the night made all the blood rush to my head suddenly."

"Let me know when you're calm and seated."

"Okay. I'm good now."

"Excellent. Would—you—like—to spend—the—night?"

"The short answer is yes. The long is I need to go to this Neighborhood Watch thing tonight."

"Nice. That'll be good for you."

"No, it won't, but I've got two old biddies who are looking into people's windows and taking suspicious adulterers cookies so they can get nosey. And there's a guy...never mind. See, that's the long part you don't need to hear."

"It's very exciting over at the Canals. I had no idea."

"Spend more time here, sweetheart."

"All right. If you insist."

"I insist, and yes, I'd love to spend the night, but I can't be there until about eight. Too late for dinner?"

"Not at all. I love that you want to feed me before, you know, you *feed* me."

"I don't want any distractions once I get you horizontal, lady, and you'll need your strength."

"I think you'll need some strength of your own."

"You've been thinking about this."

"Since your visit to the clinic."

"Wow. How you holding up?"

"I'll be fine in a few hours, thanks for asking. You?"

"I have some good days and some bad. See you soon, sweetheart. I'll bring the wine."

"Later, darling," she whispered.

24

I stood in the living room of a two-story house on Grand Canal, the fireplace crackling behind me, and the low hum of introductory and reacquaintance chatter in front. The home was newly built on a piece of property that had been vacant for twenty years. The owner, a TV producer, fought with the city for years before winning the right to build the large, but by no means the biggest, house with a great view straight down Grand Canal.

Most of the folks sitting around the spacious living room I had only a passing acquaintance with. Esther and Lou, of course, were front and center, and I knew them best, I suppose. A young couple sat behind Esther—she blond, he a shade darker. The tow-headed child on his lap was a perfect mix of the two. Next to the woman sat an older man I'd seen walking his Great Dane around the canals. We usually nodded to each other if I was coming from, or going to, and he happened to walk by. Another couple sat behind him on a loveseat. Her hair hung to her shoulders in tight curls, her warm brown eyes wandering the room as if searching out an escape. The man next to her was dark and goateed, his black hair thick and combed back off a high forehead, the silver hoop in his left ear standing out against his dark skin. He nodded to those around him and uttered an occasional 'hello' when he wasn't checking his phone. When the need arose to text or email, he let go of the woman's hand, taking it up again as soon as he was through.

A woman dressed as if she were ready to hop on the next cruise line that happened by leaned against a long granite counter that separated the kitchen from the living room. A teenage girl was behind her setting out plates of cookies and coffee cups. I heard the girl call Cruise Line *mom* once. The producer's wife, a bejeweled, thin woman used to hosting rooms-full of people she didn't know, introduced herself as Brigit, and then waved an arm in the general vicinity of her husband, Joel, who had planted himself on the arm of a long sofa and slammed away on his iPhone. The same smile he greeted me with at the door twenty minutes ago was still pasted on his face, and I suspected a plastic surgeon was to blame for that.

Growing up I knew everyone on my block of thirty houses, and most on the next block over. I'd been inside all those houses at least once, and I'd taken at least one meal in many. Mrs. Baransky, who lived next door to us on the right, baked cookies. Her kids were grown and out, her husband long gone, by the time I was coming up. If a bunch of us guys were playing stickball in the street, or maybe just sitting around on the stoop, she'd call from her screened-in porch to come and 'try out a batch, see if they taste okay'. While we ate, she showed us her husband's medals from the war, and the picture of her oldest son, dressed in green fatigues and cradling a rifle, in Vietnam.

The Parks family lived two doors down, and they scared the shit out of me, frankly. Their son, Sam, would go to jail for the murder of a local girl right around the time we all graduated from high school. A few of us, including me, saw that one coming.

The Dicksons across the street had four kids. Mr. Dickson drove a truck, and the Mrs. took in ironing. They had some pretty odd looking kids, and more times than not, you'd hear Mr. Dickson going after one or another of them, usually with his belt off.

I knew these people because most had kids my age and, on quiet nights sitting on our porch, or walking around the block to see a friend, they could be heard behind open windows and screen doors, their conversations sometimes filled with dreams and longing, and at other times filled with rage and shame. Not much was kept a secret on E. 79th street growing up. Here, with my life the way it was, and Los Angeles the way it was, getting to know anyone intimately was a crapshoot at best, and downright dangerous all the other times. These people were my neighbors, yet I knew none of them. I wondered, as I stood there waiting for Brigit to finish introductions, what exactly I had to tell these people that they would care to hear. As I stepped forward to gentle applause, I wondered how many of them I'd hear from after tonight. None, I prayed, as I stepped up and started my spiel.

MY TALK LASTED about thirty minutes, then we went another thirty with questions and complaints that had nothing to do with personal safety. After, as we stood around drinking coffee, Lou Wachley came over to me, and indiscreetly cut her eyes in the direction of the male half of the young couple who had sat behind her earlier. Their toddler was walking around, the clear center of attention. The wife did double duty keeping a close eye on the kid while she held up her end of a coherent conversation with the older man who sat next to them—the one with the Great Dane. The husband talked with Cruise Line and another man. Cruise Line was smitten. So was the other man.

"He's the one I told you about," she mouthed, ensuring that if someone had been looking into the house from across the canal, they would have been able to lip-read every word. That not a whisper came out of her mouth was moot. Luckily, the man in question was so engrossed in, not Cruise Line, but the other man, that he wouldn't have noticed Lou Wachley if she'd sat on his face.

"Does he look Arab to you, John?" Esther Horowitz asked, appearing from behind me, Lou's attempt at discretion catching her attention. "I mean, really," she hissed at Lou.

"Not him, you old fool. The one behind him," Lou hissed right back. The dark-haired man with the silver hoop in his ear came into view. He stood away from Cruise Line and listened, occasionally cutting his eyes to the young girl setting out cookies.

"Well, maybe," Esther said, patting Lou's hand. "You're sure it's *him* you saw?" Unsaid words passed between them, leaving me out of it entirely. Grateful was not close to how I felt.

"I'm going to go," I said to the ladies. I had something better waiting for me, preferably wearing very little. I'd been here for almost two hours, and I wasn't feeling what Esther and Lou were regarding any of these people. Oh, I saw a few things, but none of it was illegal.

After a longer-than-normal round of goodbyes, I made my way down the stone path from their front door to the narrow sidewalk that circled the canals. I was about to call a local pasta place and order a couple of things—light, and to be eaten quickly—when the young teenager who was setting out cookies at the start of the evening, came out of the dark side yard and across the lawn. She crossed in front of me, having not seen me come down the path, and we collided. I grabbed her arms to keep her from falling backwards. Her face was ashen and laced with fear.

"Sorry. You okay?" I asked.

"Yeah, uh...yeah," she whispered, and then stiffened as a man came across the lawn the same way she did, passed us with a mumbled 'goodnight' and headed west along the canal. It was the guy who'd been ogling her earlier.

"You okay?" I repeated as I watched the man retreat down the path that paralleled the canal.

"Yes," she said more forcefully.

"What's your name?" I asked.

"Erin," she said. "Erin Willits."

The Willits girl...

"Don't move." I hopped the short fence surrounding the yard and ran down the sidewalk. I turned the corner, but there was no sight of him. I tried to remember if I saw the wife leave earlier.

I returned to Erin Willits. "Was he bothering you?" I asked.

Her gray eyes were wide and wet. The color returned to her cheeks in a blush that ran down her neck and across her chest. Her honey colored hair was long and straight, her nose perfectly turned up, her chin strong and her body reedy and frail. The large oak tree in the yard shut the moon out completely, making it hard to see anything, the light from the living room window illuminating her face and nothing more.

"N-no. I'm fine."

"Where are your parents? Were they here tonight?"

"Yes, my mom."

"She still inside?"

The girl nodded.

"What were you doing?"

"Nothing."

"Did he follow you outside, or something?"

"No. It's...everything is fine."

I stared at her for a hard moment. This wasn't okay. Wasn't sure why but was damn sure of the what. "Okay, Erin. I'm John."

"I know. I heard your talk."

"If you're in trouble, you find me." I dug into my wallet for a card. "I'm right on the end, there," I said, turning her toward the canal and down east. "You need anything, you call." I handed her my card.

"Thanks," she said, looking at the card. She slipped it into her pocket. "I'm fine, really. Thanks...John."

I watched her go back inside the house. Things were seldom how they seemed. This could be nothing, and it could be something. It could be her, and it could be him. No matter there. She was underage. Not my problem, unfortunately, until someone got hurt or a crime was reported. And, while profiling was not a thing I'd ever admit to, I saw right away he was more 'Arab' than the dirty-blond fellow with the tow-headed toddler. I recalled what Lou Wachley said to me the other night, over cookies and wine:

...I did not like the way he leered at the Willits girl...She was serving coffee for us at the get-to-know-ya—you know the girl, John...And furthermore, I don't like how I never see that pretty wife of his.

Over and done, now, but the dude was officially on my radar. I was also fairly certain he was the guy with the glowing cigarette who took such an interest in the goings-on at my place. His size alone confirmed that for me. I stood on the path outside the producer's home and teetered between spending the evening between Karen's sheets and pursuing this. I did not like this guy, and I wondered how much Erin Willits' mother knew.

"Fuck me," I muttered to no one. I opened the gate and went back inside.

AN HOUR later I was standing outside with Erin and her mother, and I was comforted to see that the mother was as concerned as I was. I gave the usual lecture about not walking around the canals alone at night, and to watch her back coming home from school, etc. And I suggested she not engage him in dialogue—the wife, either.

"It was nothing," Erin Willits assured me for the tenth time. And for the tenth time I concluded she was lying.

I dialed Karen on my way home. "Sorry, babe," I said when she answered. "I got tied up. You starving to death?"

"No, and I was just about to call you. I've been called in. MVA coming in and they're shorthanded. I'm heading to the car now."

"Where are you going?"

"County."

"I'm sorry. You've got a long drive and a long night ahead of you, then."

"Yeah. I'm sorry, too. Not what I would have chosen tonight. How was your thing?"

"Enlightening. I've discovered I liked my neighbors just

fine this morning when I had no idea who they were. Not so much now."

"It's a beautiful day in the neighborhood, a beautiful day for a neighbor. Would you be mine? Could you be mine," the woman sang.

"Yeah, yeah."

"Cheer up, Mr. Rogers. They're lucky to have you."

"You take care tonight, babe. I guess I'll see you in a few days."

Karen sighed. "At the risk of sounding crude, I'd rather not bang one out before I go. I was looking forward to a few languid hours with you." She sounded as disappointed as I felt.

"Languid? Bang? You're an erotic thesaurus, lady blue."

"Well," she sniffed. "I try."

"When do you fly?"

"Seven a.m."

"You gonna make that?"

"We'll see. As you said, it's looking like a long night. I'll call from D.C."

"Right. Safe trip."

"Bye, sweetie," my lady whispered.

There was something keen in being denied what was right there but knowing in a few days you'd have another go at it. It wasn't like we'd never been together, yet it felt like it. I'd been nervous in the way a man who takes pride in his bedroom skills is, knowing that the first time after a long time should be memorable enough to make the lady forget her own name. Lofty goal, but I was up to it. I walked off my frustration and ended up at The Stone.

A few tables were occupied and only two sat at the bar. I didn't know either, and I didn't want to, so I sat on the end, facing the door, like usual. Mac came over.

"Usual?"

"Beer. And a water."

I knew what I could offer Karen Gennaro in a deep way I hadn't six months ago. The woman was wise and independent and spirited, and there was something about my reactive, black-and-white, over-protective ass she liked. She knew me like no other woman, and I knew her. I promised her over drinks that I'd do better this time, and I would. I was grateful she was giving us another try. Truth was, after finding her alone in her clinic with two baby criminals in the backseat of a police cruiser, I'd decided she would have little choice in the matter. And this, ladies and gents, was the side of me I'd vowed to do better with.

Mac set my beer and a glass of ice water in front of me. He leaned in. "You know who Jack Drake is, works outta Foothill?" he said.

"Why the hell would I know anyone outta Foothill?"

"Partnered with Laborteaux outta the Academy. Labby was his TO."

"Okay."

"Drake's partnered with Sebby Castro now."

Sebby Castro was Mason Laborteaux's partner the day Gonzo was killed. "I'm listening."

Mac was a retired cop out of El Paso, and he came here to L.A. to get away from an old-west mentality he couldn't wrap his head around. It was also one that almost got him killed. He's much happier now in the land of fruits and nuts, as he calls our fair city. Mac still had an eye for the job, so shit yes I was listening.

"So, one night last week three from the night shift out of Pacific were here, and Labby's name comes up. One guy who's known Drake a long time starts talkin' about this side gig Labby's got goin' on." Mac straightened up and wiped the bar in front of me, then took it down the length. He stopped in front of two guys and a woman and took their order. Instead of taking a table, they sat, and I knew that was all I'd get, for now. Mason Laborteaux was a long-term project I planned to take my time with, because when that bastard went down, I wanted it to stick—for Mark Gonzales's sake.

Mac brought the second beer over and didn't give me a glance. He needed to be careful, but obviously he thought this was important enough to take the chance. I took a long swallow and watched a tall, slender woman walk in. She stood at the door so her eyes could adjust. I wasn't in the mood. I went back to my beer and checked my phone. Karen would be at County by now, traffic being light at this hour. I didn't expect to hear from her until tomorrow, but I could always hope.

I felt someone sit down next to me. It was the woman.

"John Testarossa?"

"Yeah?" She was familiar. Dark hair cut in what they call a bob, sleek; mixed-race features, Asian mostly; forty. She was overdressed—light pants, slightly darker jacket, white blouse open at the collar. She also wore a gun. "What can I do for you?"

"Let's find out. I'm Dana Torrance."

25

I sat in an empty section of an all-night diner and sipped coffee while we waited for Alex. For a million reasons, I could not have a conversation with Dana Torrance in The Stone, a big reason being she was a cop. But maybe the bigger reason was she was the last of the adults on our victim's list.

"Captain Brennan," Alex said. He stuck out his hand while breathing hard, then glared at me and sat.

"Coffee?" I said, while working through 'Captain Brennan'.

"Yeah," to me. To her, "You took a big chance coming into a cop bar, Dana."

"I know." She looked at me. "Nothing about this is normal."

I stared at Alex the appropriate (I thought) amount of time to give him the chance to explain how he knew her, and why he was calling a Captain II 'Dana', especially when she wasn't *his* Captain II. And when I'd tired of the clinking of his spoon in his cup, I opened my hands in a classic *whatthefuck* gesture and said, "Fill me in?"

"Sorry. Dana and I went through the academy together."

"I was late to this party," she said. "I wanted to be a lawyer, I was studying to be a lawyer. And then one day I came home and told my husband..."

"Brennan," I guessed.

"Michael Brennan, yes. I told Michael I couldn't do it anymore. I told him I was going into the police academy."

"Funny, considering Mike's a firearms instructor at the Academy," said Alex.

"Anyway...I was a little older than the other recruits, but Alex was always a nice companion on those hot days on the track."

Alex laughed and nodded.

"I became a cop so I could hunt the bastard down," she said. "I became obsessed, and it about died out when I found out about your case." Dana Brennan stared into her cup, then looked at me. "My career could be called into question if that were overheard, or repeated."

"We're not looking to trip you up, Captain..."

"Dana. I think we're growing closer by the minute here, don't you, John?"

"Okay." I looked at Alex. "I'm not sure how to proceed."

"My name is on a list of victims who were abducted as children, and some of the girls on that list are turning up dead. Am I up to speed?" she said.

"Yes. The three murders we're investigating..."

"Names."

"Josie Schuyler, Clarissa Sparks and Annie Smythe... Reynolds was her name at time of death."

"And they were all abducted, molested for four days, and then released," she finished

"Yes. It looks like the other thing they have in common is

that their lives weren't too productive, and they were all in pretty vulnerable positions when they were killed."

"Give me examples."

"Josie Schuyler was in and out of rehab, had a record for solicitation. But she was in a group home and seemed to be getting things together. We also have another victim, a transient, and his DNA was under her fingernails. He didn't kill her."

"How do you know?"

"He died first."

"How about the others?"

"Clarissa Sparks was a sixteen-year-old prostitute, a runaway. Annie Smythe-Reynolds was a meth addict with an equally addicted man in her life, and two children. The man, her husband, has been cleared. Lots of shit that's not good leading up to all that." I also told her about Kristen Holmes and Rebecca Daly.

"Killer's MO?"

"Vics sexually assaulted, possibly with objects, COD strangulation with ligature—the victim's underwear."

"In every case?"

"In every case."

"Evidence? Hair, fibers, anything?"

"No."

"You won't find it, either. The man has alopecia."

"Excuse me?"

"Alopecia. It's a condition where the sufferer loses all hair. All of it. He was wearing a wig and he had facial hair he must have purchased from a party store when he took me, but for those four days he was bare as a newborn. I will never forget it."

"Were you able to describe him to police?"

"Yes." She was quiet for a moment. "I can give you information enough so you can find that police report and you'll find out everything that happened to me. This is where the rubber meets the road. I can lay low and insist you keep my information between the two of you, or I can come forward. In my position I can advocate for the others; or, I can compromise my career." She was quiet while she tended to her coffee. "How many are still alive?"

"Six, including you. One, maybe two, are still minors."

"Christ. So, the sonofabitch is still at it."

"Yeah."

She tossed her spoon on the table. "He's taking some sort of moral high ground now with his 'girls'—he's punishing them for the shitty lives they've led, thanks to him. That part, of course, is lost on him."

"We're thinking the same."

Dana Brennan reached into her purse. I saw the .22 tucked neatly into the corner for easy access. She pulled out a pen and paper, and in less than a minute I had her full name and address at the time of her abduction, and her social security number.

"Read the report. I need a day to think about how to handle this and I need to talk to Michael."

"I understand. We'll also send over a sketch of the guy, based on information another victim gave us."

"All right." She stood and so did we.

"You're a tough broad, Captain Brennan," I said.

"I'm not. I'm an angry broad. I need a day or two to put that away and get tough." She looked from Alex to me. "Get this fucker. I want him before I retire."

We sat and ordered more coffee. "I'd like to protect her name as much as possible," I said.

"Me, too, unless she wants to come forward, like she said."

"Women have enough trouble getting into the supervisory ranks without this kind of thing hanging over them."

"I think she knows that, John, and if she decides to go public, then she'll handle the fallout. Like you said, she's tough, no matter what else she says." He rattled the spoon around his cup. "And another thing: how the hell did she know you were at The Stone. She's the CO out of Foothill division."

"I don't know. I was wondering the same. Foothill, you said?"

"Yeah. Why?"

"Mac started jawing about Laborteaux and someone from Foothill, but he couldn't finish, mostly because she walked in."

"Fuckin' cockroach will not die, and people keep trying to help you let him not die."

"Don't worry about it."

Alex drained his cup and placed his hand over the rim when the waitress came by to refill it. "We got two women who chose professions so they could find closure in their own way," he said. "One wanted to connect with the other victims, and the other wants to find the asshole who ruined her life."

"Yeah, both of them balls-to-the-wall survivors, too."

"Not good, Johnny. We don't need these women interfering."

"Now you're talking, pal."

"I saw your point before."

"You're attracted to Grace Dashiell."

He got quiet. "Yes, I am," he finally said. "Never happened to me before. Never. I've never gone out on Lisa—never wanted to. This is foreign territory for me, *güey*."

I'd known Alex for ten years, and in that time our

conversations rarely got personal. When they did it was two words out of him, and twenty-two hundred out of me. He'd said quite a bit in the few he'd just uttered.

"Let me have this. Let me just...sit with this a while," he said. "It feels good."

"Lisa's like a fuckin' sister to me," I reminded.

"Yeah." He set down some dollars and we walked to the parking lot. He turned to me before getting into his car. "Small fuckin' world, huh?"

I looked around, wondering where Dana Torrance, nee Brennan was now. Talking to Mike? Taking a drive? Loading her .22, pulling out the vodka, and getting good and comfortable? Cop as victim. Cop as victim and the CO at Foothill. Mac at The Stone, talking about cops at Foothill. Laborteaux, partners of Laborteaux, talking heads who know both in drunk conversation at a cop bar, where the ears all have eyes, and vice versa. The world was indeed one small fucking place. I had work to do. So much fucking work to do.

"You'd think that'd make our job easier, wouldn't you?"

"You mean our job ain't easy?"

I laughed at that. "Night, Alex."

———

WITH THE INFORMATION Dana Brennan gave us, and after a lot of archival digging, I located the file on her abduction, back in 1989. I also found Annie Smythe's file. I dug a little further, and soon I had the file of Grace Dashiell in my hand. The first three abductions, as far as we knew.

"I want to compare what these three said against what our three latest victims had to say. We have ..." I paused to consult the list still posted on the white board. "...twenty-nine years between the first known abduction and the last."

"Good idea," Alex said, opening the file on Grace Dashiell. Okay, I'll give him that. I took Dana Torrance. "Twenty-nine years," he noted.

"Molesters can go unchecked for a long time," I said.

"I know. But he's not molesting anymore. He's killing. Why?"

I shook my head as I read the report taken when Dana Torrance, age ten, was returned after she went missing for four days. "Jesus."

"What?"

"Same things. The smell, the burning eyes." I read on. "The strangulation that stopped just before she passes out, then she's allowed to go home. Quote, 'He told me I was a good girl and said he'd take me home'. Question, 'Where did he drop you off?' Answer, 'In the park. I walked home'. Interviewer asks which park. She answers and he says, 'That's over two miles from your house. How did you get home?' Answer, 'He told me how to go.' So, he's a friendly molester."

"Listen to this," Alex said. "From Grace Dashiell's interview: 'He said my name. He knew me. He said he knew my father and said if my father knew what I was doing with him, he would be mad at me'."

"So, maybe Grace was right; it was the same man who worked for her family when she was younger."

"We can check the other interviews, see if he pulled that with the other girls," Alex said. "That's one way that molesters get kids to go with them, right? 'Your mom's been in an accident. You need to come with me'."

"Yeah. Trust in familiarity." I read through every word of Dana Torrance's interview with police after she was found.

In this case, it was Ventura Co. Sheriff's Department who took this case. For a traumatized little girl, she gave them an incredible amount of information. Of all the cases, hers was investigated most aggressively. I understood that. The more you had to go on, the more invested a cop stayed.

"You know, Alex, I think part of the reason why we don't have consistency here is because some of these abduction cases were handled through LAPD and some through Ventura County Sheriff's Department. Like, no one was taking responsibility for jurisdiction in that particular area. Maybe that's how this guy went unchecked for so long."

He looked up from the file. "And who would know that and take advantage of that fact?" he asked.

"I said it before, and you almost swooned."

"Say it again."

"A cop—or someone with a good working knowledge of cops. Better?"

"Not really."

I read through Annie Smythe's file. Same MO, much the same story as the others. "Not a word about a uniform, or a badge, or weapons. If our guy was a cop, wouldn't he dress the part? Easier to lure a kid into a car if you're dressed like a cop, no?"

"Even if he wasn't a cop, it's not hard to get a uniform, at least one good enough to fool a kid."

"Okay, so he didn't need the props to get a child into his car. In Jane Dobson's case, it was a puppy. In Dana Torrance's case, he simply drove up and lifted her into the truck. By the way, she describes the same blue truck."

"Hey."

It was Alex's tone that brought my eyes to his.

"Grace says that while she was being held, there was another girl." He looked at me, then went back to reading.

"She says, quote, 'She looked a little like me, but my skin is darker. She had the same hair as me'. Interviewer asks, 'How old was the girl?' Grace says, 'Older. She had...these'. Interviewer notes victim touches her chest. 'She had breasts?' the interviewer asks. 'Yes. She was Bobby's age.' Interviewer notes that Bobby is Bobby Dashiell, victim's brother, who is sixteen. Asked, 'Was this girl being kept against her will?' Answered, 'No. She left and came back. She knew my name, too. She was nice to me.' What the hell, John?" Alex had the phone to his ear and was dialing Grace when my cell phone vibrated across my desk. It was Karen. I got up and stepped into the hall.

"Hey, sweetheart."

"Good morning."

"You sound beat. When did you get home?"

"About four. I'm on a flight at three this afternoon. I'll get into D.C. at about eleven-thirty."

"When's your gig?"

"Tomorrow night. I'll sleep in."

"Good. How did it go last night?"

"Rough." She sighed. "Three of the six brought in were DOA, and I lost one in the OR."

"Aw, baby..."

"Yeah. How's your day going?"

"Busy, but better than yours. Nothing but live bodies today."

"I'll let you go. I just wanted to hear your voice."

"Thank you. Made my day, babe."

"Call Jada if you can't reach me. I'll be home Thursday."

"We'll get together then."

"Yes. Bye, darling."

Alex was off the phone when I came back in. "Grace said

she has no idea what I was talking about and doesn't remember telling the interviewer about a girl."

"Shit."

"I know. She said not to lose hope. She remembered about the guy when she was three or four..." Alex paused.

"What?"

"Hang on." He picked up the phone, asked for Grace again, and started talking as soon as she came on.

"Grace, when this guy was working for your family... remember? Well, did he have a child with him, a daughter... someone?" Alex paused. "Yeah...was there another girl, a friend, older than you..." Alex pulled the file toward him and read. I had an idea where he was going.

"...she could have been eight or nine at the time?" Pause. "Another girl, a visitor, a friend...came and went, like this man did..." Alex's eyes got wide as he listened to Grace talk. Then he banged his hand down on his desk. "Yeah...yes. You told police that this girl at the house where you were kept was 'Bobby's age'...your brother, right? Sixteen. Well, if this was the same girl with the man who worked at your house, she'd have been eight or nine at that time. You remember her." He listened. "Okay. Okay, that's fine." After another five minutes or so, Alex wrapped it up. "Thank you, sweetheart. You did good. Real good." He hung up the phone and sat on the edge of his desk.

"There was a girl. Only came a couple of times, Grace said they used to play the 'hiding game'. Said this girl told her that every time Branch was around, to go hide. The girl taught her how to hide from him. She'd say, 'No matter what, don't let him find you.' That girl, five years later, was at the house where Grace was kept."

"She was trying to protect Grace back then. What the hell happened five years later? How does this sixteen-year-old girl go in and out of a house where a child is being held against her will, and not get help?"

"John, you know how trauma and abuse works. How many captive people go in and out of society every day and don't say a word to anyone, or ask for help, or run off, and instead return to their captor? And if you're sixteen, and scared? Or you're sixteen, and this guy means something to you and you don't want to see him get into trouble, you try to help the victim, maybe, but you don't fucking tell."

"Who was it?"

"Well, if the guy at the time was eighteen or twenty, and the girl was ten years younger, it's not a daughter."

"Sister?"

He shook his head. "Grace said she thought the guy called her Betty. Or Benny."

"Okay. That's good, Alex. That's good.

"Felt good."

"Yeah...sweetheart."

"Bite me."

26

"So, I think I found your BJ," Preston McConnell announced.

"And before I've had coffee, Preston. That's impressive."

"No. BJ Mardigan." And then he laughed as the whole joke came together for him.

"Go ahead, kid. I'm listening."

"Okay, so I searched BJ Mardigan, and I came up with a few hits, naturally."

"Naturally, given a name like Mardigan," Alex said.

"So, I tapped in to the DMV database..."

"Uh..." I straightened up and held my hand up like a traffic cop. "You what?"

"No good?" he asked with all the innocence of a baby scorpion. I was gaining new respect for this boy.

"After this, you and I are going to have a chat about what we do and do not need to know, okay, Preston?"

"Yes, sir. I'd like that. Anyway, my research uncovered that BJ Mardigan was the legal registrant of the 1978 Ford F-150, license plate XJA 665, and that the registration expired in 2002. I traced the name via SSN..."

"SSN," I muttered to Alex.

"...and found out that BJ Mardigan also goes by the name BJ Shay, and she is the current owner of a 2011 F-150..."

"Brand loyalty; that's good."

"...white..."

"Okay, Preston. I don't need the rundown. Your notes are impeccable."

"Thank you."

"So, BJ Shay..."

"Right, aka Beverly Shay and Beverly Jean Shay."

I looked at Alex. "Okay."

"And the clouds part," said Alex.

"What? Whaddya mean? What am I missing?" asked Preston, desperate to be kept in the loop.

"She's tied into this somehow," I said.

"Explains Henry McLaren's involvement. Gimme Shelter."

"It doesn't explain, it..."

"Gets us into the neighborhood," Alex said.

"I'll take that."

"Hey. What's going on?" Preston whined.

"Preston, are you sure you want to go off to that fancy school with all those nerds?"

"Uh, Detective Testarossa...I'm one of those nerds."

"We need you, Preston, but I understand. You go off and do. But don't forget us while you're holed up in some underground bunker at MIT developing the next spy satellite, huh?"

"I won't. Can I go with you to hunt this BJ down?"

"No," we both almost shouted. It turned heads in the hall all the same.

I sent Preston off to search Branch Mardigan and Branch

Shay, taking the chance that he and Beverly somehow shared the same name. After some more digging, we found out that Beverly Shay, aka BJ Mardigan, aka B. Shay, studied at Pierce College and CSUN, got a degree in social work, and then worked for the city as a case worker from 1983 to September 1995.

"Look at the list, Alex," I said, pointing up at his handiwork on the whiteboard. "We have a break in the abductions from 1989, when Dana Torrance was abducted, to 1991 when Annie Smythe was taken."

"Beverly Shay was working for the city during that time," he said, "And she was still a case worker in ninety-five when Jane Dobson was abducted. Then nothing again until Brenna Delacroix in ninety-eight."

"Breaks happen all the time," I pointed out. "Marriage, job, jail time."

"Or a job with the city."

I thought about that for a moment. "So, she takes a week off and snags Annie Smythe for four days then goes back to work?"

"She's not our molester."

"Maybe not when she was sixteen, when Grace Dashiell was in a house getting raped for four days. She was in and out, living her fuckin' life, but right then she wasn't molesting little girls, no." I pulled the file on Emily Knox, who was eighteen now, and Jade Warren, who was twelve. We hadn't talked to them yet. We wanted to make do with what we had in the files regarding their abductions. No reason just yet to bring them into this.

"Both girls describe a man, the smell, the underwear tied around the neck, being released after four days...it's all the same. Beverly Shay isn't molesting kids."

"But she has access to those who were molested, based on her career as a case worker, doesn't she?" Alex said.

"A caseworker would get involved if there was follow-up after an arrest or removal from the home because of abuse, or if the kid was a runaway…"

"Nothing to follow up on, no way or reason to follow up if the girls went on to live their lives with no trouble—like Dana Torrance, Grace Dashiell and Jane Dobson," he noted.

"Right, and very easy to have access to records, including addresses, if the girls are getting arrested or running away as juveniles. So, why kill them, Alex? She's not molesting these girls; we've established that. What motive does Beverly Shay have for killing girls who have already been victimized once?"

"Maybe she's not. Maybe she's talking about them with the killer," he said.

"Let's ask."

IT WAS a quiet day for a Friday on the Walk. A breeze blew, and noises from the shops along the stretch between the basketball courts and the end of the walk, where t-shirt shops gave way to cafes and courtyards, mingled into a long chorus of slow talk and Billboard-100 pop. Tourists, normally out people-watching or t-shirt-buying were elsewhere. Two patrol cars were standing by as backup, one stationed behind Gimme Shelter. We had no idea what we had with Beverly Shay, but we were going to question her today—either where she stood, or in our house.

As we approached Gimme Shelter, the normal group of displaced persons who mingled outside the squat building was elsewhere, too. The area was usually crowded with people, between the shelter, Phoenix House—a place for recovering addicts—and a voucher hotel, where a lot of transients stayed for a night, or a year, depending. Today, the area was deserted. As we approached, we could see why. Gimme Shelter was locked, and a steel gate had been pulled across the door. Over the ROVER, the Adam car announced code 6—they were in place and standing by.

"Okay," Alex said, staring at the gate over the door.

"All of a sudden?" I put in.

"No. Not all of a sudden." Alex turned from the building and worked a 360 of the area. I did likewise while I spoke into the ROVER.

"Fourteen-William, copy, show us code 4, shelter closed and locked, POI unaccounted for." I snapped off the ROVER. "Fuck." Homeless people blended in, some resting under palm trees, others shuffling along the sand beyond the Walk. A hundred feet down, and clustered around a cement table under a wood overhang, a group of homeless men stared, then averted their gaze once we took notice. I headed in their direction. Three stood and headed toward the water, wanting no part of us. The others stayed, their remaining brain cells unable to fire rapidly enough to tell them to get the hell outta Dodge.

"Hey," I said when I got to within twenty feet of the group.

"Hey, there, Captain," one said. He was bald as a Bocce ball and wore a woman's bathrobe. His face was scarlet from too much sun and not enough vegetables, and his red eyes advertised recent use of something mind-altering.

"Hi, there. What's your name, pal?"

"Seymour. Uh...Yeah. Seymour."

"Seymour, you know about the shelter over there? Why isn't it open?"

"Beats me. I tried to get in last night and it was...it was closed...closed up..." Seymour stared at his fingers, then spoke to an imaginary friend next to him. "Closed up tight," he finished.

"Since last night?"

"Yeah," another man said. He looked drunk, but in fairly good condition otherwise. He also looked about sixteen. "I tried to get in last night, too. Afternoon, maybe. Fuck, yeah."

"Your name?" I asked.

"Who's askin'?"

I pulled out my badge. "This guy."

"Sky," he said.

"Nice. Anyone see anything, see anyone leave... anything?" They all shook their heads. I tried to make eye contact with each of them. "You all have somewhere to go tonight? Supposed to rain." They all mumbled something about being okay, thanks. I gave them all one more stare-down, then turned to go. We got a few steps away when I heard, "Hey. You Simple Man?"

I turned to face a large black man with a graying beard. His equally gray hair stuck out of a brown bowler hat. Light khakis that were fairly clean hung on thin hips, and a blue LA Dodgers hoodie clung too-tight to an extended belly.

"You friends with Tree Top, yeah?" he continued.

"Yes. You are?"

"Jenner." He turned around to see if his pals were taking notice of his sudden defection, and when he felt safe, he turned back to us and started walking in the direction of the cafes and courtyards. We followed.

Jenner sat at a wooden table outside a frozen yogurt shop sipping a cup of coffee and munching on a blueberry muffin. A pack of Starbursts, already half gone, lay open next to the muffin. All, thanks to us.

"Somethin's up with that damn place," he said between bites of muffin. Juice from the Starbursts dribbled out of his mouth, and he wiped as he alternated between the coffee, the muffin and the candy.

"The shelter, you mean?" I asked.

"Yeah, the shelter. Too much shit, and it stinks."

Alex sat. "You wanna elaborate for us, Jenner?"

"Look," he said, coming up from his coffee for a minute. "It's different out here. We look out for each other, and we don't talk, you get me? I've been out here with these people off and on for years, and for the most part, I've felt safe. But somethin's not right lately...no, not lately. For a long fuckin' time." We waited and watched Jenner work his food: A two second sip of coffee, followed by a small piece of muffin that he tore off with his fingers clockwise from where he'd torn off the last piece, followed by a small bite of a Starburst. He finished each piece in three bites, then opened another and laid it on the wrapper, then he moved on to the coffee. And so it went.

"When were those bad fires in Malibu, how long ago?" he asked.

"Last August," Alex said, looking to me for confirmation. A nod gave it to him.

"Yeah. Well, that's when things got strange."

"How so?" I asked. I had to wait until he'd unwrapped another piece of candy—green this time—and laid it out like an offering to himself.

"First, a gal named Orliss turns up dead, under one of the lifeguard towers. Now, she never bothered no one. A few of us shared her, and she whored for drugs near the pier. A bunch of us think that maybe the wrong trick got to her, you know? So, cops come sniffin', but that ends quick because who cares about a black whore in Venice? Problem with

Orliss is she's a nosey bitch, and before she goes the way of the not-breathing, she tells a few of us that this new cracker hangin' around is a bad motherfucker. Only comes out at night, that kind of shit. Then another sand camper loses life. Wanna know why?"

"Sure."

"Knew too much." Jenner took a too-big bite of the lime Starburst and realized there was no way he'd get three out of the tiny square, so he swore and tossed it over his shoulder. He stared at his carefully planned meal, grunted, and carried on. "And the too much these people knew, and know, is too fuckin' much. Ain't good, Sipowicz. Aint good at all."

"And what is it that everyone knows?" I asked.

"Huh...no. I say, I'm next, you know? I will say this: it ain't over. Check your files. Tree Top been talkin', and I told him to zip it."

"Talking to who?"

"To too many. He knows some things too, but sometimes that tall fool gets confused. Like, he thinks that little girl used to sell the jewelry was on to something."

"Josie Schuyler?"

"Little Asian chick. Don't know her name."

"The sand camper you mention, the one who knew too much. His name Henry McLaren?"

Jenner took the last sip of coffee, tipping it to get the last drop, then ate the last bite of muffin. He finally turned to the light pink third of the last Starburst in the package, laid out on the wrapper. He stared at it, then popped the candy into his mouth. "You might know too much, yourself, Simple Man. Careful with that."

"It's my job to know more than the others, Jenner."

"Well, anyway..." Jenner stood, gathered his trash,

walked two steps to the trashcan, and disposed of his garbage. "Thanks for the snack."

"Hey, Jenner," I called to him as he walked away. The man turned. "What does this bad motherfucker look like?"

Jenner tossed his head back and laughed hard. Hands rested on narrow hips as he looked out past the trees and the skaters and the tourists. He stared at the clear blue Pacific as the sun began to sink toward night. Off in the distance, Bob Marley sang about crying women and sharing a single bed. Someone upwind was smoking a joint. A couple argued in Spanish as they sat at a mesh table eating chilidogs. Jenner's bowler hat sat askew on his head. A stain began to spread at the front of his pants.

"Jesus," he whispered, turning to me. "Sombitch looks just like Jesus, man."

27

*A*fter questioning people inside Phoenix House and The El Dorado, the voucher hotel, about any odd comings and goings at the shelter—and Beverly Shay in particular—I updated the BOLO I'd put out on Beverly Mardigan Shay and the white F-150 registered to her. Alex and I sat on a low wall as the sun set over the Pacific.

"And we're back to Jesus."

"Beverly Shay is Jesus-ish," Alex said.

"Be serious. Beverly Shay is the girl Grace saw in that house, and at her own when she was three," I said. "Bevy."

"Not Betty or Benny."

"Nope. Bevy. So, who is she protecting?"

"I'd say someone with Alopecia."

"Last I checked, Jesus didn't have it. Fuckin' hair for days."

"Uh huh," he said. "But looking like him would allow this fucker to hide in plain sight. Why did Bev Shay leave social work, do you think?"

"To open a shelter. So she could keep an eye on him."

"And why become a social worker in the first place?"

It took me a minute. "To keep an eye on the girls."

"Beverly Shay tried to protect Grace Dashiell all those years ago when she taught her how to hide from Branch," Alex said. "And she was there eight years later when the sonofabitch grabbed Grace."

"There was nothing she could do about it."

"Yeah, but she sure as shit can now."

In police jackets, armed with wire and bolt cutters, battering rams and guns drawn, we entered Gimme Shelter at two a.m. We pulled files and records, hoping we'd find something that would give us a clue who Beverly Shay was, and more importantly, who Branch Mardigan was.

WE WERE ALL BACK at it early, after the two-a.m. raid on the shelter. What we found in the shelter didn't yield much more than what we already had. There was nothing personal in or around Beverly Shay's office to indicate she had a family, or friends. No invitations to parties she forgot to toss, no pictures of brothers, sisters, husbands or kids. Not that everyone had, or needed those things, but still. It was odd.

"They're brother and sister," Preston boomed, still in the hallway, as I was taking my first sip of coffee. I dribbled.

"Goddammit, Preston."

"Sorry. Siblings. Beverly and Branch are siblings. Look at this: she put him as a contact on her application for college in 1989. After that there was no mention of him on anything she filled out or filed—from what I could find."

"Breathe, Preston," I said, taking the cream-colored file out of his hand. "And sit down. You've earned it."

"Thanks."

"So, Branch Mardigan worked at LGS Labs, a private forensics lab, from 1990 to 2005," I said as I looked up at the list on the whiteboard. "That was after Dana Torrance."

"She gave police a ton of information after she returned home," Alex said.

"And he decided to hone his evasion skills because, I bet after her, the cops came damn close to finding him." I kept reading. "You know, he was working for this company when DNA tracing was still cutting-edge. He learned right along with everyone else, including what worked and what didn't. He got better, right along with the science."

"When did he leave the company?" Alex asked.

"Two-thousand-five, when Josie Schuyler was abducted. Then no abductions again until oh-eight, and then two again in oh-eleven."

"Odd breaks."

"Again, criminals take breaks. And sometimes what looks like a break to us is simply a change in MO or location."

"This forensics company still around?" he asked.

"Check on that, will you, Preston?"

"Sure." He slammed his fingers across his laptop keyboard while I talked some more.

"Bottom line, this guy looks like Jesus, the folks around the shelter seem to think he's hinkey. Makes sense he's hanging around the shelter. The sister can keep her eye on him..."

"And fail."

"But what happened with Henry McLaren?" I said.

"Maybe he got too close, knew too much. That's what Jenner said."

"Yeah. I worry about Tree Top now. Maybe I'll take a walk tonight."

"Careful, *güey*."

"Yeah. And Karen's coming home."

"Huh, let's see: take a walk to look for nutty Tree Top, or have some wine and woo-woo with the lady love. Hmmm."

"Woo-woo? What are you, five? And I can do both."

"Good luck to you, jackass."

Preston spoke. "Company's out of business, it looks like, Detective."

"You're a star, kid. How much longer do we have you, again?"

"August. Maybe I'll take another gap year, stay here."

"No, you don't. Come back to us summers and holidays, buddy. You gotta learn to keep the enthusiasm to a minimum, though. That shit works Mrs. Armstrong's last nerve. And you'd better not be looking at porn."

"Uh...what?"

Alex chuckled. "T, leave the kid alone. You'll give him ideas."

Preston stood. "Just so you know, the mainframe logs your IP address, your location, and your sign-on and password the second you enter a porn sight, and after it sends all your information to the tech people, who will pass it right on to your boss, it will lock you out of the computer."

"Good to know. How'd you find that out?"

"I wrote the program."

KAREN WAS SCHEDULED to land at eight p.m., but I knew she was looking into an early flight out of D.C. We'd both been so busy that we hadn't talked except through text since she flew out earlier in the week. After taking my promised stroll down the Boardwalk and not finding Tree Top, I went home, changed out of the suit and into jeans and a sweater, grabbed a nice bottle of Amarone and headed to Karen's. I stopped at the store below her place and picked up two-dozen fresh clams, clam juice, fresh herbs, a leek, some fresh garlic, an inexpensive bottle of white, and a pound of linguini. If she was home, great. I'd seduce her with food. If she wasn't, I'd get it half done and we'd eat...whenever.

I parked in a visitor's spot and entered the lobby. The security guy wasn't at the front half-moon counter where he's usually stationed. Six months ago, that guy's name was Billy. I had no idea who was in charge of keeping everyone safe in this place now.

I took the elevator to the 19th floor, Penthouse. Her place was on a corner with city as well as marina and ocean views. I walked down a short hallway and turned the corner toward Karen's. Billy was no longer missing. He was standing outside Karen's door with the concierge, a guy named Rocky. Both men I'd gotten to know well when Karen and I were together during what I like to call Round One.

"Hey, guys," I said, waving my bag of groceries. Karen's face peered around the doorframe.

"Johnny." Breathy, and not in a good way. The demeanor of the two men outside her door communicated that this was not a casual call-upon.

"Everything is fine, gentlemen," Karen said, but I knew better.

"Detective Testarossa," Billy greeted. "Good to see you again, sir." He stuck out his hand, seemed glad I was there. I gave it a few pumps and then took Rocky's. All of this killed just enough time for me to see Karen raise her eyes to the heavens and turn pale. It also gave me a chance to peek through her door.

"Oh, fuck no. Really?" I pushed past Karen and set my groceries on a side table in the foyer. Adam Shapiro blocked the end of the short hallway into the living room.

"John," Karen said behind me.

I ignored her and stared Shapiro down. He had the good sense not to get cocky. "I'm guessing it's time for you to leave," I said.

"I don't think so," he said.

"Rethink."

Shapiro looked around me and addressed Karen. "Is that what you want, Karen?"

I wanted to hear the answer, too. I turned around and met her eyes. Scared, angry, embarrassed. It was all there.

"Yes," she whispered.

"Big mistake." Shapiro snatched up his keys and brushed past me. Touching me—even a little—was a bigger one. I grabbed him by the front of his shirt and slammed him against the short wall outside the kitchen. A picture fell to the floor and the glass shattered. In an instant Billy and Rocky were on me.

"He's not worth it," one of them said.

"I see you near her again," I hissed into his face, "and I'll kill you. You hear me? I'll fucking kill you. Threaten her again, or admire her from afar, and I'll do it slow."

As any good cop knows, threatening to kill someone, even if the threat is an idle one, doesn't bode well if the threatened turns up dead. I'd just said a whole lot of bad in front of three people. With all that legal knowledge sitting in my head, I still didn't care.

I slammed him against the wall again and hauled him through the door and into the hallway. I turned back to Karen.

"Get inside and don't move." I shoved Shapiro down the

hall, with Billy and Rocky following. When the elevator came, I didn't get any gentler.

"There are cameras in here," Shapiro informed. He should know—he built the damn place. In a city this size she couldn't manage to get farther away from this asshole? I stared at the descending numbers until the doors opened again. I showed him the way out via a three-person escort through the door and into his car. I noted the make, model and license plate in case I felt the need to chat with him again. After he peeled out, I turned to the two men, both built like tanks, but neither, it appeared, was watching the store.

"How the fuck did he get in, boys?"

"He came, asked for her, I called, she gave the okay to send him up," Billy said.

"Great."

"You know he built this place," Rocky said.

"Yeah. So?"

"Well, I'm just sayin' Gives him access and all that."

"No, Rock, it doesn't. You treat him the same as everyone else who comes through here."

"Yeah, well…"

"What were you two doing up there just now?" I asked.

"Someone on eighteen complained of shouting coming from the balcony above them—Doctor Gennaro's place," Billy said.

"Great. And she was trying to convince you all was well."

"Yeah. Uh, something else: she was gone earlier this week…"

"I know."

"Well, Mr. Shapiro came by, said he was watching her place while she was gone."

"So, you let him up."

"I let him up," Billy said.

"Why?" I asked. "Wouldn't Karen have told you if that was the case?"

"Probably."

"What aren't you telling me?" I said.

Billy looked at Rocky, who shrugged. "He, uh..." Billy blew out a big breath. "He has something on me."

"Of course he does. What?"

"About a month ago I was, uh, not manning my post and someone got up, went floor by floor and robbed a bunch of places. You'd be shocked at how many people leave their doors unlocked..."

"Because you're here, protecting the fuckin' world," I said.

"Yeah. Anyway..."

"He found a way to get the surveillance video so you wouldn't be seen...*not here*," I guessed.

"Something like that."

"So, you endangered someone I care about, as well as all her neighbors, because you were, what, getting a blow job from the Chunky Chicken delivery girl?"

"It wasn't like that, but, still...I wasn't here, and I should have been."

"Damn right. And, where were you?" I asked Rocky.

"With him. We were involved in a personal matter with another tenant."

"Look, you two clowns: I don't care what the fuck you were involved in. This is not good. I've got a problem now, and it's one the two of you are familiar with." Both men knew of my history with Shapiro.

"Okay, you're right," Billy said. "It's all bad. I'm going to management tomorrow. I'm not going to be that fuckin' guy's bitch, that's for sure."

"You'd rather be mine?" I stared at the two men, decent guys who felt the need, for whatever reason, to abandon their posts resulting in bad all around. I'd find out another time what the hell was so important that they both had to help out on this 'personal matter' allowing a crime to be committed; and it could have been so much worse.

"Sure," they both said.

"Okay. You don't go to anyone. It's over and done with. But the lady in nineteen-ten becomes your life, as of right now. She is your priority."

"But how...?"

"You'll figure it out. You find another way to be everyone else's special helper, but you are her server and protector from now on. And I want to know whenever Shapiro shows up. I don't need you calling me every time the woman breaks a nail, but I want to know about him." I pointed out the glass doors to the underground parking. "And I want her moved to that parking spot right there," referring to the tandem space right outside the glass doors, where she could be seen coming and going. A white Tesla was occupying the spot at the moment.

"That space belongs to..."

"I don't care. Find a way."

Billy closed his eyes and nodded. "Is that it?"

"Yes. Not so bad, right?"

"What do I do about Shapiro?"

"You deny him access to her place, no matter what. If she's home and he asks you to call up and announce him, hold your goddamn finger on the hang-up button and lie your ass off. She is not home to him, not ever. Then you call me. He gives you any trouble about the other stuff, call me."

"Okay, Detective."

"We're old friends now, kid. Call me John." Billy rolled

his eyes and huffed out another breath. "Figure out a way to get the guys on the first shift up to speed on this."

"How do I do that?"

"Not my problem."

"Shit."

"Yeah, shit. You like working here?" Billy nodded. "You?" I asked Rocky. He nodded, too.

"Then you'll figure all this out. Please understand, boys: you don't want to cross me up on this. Shapiro will be like dealing with your sweet Aunt Sally compared to me. Got me?"

"Yeah," they said.

"Put Karen at risk again, *ever*, and you'll answer to me, and I'm a hell of a lot more dangerous than Adam Shapiro is."

"I get it."

I looked at Rocky. "Me, too," he said.

"Good." I started toward the elevators. I was far from finished with this woman.

28

I took the elevator up to nineteen and walked through Karen's unlocked door. The kitchen light, on when I first arrived, was off. A lamp in the living room was the only light burning.

"Karen?" I moved through her place, starting with the master. The white capris and blue sleeveless top she'd had on earlier were spread neatly on her made bed. "Gennaro!" I searched the living room and moved to the kitchen. The groceries I'd brought were still on the side table in the foyer. The kitchen was clean and unoccupied. I strode down the hall to the guest bedroom and bathroom. No sign of her.

The French doors to the balcony off the living room were unlocked. The balcony lights were on. No Karen.

"Goddammit!" I leaned on the balcony and wondered how long I would sit here like an asshole and wait for her to come back. Leaving, walking away, going home was the best thing I could do for myself, and her. If she'd had an explanation worth hearing, she would have stuck around and offered it to me. Instead, she ran off like a guilty child.

She gave the okay so I sent him up.

"Yeah. Great," I said to the cool night air. I went inside, stepped behind the small half-circle bar tucked into the corner of the spacious living room, and poured myself a Balvenie, neat. The gray micro suede couches of six months ago had been replaced with deep red leather, oversized and overstuffed. The square coffee table was heavy black granite. A tall red vase sat in the middle, filled with a dozen white roses. Squat lamps with black glass bases and white oval shades rested on glass end tables. Glass and metal sculptures on black columns were tucked into corners throughout the room. A tall white vase with red roses sat in the middle of the black granite dining table, which was the only item in the room she had not replaced—probably because it couldn't be lifted.

"Love what you've done with the place, sweetheart." I refilled my glass and took it outside. The night was cool, the marina bright with lights and motion on a rare, fogless evening. Voices echoed up from somewhere below—an argument through an open window. Happened a lot here, apparently.

Doctor Gennaro was gone earlier this week, and he came by, said he was watching her place while she was gone.

And you let him up.

I let him up.

"Yeah, man. You did, Billy-Boy," I said out loud. In addition to all the other shit I had to think about, I hadn't stopped obsessing over what the hell Shapiro was doing up here when she wasn't home. I knew this much. No matter where Karen was right now, she would not be staying here tonight. Cameras, listening devices...I put nothing past the motherfucker.

The pool, eight stories below, shimmered with movement as a lone figure glided through the water. The outdoor area, illuminated by strategically placed lights in yellow, green and blue, was the water worshipper's only audience— or so he, or *she*, thought. Half the complex was witness to the smooth, sleek movements of a body in motion. The swimmer reached the far edge of the pool, stood and turned around. Elbows rested behind a slender body on the edge of the pool, head thrown back, breasts thrust out, white tank suit shining like a beacon under the moody lighting of the pool area. Even from eleven stories up, I knew it was her.

"Good to see you, lady blue." I went inside and rinsed my glass in the sink. I went into her bedroom and folded the clothes on her bed, chose an outfit in case she had to work tomorrow, including under garments, and shoved it all into a bag I found in her closet. I grabbed what appeared to be her face paints as well as other shit off her vanity and stuck that in the bag, too. The woman was stuck with what I chose, and she sure as hell wouldn't be coming back here until I had the place scoured for electronics. I'd figure out how to accomplish that between now and tomorrow.

Finally, I grabbed the groceries and her purse, which was on the side table near the front door, her keys beside it. I locked the door, preparing my words for her carefully on that fucking subject.

I watched her fluid strokes, the rhythm of arms reaching out, head turning, breaths being taken, feet kicking up tiny splashes as she moved across the pool. I should have known this was where she'd go. It was where she came to blow off stress, or to think, or to pout. I imagined she was doing all three at the moment. She gasped and choked on pool water when she picked her head up and saw me standing at the edge of the pool.

"Come out of there," I said. "I'd like a word with you."

She met my hard look with a sultry one of her own. "Just one?"

"I said get out of there, Gennaro."

"I don't think so, dear."

"Now, or I'll come in there and get you"

One corner of her beautiful mouth turned up as she stood in four feet of water and crossed her arms over her chest. "Do it."

I pinned her to the spot with a look that said in no uncertain terms that I was not fucking around. I felt my face grow hot—lust, anger, and a dozen other emotions she'd feel the brunt of in a minute. She asked for this; now she was going to get it.

I toed one shoe off and pulled my sweater up over my head while I kicked off the other. She kept her eyes glued to mine as I went for my belt. I took my time unbuckling it, and I grew hard as I watched her suck her bottom lip between her teeth as I pulled it from my pants. This dance was a familiar one, choreographed to test my endurance, my level of investment. My love. I tossed the belt carelessly to the floor and unbuttoned my jeans. Her eyes got moist as the tip of her tongue came out and licked her upper lip. My pants were halfway down my legs when she started to back up. As she turned to swim toward the deep end, I jumped in and gave chase. Karen was a good swimmer. I wasn't too terrible, either. I had her by the ankle before she got ten feet. I pulled her back, turned her around, and took her ass in my hands. I lifted her up.

"Wrap your legs around me."

"No."

"*Now.*"

Her feet left the floor of the pool and she wrapped her strong legs around my waist.

"I'm taking you to my place and we're going to talk."

"I'm not..."

"You are." I walked the few feet to the stairs and carried her out of the pool, setting her on her feet next to a lounge chair that held what looked like two towels, and turned out to be a towel and a spa robe. I wrapped the robe around her and pulled off my wet underwear. I used her towel to dry myself off, then gave her the wet towel for her hair. I threw my sweater and pants on, not bothering with shoes or my belt.

"Move," I said.

"I said I'm not..." She got no farther. I had her off her feet and over my shoulder before she could string the rest of the words together.

"Put me down! John, goddammit, put me down."

"When I get you to my car, I'll put you down."

"I'll walk, dammit! Johnny, please."

It was a silent walk to my car. "I need a change of clothes," she said as I opened the car door for her.

"I have clothes for you. Get in."

"Why are we doing this?"

"I'll explain that to you. Get in the car, Gennaro."

"Look, I know you're angry," she began when I got into the driver's seat. "But I am my own woman, John. Let's get that straight. I do not and will not answer to you or anyone else when it comes to my personal relationships. What I do, I do for reasons that are my own, and I don't need to explain myself to you. I realize that you have a serious problem with Adam, and I appreciate that, I really do." I let her go on as I pulled out of the garage and headed down Lincoln Blvd.

"I need to handle this my own way. You barging into my home and slamming him around like you are on the school playground is not okay with me." She waited for me to comment, to object, to argue my point. When I stared at the road, she sniffed righteously and continued.

"Obviously, this is something we haven't addressed, but now is as good a time as any." She cleared her throat, uncomfortable with my silence. When I didn't respond, she was quiet the rest of the drive to my place.

"I cannot believe that I agreed to do this," she said when I stopped the car inside my garage.

"But you did."

"Not really."

I laughed. "Okay." I grabbed the bags out of the back— her stuff and the groceries—and moved her through the garage and into my house. In her robe, hair wet and ropy, she was still gorgeous.

"I...love that you are so...so..." She stared off into space in search of the right word. "Protective," she said as I set everything down on the kitchen counter. "But I do not need rescuing, John. I am a capable woman who can, and would prefer, to take care of herself. Now, on occasion, your *way* is...somewhat appealing."

I leaned against the counter, folded my arms and nodded.

"But please don't confuse...*foreplay*...with everyday life." She said that last part with a stern shake of her finger.

"You done?"

She folded her arms and stared out the large picture window over the kitchen sink. "Yes, I guess so."

"Good." I untied the robe and shoved it off her shoulders. It pooled on the ground at her feet. I felt a shiver run through her as I jerked her hard against me. "First, don't ever run from me again."

"I beg your..."

"I asked you to stay in your place..."

"You *ordered* me to stay..."

"You ran away..."

"To the pool, for God's sake..."

"Because you knew I'd have one or two things to say about your house guest. Right or wrong?"

"Right," she whispered after a long mull-over.

"And while you were busy handling this *in your own way*, he went up to your place while you were out of town. Did you know that?"

"No. What do you mean?"

"I mean, Shapiro came by while you were gone, told the boys in the lobby he was taking care of your place, and they let him up. You're not going back there until I've had the condo swept for cameras and listening devices. You understand?"

She searched my face for further explanation, knowing I'd only be repeating myself. She took her time with it all. "I don't know what to say."

"I think you've said enough."

"I've probably said too much."

"Well, I've said very little, but that's about to change. I love you. I will stand in front of you and take a bullet. I'll stand beside you and hold you up, I'll get up your ass when you piss me off, and I will sure as shit jump into a pool and drag you out, especially when you dare me. That won't change. Not ever. It was this way six months ago, and it'll be this way fifty years from now, if you'll have me. You have a problem with that, let's say goodbye right now. I'll understand. No—actually, I won't. You want me this way, or you wouldn't be standing in my kitchen in a wet bathing suit.

"You want to get mad, call me overbearing, drone on

about you're mad as hell and you're not going to take it anymore, have at it. I'll listen, and I'll sympathize about how shitty it must be being loved so hard, and then I'll turn right around and love you. *Hard.* I'll love you so hard you'll forget your own fucking name. I'll love you so hard you'll think twice about taking risks that will take you from me. I'll love you so hard you'll beg me to set you straight again when you get all twisted. Arrogant? Really? Is that what you're thinking? How hard did that motherfucker love you, Karen? Huh? Did he fight for you? Where is he? I don't see him. He ran you off the road last year as, what, some sort of weird foreplay? He fucks with your family and you *invite* him up. Why? To be nice? Don't be nice. Be done, like you said you were the other night."

I slipped the straps of her bathing suit down her arms and peeled it to her ankles. She stepped out of the garment. I picked up the robe and put it around her shoulders. I grabbed the front lapels and pulled her to me. "How hard do you want to be loved, lady?"

She swallowed past a dry throat. "Hard."

"How—hard?"

Moisture swam in her eyes, lips parted, and that stubborn thing sat low inside her, that thing that would not let her own what, and who, she was. "Fight through, babe, and tell me how hard you want to be loved."

"I...I..."

I pressed against her naked body. "*How hard?*"

She brought her hands up and cupped my face. "So hard I forget my own name," she whispered.

I lifted her up and she wrapped her legs around my waist. The robe fell to the floor once again. This time I left it. I dug my hands into her flesh and carried her to my bedroom.

On her back, on my bed, I had her. I had the girl. Naked, unencumbered by clothing or commitments or enemies, I had her.

Karen wrapped her arms around my neck and pulled me down. She took my mouth while she yanked my sweater off. My pants came next, and for the first time in six months I was skin on skin with the only woman who mattered to me. She arched her back as I took a taut breast into my mouth. She tasted like honey, smelled like the pool, felt like satin to my sandpaper. My hands roamed her body like a blind man reads braille. I kissed every inch of her. I saved taking her mouth until the end, so she could taste herself on my tongue. And when I entered her, she arched up and hissed my name.

"I want more than tonight. I'm not giving you up again." I eased out and plunged deep.

"*Johnny*."

I inched out of her and brought it home again. "You—are—*everything* to me." She sucked me deep inside her as the end of one orgasm bled into another. She thrust her hips up and I went deep again, her muscles working like a fist, sheathing me from tip to root. I knew of love, I knew of good sex and explosive orgasms, the kind that make you weep, make you weak for her in ways you never dreamed. I was there. I was weak with her. She owned me. I was done-for. I would do anything for her now: kill, maim, grow gills and move to Atlantis. How did I get to this place, where I felt myself slipping away? She said that loving me would make her lose herself. I knew that loss. I was there.

Eyes closed, face slack, breath jagged, hands fisting my hair, she came hard beneath me, my name spoken on a cry, tears moistening the pillowcase under her head. And with one final thrust I released, my mouth against her ear,

"Mine," I growled. And then I took her mouth and spoke the three words I would never tire of, and I spoke them like a prayer, like a promise:

I love you. I love you. I love you.

29

I floated up from sleep as a warm, naked body molded against my side. My arm found a route around her and I pulled her close.

"You smell good," I mumbled.

"Shower," she whispered, nipping my earlobe.

"I like the pool smell." I opened my eyes. Her hair lay damp across her shoulders.

"Nevertheless, it is not good for my skin."

"Your skin…" I rolled over and settled her onto her back. I kissed along her jaw, down her neck and across her chest, greeting each beautiful orb with a gentle hello.

"Do you have to go in today?" I asked.

"I'll go into the office for a couple of hours later this afternoon."

"Don't go back to the condo until I've had it checked out."

"I won't. What will you do?"

"Get someone in there."

"How does that work?"

"Someone goes in with a detector that beeps if they come across something. Very CSI."

"I can hire someone, honey. Don't use..."

I set a finger over her lips. She had the gall to kiss it. "We'll see. Don't worry about it today."

"Okay."

"And lock your damn door. I don't care if you're going to the laundry room. There've been a few B and E's in the building..."

"I heard."

"Well, the folks who got screwed left their doors unlocked."

"I wondered about that. How did they get past security?" she asked.

"I'm working on that," I said, keeping her out of that issue for the time being. "And another thing..."

"Oh, dear."

"Why? Why did you let him up last night?"

"Do we have to talk about this?" she asked, twirling a finger over my chest.

"Yeah."

"I don't want to make things worse for my dad, so I was trying to be...reasonable."

"Stop being reasonable. As one of the largest construction firms in the country, I'm assuming Dunn/Gennaro has lawyers."

"They do."

"Then your dad can use them. Nick doesn't need his daughter fighting his battles, and you don't need to placate that asshole for another second. I won't allow it."

"Oh, you won't?"

I pulled her on top of me and swatted her ass. "No, I won't."

"Mmmm, well," she said, straddling me. She ground down on my building erection. "If you...won't..." She rose up and took me inside her. "*Allow* it..."

"'S'right," I murmured. "Teach you to sass me..."

"Mmm hmm," she said, capturing me in a velvet glove. "I've learned my lesson." She gasped and threw her head back, holding me against that secret spot inside her. "You're the boss."

And then she came.

———

I left Karen asleep in my bed and I was at the station by eight a.m. I called Amelia Carter at the Scientific Investigation Division and asked her for a referral from her department. Sweeping for bugs and cameras was their specialty.

"I'll have someone call you, John. What's this about?" I told her. Amelia was quiet for a moment. "I'll see to this myself," she finally said.

"Carter..."

"It'll take half an hour, John. Whatever it takes to keep you with that woman. Jesus, we've watched you mope for six freaking months. Let me do this for you...on behalf of *all* of us."

"You're sweet, Carter," I said. I gave her the address.

"I'll call you when it's done."

I thanked her, hung up and called the security guy at Karen's condo. If Shapiro planted anything in Karen's place, he was done. *Done.*

———

I was working the files of some of our victims when Alex

arrived. It bothered me that so much had gone on in this one area near Chatsworth, and no one seemed to work hard enough to find the asshole who had taken twelve girls over thirty-plus years. And now it appeared the same asshole was sorting through the most vulnerable of his victims and killing them. Tiffany Funk was the last of the abduction victims, and we knew nothing about her.

"I want to talk to Grace again," I said to him after sharing my thoughts. "Maybe she can help us with this person. If Tiffany Funk is set to be our next victim, maybe we can stop that from happening."

"Yeah, good," my partner said, a bit of sarcasm dripping from his fangs. "What happened to not letting Grace help? To not involving her?"

"Since I'm the one calling her, she'll actually be helping and not giving you a boner."

"Fuck you," he growled.

"Grace," I said when she picked up the phone. "We need some help."

"Of course," she said.

"We have one victim out of the twelve we still haven't located. If social services or DCFS has ever been involved with her, could you tell us?"

"I think I could dig something up. Give me her name."

"Tiffany Funk."

"I'll get right on it."

"That was good thinking," Alex said after I hung up.

"You're sorry for the 'fuck you', now, aren't you?"

"A little."

"Well, it's worth a shot, because we can't find Tiffany Funk on our own." I stared at the whiteboard. "Bubba, I want to understand this area, where these kids were taken."

"You think it matters now, when he's probably hiding out on The Walk?"

"Someone, somewhere—either with LAPD or VCSD—knows about this prick. He can't have gone unnoticed for this long."

"Seems that way, though."

"When I worked detectives back in New York, there was a guy who was setting himself up in abandoned buildings, and on rooftops, and taking out street whores with a rifle. It went on in Harlem, and it went on outside The Plaza. It didn't matter if she was a two-dollar whore or a thousand dollar a night escort. He knew about them, and he shot them, sniper-style. He'd been doing it for twenty years. Twenty years taking out Ladies of the Night. No one knew him; no one could catch him. There were two-year breaks between the killings, and there were two-hour breaks between the killings. He was hiding in plain sight, except he wasn't leaving anyone alive. No one could ID him, describe his voice, or describe how he smelled. We have so much more on this asshole, but we can't seem to fucking track him." I stood and slammed my finger against every name on the list of victims. "We can't fucking find this sonofabitch, but there sure as shit is someone out there who can."

Alex let out an exasperated sigh, but he didn't mean it. He saw where I was going.

———

"I REMEMBER THAT CASE," said Steve Pauling. We sat outside a burger stand on East Los Angeles Street in Santa Susanna, west of Chatsworth. The small community nested between the 118 and the 101 freeways. Parts of the surrounding areas, Pauling admitted, were a no-man's land, where VCSD and

LAPD fought often about who was in charge. Neither side was in a hurry to take responsibility. I got it. When you already had a caseload of dead bodies and unsolveds, the last thing you wanted to take on was an area of the city where dead bodies stayed well hidden, and people broke bad without detection.

"I was a detective with the Sheriff's Department back then, I remember that little kid—Dana Torrance. Physically, she had all the earmarks of rape and abuse, but no evidence—no semen, no hair, no epithelial. But that kid sat with us for days and described what happened to her, gave us so much detail. We knew there were others; at least two. One disappeared and was never found, I understand." He took a bite of his chiliburger and washed it down with a beer.

"Kristen Holmes," I said. "Her body was found a year after she disappeared. LAPD was on it."

"See? Between LAPD and the SD, no one knew who was supposed to scratch your watch and who was supposed to wind your ass. Not good."

"Agreed. I think this guy knew that—*knows* that. He seems to have a good working knowledge of forensics, and I think he knew something about cops and jurisdiction."

"Makes sense," Pauling said. "I moved on after the Dana Torrance case. We were getting nowhere and had no help, no support. Too many swinging dicks trying to be in charge. It wore me down."

"Where did you go?" Alex asked.

"Sheriff's Department out of Malibu. Now there's a hotbed of crime. We got Mel Gibson going on drunk rampages about Jews and Nazis, we got rock stars breaking up their houses over who got caught doing whom, and the occasional speeding Lamborghini along Trancas Canyon. It was a great place to retire from. But I know this area best. I grew up here, when the one-eighteen wasn't, and Charlie Manson was busy raising a stink up at the Spahn."

"We're trying to figure out where this guy operated from. We have a name."

"Well, I might still have some connections. What name ya got?"

"Branch Mardigan."

Steve Pauling's eyes got wide, and then he started to laugh. "Well, if the name really is Branch Mardigan, you won't find him unless you dig deep."

"What do you mean?"

"Branch Mardigan was the Mayor of Simi Valley during most of the sixties. He was murdered in seventy-seven."

"Murdered?"

"Yeah. Big deal. Comes out after his funeral that he fathered a child by some woman who worked for him."

"Was the child a girl?"

"Seems to me it was. I never met the man, but I remember the murder, and the scandal. Let's take a ride."

WE SAT IN A CLOSE, windowless room at the Ventura County Sheriff's Department station, while Steve Pauling worked the computer. "See, here's the story of Mardigan's murder, and then...here's stuff about the girl." Even at the young age of seven, I recognized Beverly Shay.

"That the kid was half-black was just the beginning. Turns out Mardigan had a son, but no one ever saw him. Rumor was he was in some sort of institution. Kid had problems."

"One of the victims, abducted in eighty-eight, thinks the person we think is named Branch Mardigan worked for her father. She thought he was eighteen or twenty at the time, and this victim remembers a young girl there sometimes." I gave a basic description. "We are looking for that girl now. We know that Branch Mardigan and Beverly Shay are siblings."

"Then you are looking for Mayor Mardigan's son and illegitimate daughter."

"How was the Mayor killed, does it say?" Alex asked.

It took Steve Pauling some time, but he found it. "He was beaten to death. No evidence. No nothing."

Pauling thanked the on-duty deputy for the use of the computer. "That was a solid he did me," he said as we walked out into the afternoon sun. "He could lose his job for what he did just now. We stick together, the SD."

With Pauling behind the wheel of an inconspicuous SUV, we drove up through the hills and the new neighborhoods in and around Santa Susanna, Chatsworth and a town called Callahan, where a few movie ranches were still in existence for tourists and filming the occasional western. As we drove, Steve Pauling explained the expansion the area enjoyed through the last twenty to thirty years. We drove by what used to be the Spahn Ranch, where Charlie Manson holed up with his troop of teen degenerates in the sixties. He took us past the house Dana Torrance lived in when she was abducted. I wondered if she ever came back, drove by, recalled better times. I know that whenever I went back to New York, I always drove past my old house, the one I grew up in. It kept the past in its proper place.

Pauling drove on, retracing the steps he thought Dana Torrance took before she was abducted. The town had changed, he said. There was a Wal-Mart now, and an Appleby's. And when he drove out of town and over Santa Susanna Pass and across to Box Canyon, the sweet smell of sage and fennel and pine and eucalyptus slipped through the windows of the car like a familiar friend, and I wondered what it would have been like to grow up in what I could only describe as country, instead of the steady diet of blacktop I enjoyed.

Getting the feel for where our victims and our killer spent time was helpful. I wasn't sure how yet, but I felt like we were closer to getting him. The key to him was Beverly Shay, Mayor Branch Mardigan's love child.

WE WERE ABOUT to clock out for the day when Ginger set a piece of paper down in front of me, her look all smart-ass.

"Your day's not over yet, darlin'."

Just when I thought things were getting dull on the job. "This isn't the way to score points with me, woman," I said, tossing the note in front of Alex.

"Don't I know it...*honey*," she said as she walked out, purse in hand, *her* day over.

30

"*Well*, if it isn't my two favorite police-type folk in the world! Hmmm mmm, honey," cooed Junie Joo. She sat at a table outside a burger stand where Washington Boulevard ended at the beach. A paper boat filled with Buffalo wings sat in front of her, the vinegar-heat from the sauce catching on a wind and making my mouth water. We hadn't heard from Junie in a while, the last time being when she helped out on a case involving a murdered college kid, David Crane. Junie had done us a solid that time.

Today she was in a sunshine-yellow dress and a matching wide-brimmed hat decorated with feathers in all the bright shades. Despite a decent figure and a walk to match, Junie Joo's sculpted face and prominent Adam's apple gave her gender away to anyone half observant. Still, Junie was harmless to everyone except herself, and for that I was always sorry.

"What's up, Junie?" Alex asked with impatience.

"Mmmm," she said, finishing up the last wing. "One minute, honey. These things are hotter than little sister's pussy in July. Lawd." She took a swig from a plastic water bottle, dabbed her mouth, then stood and tossed her trash. She crossed Washington, walked down a concrete path in front of condos and multi-million-dollar homes, and sat on a low wall with a bed of flowering plants behind her.

"Honey, a lot of the no-good is afoot, and Junie is not foolin'."

"What do you mean?" I asked, and I did it before Alex did in less gentle fashion.

"Well, I will have you know that Junie has relocated to these beautiful parts you see before you." She looked around. "Oh, not here, honey, per se. My sugar daddy ain't *that* sweet." She tossed her head back, exposing a long neck and a three-inch scar. A masculine laugh escaped before she caught it and femmed it up a bit.

"Junie," Alex growled.

"Now, before you get your tighty-whities in a twist, Alejandro, allow me to preface, honey. Junie has relocated, and with her, a fine sense of what goes on around her came right along with, honey. So, per usual, I have been mindin' m'own business and I been watchin', and I am a pro at both, if I do say so m'self. Now, you know me well enough to know that I try my best not to get too downwind of the seedier side of The Front, sad as their lot in life is, honey. But I have heard talk, and most of it comes from that tall ice cube who refers to you as Simple Man." She winked at me. "Se-ex-y."

"Tree Top," I said.

"The very one. Anyway, he was in a state last night, honey…"

"I thought you didn't hang downwind of these people, Junie," Alex said, perching himself on one of the cut telephone poles that separated the walk from beach parking.

"I do not, Rico Suave, but I have made an exception, and

thank heavens I did. Ignoring that sorry sot would not be *de rigeur*, honey; therefore, Junie took a deep cleansing breath, held it, honey, and heard him out."

"And for that, we're grateful," he deadpanned.

"*Gracias*, my favorite hot Latin. Mmmm. A dear compadre of mine passed in a nasty way recently, so I admit I have had my ear closer to the earth than usual, so to speak, honey."

"Was the compadre's name Orliss?" I asked.

"Indeed it was."

"Keep going," I said. "We'll get back to her later."

"Touché. So, anyway, this Tip Top fellow is in a state, like I said, and he is talkin' about dead children from years ago, and then he says that some under-the-bridger that trolls The Front is carryin' round a wallet full of pictures, and I spent every resource I have available to me, honey, to extract out of that Jolly Green Giant what types of pictures he is referrin', because he was of a certain mind, and I was getting' a bad feelin', you see."

"Okay," I said, after it was clear she would say no more, but before Alex blew an artery. I dug into my pocket and pulled out a Jackson.

"Oh, honey, that's thoughtful, but this is so disturbin' I'd have shared for free." She slipped the twenty down the front of her dress. "The pictures are of children, don'cha'know. Little girls. Twenty, thirty pictures, according to this poor fool. Now, looky here: Junie can be a naughty lass when she sets her mind, but my antennae go up when *chillins* are afoot." She wagged two fingers above her head like a bug. "And furthermore, this Tall Collins is all a-dither over this nefarious goin's on—not sure why, honey."

"He used to be a cop, Junie," I said.

"No kiddin'. Isn't that sad?" she tsked. "Well, that might

be why he kept sayin' he needed to talk to you, honey," she said to me. "Somethin' you and Ricky Ricardo here are working on. He said he needed to tell you about this cracker, but he didn't know where to find you, honey. I did, of course —not that I volunteered this fact, rest assured. I like to remain stealth in our dealings." She pursed her lips, inspected her nails, and fanned her face with a bony hand.

"Did he tell you anymore, Junie? Give a description —anything?"

"I'm sorry, honey, he did not. It's a wonder I got out of that fool what I did." Junie stood. "I have shot my wad, so to speak. As always, Handsomes, you can count on *moi* to be your eyes and your ears." She waved a hand over her shoulder and sang her way down the walk and out of sight. "...*If ya liked it ya shoulda put a ring on it...all the single ladies... all the single ladies, uh oh uh oh...*"

———

"I SAW IT ALL," Tree Top said. We sat on the concrete steps that served as bleachers while men played a game of four-on-four, the smell of fries and pizza coming off the greasy spoon behind us like a sweat. "Motherfucker whips out this wallet and the pictures just pour out like a waterfall, all slipped into plastic holders. No motherfucker on this walk should have that many pictures of little girls, Simp."

"Agreed, Toppy," I said. "Can you find him for us?"

"Yeah. Yeah, I can. Things been better, Simp. I can help."

"Good. That's fine, Toppy."

"How do I get in touch?"

I handed him another one of my cards. I wrote my cell number on the back. "You get to a phone, Toppy. You can't find one, you get to Junie Joo. She'll find us."

"That tranny's more trouble than she's worth," he said.

"She's the one got us to you, Top. You can't reach us, you seek her out. Got it?"

He nodded. "This is the kind of trouble I'm talkin' 'bout, Simp. Whole shit-load a no-good hap'nin' right now."

That's just what Junie said.

———

I LAY NEXT TO KAREN. Her fingers played a tune against my hip. As something deep and sultry and made for sex played on the stereo, I thought about life with her. I wanted to do it different this time. I wanted our time together, our *life*, to be about us, and not filled with war stories of the streets and of the messes that rubbed off on me every day. I did not want to share Branch Mardigan with her, or Tree Top, or the fifteen-year-old baby gangsta we found in an alley a week ago, his brains all over the asphalt and his mother screaming behind police tape. I did not want to taint her with that grime.

I'd been able to report to her that Shapiro had not planted cameras or listening devices or anything else in her place. What I didn't report was my plan to find out what the fuck he thought he was doing going up there when she was gone.

Another day.

"Tariq's last day of school was today," she said. Karen had arranged for Tariq Williams to enroll in a small, progressive private school in Santa Monica, tuition paid by her. He took the city bus every day to and from. She had kept tabs on him, had no intention of letting this kid go. I was reluctantly hopeful.

"Yeah?"

"He did well, Johnny. I'm so proud of him."

"I am, too, sweetheart. This went far better than I thought it would."

"It went exactly as I thought it would," she said. The slow circles she made over my hip continued up along my ribcage.

"I'm going to give him a job at the clinic this summer," she finished. "I know how you feel about that."

I pulled her close and held it. "You have no idea how I feel about that."

"Yes, I do."

I knew how much she wanted me to be okay with it, because it was a drag to have a lover who thought you made shitty decisions all the time. "How much are you willing to lose?" I said after enough quiet passed.

"What do you mean?"

"You know what I mean."

Karen rose on an elbow, so we were eye to eye. "No, I don't."

"Box it up, get it contained—what you're willing to lose —because when that kid remembers what he is…"

"He's a kid, John, and a human being." Vehemence swam in her tone.

I pulled her back down and positioned her against my side. "Don't misread what I'm saying. You don't really know anything about him. Kids lose their mothers all the time, and it was obvious he was taking care of his until close to the end, but you don't know what his life was for fourteen years. What he makes of himself remains to be seen."

She was hurt that I didn't share her humanism. "He's done well so far."

"I know that, and the odds were against him."

"Yes, they were."

"Baby, I like the kid. I want to see him do well. But mostly I'm invested in him because you are." I stroked her bare arm. "Decide what you're willing to lose over this. You're bringing him into an environment that's new to him, and there's temptation—drugs, money, equipment, access."

Her face contorted into something that looked painful. I was killing her now. "God," she hissed, and tried to pull away.

"Stop." She put up a half-hearted fight. "Stop, Karen."

"I don't want to look at the world like this. I am not naïve, John, but my God. I'm not happy looking at things this way."

"I know that."

"I've seen the bad, too."

"Babe, I know you have."

"Feeling this way doesn't *feel* good."

"I know." I managed her back into my arms. It wasn't easy. "*Prego capire, amare.*"

"I'm trying," she said. "I'm trying to understand you."

I turned her face up to me, and I pushed her hair back. "Tell me what you're willing to lose when...*if* this kid turns south. Your stuff? How important is your stuff?—computers, scanners, medical equipment...?"

"Stop."

"How important is it? You're insured, right?"

"Yes."

"Stuff's unimportant, then?"

"I don't want to do this."

"I know. Let's do it anyway."

She sighed. "I'm insured."

"Good. How about your trust—in him, in kids, in people in general. How important is that?" I pressed my hand against her heart. Its beat was strong. Still.

"Very." Tears sat in her eyes.

"You willing to get hurt with that, over this kid?"

"I understand what you're trying to do..."

"Good. Answer me."

"Obviously, if something happened where Tariq betrayed my trust, I'd be hurt."

"Yes." And that's when the kid would feel me crawl so far up his ass he'd need an earth mover to get me out. I didn't tell her that. She already knew. "I'm not saying don't do this. I think working in the clinic will be great for him. All I'm asking you to consider is what you're willing to lose, and then get that straight in your head. Don't give any more than you're willing to lose." I tightened my arms around her. "I've made you mad, sweetheart. I didn't want to do that."

"No. I just..."

"This is going to work out. You know why?"

Tears moistened my neck as she buried her face there. "Why?"

"Because he adores you, and he will not want to disappoint you. That's the good news. The bad news is where he's come from. If he can keep heading toward where he needs to go, it'll be just fine."

"I understand," she said.

"I'm sorry."

"For what?"

"For my fucked-up view of the world."

"Will you let me show you a different side?"

I slid down and took her with me, my arms around her shoulders, my hips between her open legs. I glided my nose over hers and kissed her with reverence and with passion and with gratitude, and then I slid inside of her, because that was where I saw the world at its best, at its most glorious and Godly. That's what she did for me; that was the other side she offered, every time she opened herself up for me. I tried to remember good things I'd done in my life to deserve this moment, and moments like it, and when I'd find one, boy did I hang on to it, remembering to give myself a little break, one small break, because whatever it was I'd done that was good, it must have been fucking spectacular to bring her back into my life.

It had to be over-the-fucking-top spectacular.

31

*I*t was after midnight when my cell vibrated itself right off the nightstand on my side of the bed. Karen stirred and reached for me, her hand settling on my hip.

"Arrung," I grunted into the receiver.

"Simp, it's Joe...uh, Tree Top."

"Toppy, hey," I said, sitting up. I listened for a minute, then I hung up and called Alex.

"IT AIN'T MINE," was all he kept saying. He was shaking so bad that the steel cuffs rattled a steady beat against the chair he was anchored to. The wallet lay open on the table, the twenty-seven two-by-three pictures, each encased in plastic picture holders, lay face-up. Some were old, obviously taken in the seventies and eighties. Others were newer, the clothes, the hairstyles, the quality of the school-enforced pictures so familiar to anyone who attended the institution as a child. These were the sweet, smiling faces of what appeared to be second to fourth graders—ages seven to ten or eleven.

"We're getting nowhere," Alex said.

"I have an idea." I left the room and pulled the night watch commander aside. After some convincing, he nodded agreement.

"WE'VE CLEARED the place out, Top. All the coppers are out on duty. No one will see you."

Tree Top sat in my car. His eyes were moist as he looked around the parking lot of Pacific Station, as if he were about to take the long walk to the electric chair.

"I loved police work," he whispered. "I fucking loved everything about it." He turned to me. "What happened?"

"The job happened, Joe. The fucking job happened. It kills the best of men and wounds the rest so that there's no life to live after it's over. It gets to some harder than it gets to others."

Tree Top opened his eyes wide to stem a flow that had started a while ago. "I'm never getting this back, am I, Simple Man?"

"You are tonight, Detective Treach. We need you tonight."

He wiped his eyes and nodded, and then I led him through the back door of Pacific Station. It was two a.m. and the place was quiet. Alex and I stood by while Tree Top talked the man down. What came out was that the transient Tree Top saw with the pictures, Shane Donner, occupied room twelve at the El Dorado Hotel, and he found the wallet on a high shelf in the closet. He thought the little girls 'were pretty'.

SHANE DONNER HAD BEEN the occupant in room twelve of The El Dorado until two days ago. He'd been at the voucher hotel for a month, courtesy of Gimme Shelter. The room had not been occupied since. Had a crime been committed in this room, we'd be fucked. It had been bleached, scrubbed and pine-cleaned, as it was after each resident vacated. Faded linens were folded and set at the foot of a stained twin mattress.

SID arrived, and Alex and I started moving furniture. We moved the white metal pipe-framed bed out and checked the floor and surrounding walls for blood. All stains were swabbed and packed up as evidence. Then we moved a cheap six-drawer dresser away from the wall, and I could see the variation in the floor right away. With a gloved hand I pressed against the faux-wood and it gave. With a little work, I lifted the one-by-one-foot tile and set it aside. Alex shined a flashlight into the hole.

I reached in and pulled out a three-by-five box, six inches deep. Inside the box were hair ribbons in several colors, folded into three-inch lengths and banded. Jeweled and cartoon-themed barrettes were placed in rows. Four braided string friendship bracelets lay side by side, like dead soldiers. I knew what these were: Alex's daughter, Celeste, wore one, and she had made one for me, which I kept on my dresser in my bedroom. I saw it every day, and I thought of her.

I set the box aside and looked into the hole again. I pulled out two pairs of sneakers; the kind little girls wore.

"He keeps souvenirs. The motherfucker keeps souvenirs." There would be hair on the ribbons and barrettes, sweat on the shoes—maybe. I handed everything over to SID. No one spoke as we checked every inch of that room. We found nothing more. The predator's hiding place produced a small treasure that I hoped would be enough.

"All the ribbons, the barrettes, Alex."

"Yeah, *padna*," he said.

The pine smell from the last cleaning seemed to get stronger and my stomach roiled. Paint was peeling from the ceiling, and a small pile of flaked-off paint lay in one corner of the room. The single bulb further dulled the dingy yellow walls. The bed and the cheap dresser still took up space away from the walls and out of their element. I wondered how long it would take management to put it all back together for the next resident, or maybe they would forget about it, and the next sand napper looking for a clean bed for a few nights would have to move it all himself. Sweat stained the underarms of Alex's blue chambray shirt, his badge hung around his neck instead of a tie, his suit pants replaced by worn khakis he'd tossed on in a hurry after my phone call from Tree Top. He looked beaten, his eyes heavy, his mouth set into an angry line. I knew I looked the same. No mirror needed to confirm that fact.

Did Branch Mardigan stay in this room prior to Shane Donner taking it over? The two did not know each other, according to Donner. Donner found the pictures. He knew nothing more.

"There's more," I said, looking over at the box I'd given up to SID. "Those ribbons belong to..." Alex's eyes met mine. They were haunted.

"We have more to find," he said. "There's more."

"DON'T REALLY KNOW HIM," the manager of The El Dorado

said after confirming that Branch Mardigan occupied room twelve. "Couldn't pick him outta a crowd a one. My records show he's stayed here probably twice since I've been here, going on two years now. Not to say he doesn't stay else-where. Just not here."

"What other information do you ask for?" I asked.

"Well, not much, since they don't come here with much." He shrugged. "It's why they're here, I guess."

"So, no car, no other address?" I asked.

"What, like a second home, in Palm Springs, maybe?"

"Okay, so...no?"

"Uh...no. The shelter down the street refers most of 'em here. I get some referrals from the one in Santa Monica, one or two a year from Culver City and points east."

"Can you tell me anything about this guy, like, is he...all there?"

"You mean does he pick at the air and babble to someone ain't there to you and me?"

"Yeah."

"No. I don't remember him much, but we can't take those types anyway. Gotta have half a brain cell to stay here. What he do?"

"Nothing," I said, taking a business card out of a yellowed plastic holder on the counter. I returned the favor. "Call us if he shows again." The man nodded and was still studying my card when we walked out.

"Fuck could be watching us right now, Alex."

"Yup. You think Mardigan killed his father, the Mayor?"

"No evidence, right? Master of disguise. Who knows?"

"I hate standing around waiting for the other shoe to drop, Johnny."

"Yeah." We stood on the walk and watched the rising sun behind us reflect off the Pacific. Hours ago I was in my warm bed next to Karen, the coffee pot set to go off at five a.m. We'd take some time, sit, go over our day, and maybe plan what to do tonight. Now I'd be lucky to see her at all before the sun rose again. I'd call in another hour, tell her I wish I was having coffee with her instead of standing where I was standing, on The Walk at sunrise, trying to figure out a killer's next move.

"Tiffany Funk is the last name on our list, other than the two minors."

"And we know nothing about her," Alex said.

"We need to find her. If she's been in trouble we'll be able to find her."

"If our guy doesn't find her first."

———

THE DUSTY TOWN of 15,000 people was shadowed by the San Gabriels, which still had a cap of snow on top. East of Pearblossom in the middle of the Mojave, the town of Phelan was as faded as the dust that blew across the colorless street. The only schools in town sat side by side up a hill, and on days when the teacher's voice became a low hum in a kid's ears, he could look out the window and down on the strip mall across the street; Martha's Nails, Pico's Tacos, a Quik-Chek check cashing center, and Nia's House of Massage took up space next to a weedy vacant lot on one side, and Gunther's Auto Haus on the other. Three of the four businesses were boarded up. There were two cars in the lot, both in front of Nia's.

A visit with the San Bernardino Sheriff's office in town confirmed that Tiffany Funk was a kid on the edge. She had been arrested twice for shoplifting, and she'd been hauled in too many times to count on truant violations. She'd run away from home twice, once settling comfortably for a week in a dark alley in Torrance before cops picked her up and brought her back home. Tiffany's mother was single and worked two jobs. The kid was ripe for the idiot we were in pursuit of. In light of what happened to her a few years ago at the hands of Branch Mardigan, her path to a life not-so-great was no surprise.

A bell sounded and a crowd of six-to-twelve year olds poured out of the elementary school. Most boarded yellow buses. Some got into cars parked between the curb and a line of orange cones. Ten minutes later, slightly larger kids from the middle school came out, mingling in groups before dropping skateboards to the ground and taking off toward town, or boarding buses for home. When the high schoolers came out, they did it slower, less eager to part from friends. Many lit cigarettes once on the sidewalk; a few dropped their backpacks under a large tree and sat on the ground, smoking and laughing.

A group dressed in black came out, hair matching their clothes and hanging over their eyes, big rings stretching earlobes to the size of quarters, boots and jackets or hoodies covering everything from neck to toe, skin pale, mouths turned down, all joy gone.

She walked in the middle of the group, surrounded by three boys and another girl. Her hair was black and uneven, as if a lawnmower had missed a turn somewhere. A long piece of her hair hung down between her eyes. It was dyed fuchsia. Her eyes were ringed in black and red; she looked diseased. She wore a black metal-spiked collar around her neck and a bright green beret-type hat with an orange puff-ball on top. She carried nothing in her hands except a cigarette. The picture I held in my hand, provided by the San Bernardino Sheriff's Department was on target. That the girl went by Tam O'Shanter instead of Tiffany Funk was the only reason why she was still alive, based on our killer's MO.

The group moved as a unit, heading down the street toward the main drag, and the Starbucks on the corner. A tall, lanky kid whizzed by on a skateboard and jostled the slight, black-shrouded boy on the end, sending him spinning like a dervish. Swearing and raised fingers followed the skateboarder, who was down the street and around the corner before anyone could get their bearings. We watched them go into the Starbucks and come out a few minutes later carrying their drinks. They walked across the main street, then down a small side street, where they entered a deserted park and planted themselves on aged and rusted playground equipment. Alex parked under a tree and we watched.

"You think our asshole even knows about her?" Alex said.

"I don't know. The name change helped her, I think. She's lived in the community here since she was about twelve, so they moved out of the Chatsworth area soon after her abduction."

"Move away from the pain, and it changes nothing."

"Yeah."

The kids hung out until the sun started to go down, and then two of the boys left, leaving Tiffany, the other girl, and a boy. He lit something and passed it around, while the other girl walked over to a small, leaning barbecue next to a concrete picnic table and some dying oleanders. She lifted the grate on the barbecue and pulled out a bottle of something. She returned to the group and they passed that around, too, until it got dark.

It was well past eight when they separated, and we

followed Tiffany Funk home. She walked down a dark street past same-looking box structures plastered in stucco and decades old paint. Chain link fences, rusted from years of dust, wind and rain offered a sense of protection from whatever lurked outside, yet I got the feeling those outside the fences were the ones needing the protection.

"My half-brother, Chris, lives in Palmdale. Nicer than this, but you kind of get the picture," Alex said as we kept a good distance so we didn't spook her. She made a left on Pine Street. We did likewise. I remembered Chris from the communion party for Stevie at Alex's house. Nice guy; firefighter...

"Shit!" Alex said, as stunned as I was. Tiffany stopped in the middle of the street and stared into the intense light as I jumped out of the car and raced down the street to her. I caught the beginnings of Alex's call to firefighters and local coppers, and as I got closer, Tiffany broke into a run toward the house.

"Hey...hey, hey," I said as I headed her off and pulled her to me.

"My house! My fucking house! Fuck! Let go of me. Who the fuck are you?"

Neighbors emerged from dark dwellings like zombies. There was no urgency, no excitement about the fact that the home at the end of the block was engulfed in flames, kissing the dark night sky, electronics and dead wood popping and crackling like a Fourth-of-July show at the park.

"Tiffany," I said, taking her shoulders and turning her toward me. I introduced myself, showed her my badge. "I need you to come with me."

"My house. Oh, my God, my fucking house! What the fuck?"

Wonderful. "I know. We're going to help you." Alex came

up and placed his hand on her shoulder. He introduced himself.

"Fire on their way," he said.

"My house," she said.

"Get her to the car," I said. "And find a parent." I walked toward the house, holding my hand up, badge attached, to anyone attempting to venture outside their rusted fences. The house was fully involved now. I ran back to the car as the fire trucks came screaming down the street. There was nothing more to be done.

"I had Tiffany call her mother. She's on the way," Alex said.

"Good."

The girl sat in her mother's car while I filled Sheriff's deputies in. They would get back to us about the cause of the fire. In the meantime, we needed to talk to the girl.

32

The interrogation room at the San Bernardino County Sheriff's Office was as cramped and stuffy as ours, and no less attractive. Two deputies joined us, along with Tiffany and her mother, Roxanne. The heavy-set woman sat motionless in a plastic chair, a defeated scowl on her face.

"I don't know where to begin," she said. "What do we do now?"

"Uh...not live in the house?" Tiffany said, her upper lip curled in disgust at the woman sitting next to her. We got out of Roxanne that they were renting the house.

"We'll find you a place to stay for the night, Mrs. Funk," said one of the deputies.

"What happened? What caused the fire?" She turned to her daughter. "Were you smoking in the house this morning? Lighting incense?"

"Even if I was, I think I know how to deal. Fuck off."

"Okay," I said, trying to reign in my initial response, which was to smack the kid right out of her chair. "You can deal with the fire department on the hows and whys later. I want to explain to you both why we're here, and why we were following Tiffany."

"You were following me?"

"Yes. We watched you come out of school, go to Starbucks with your friends, then go to the park."

"What friends? You were in the park?" Roxanne said.

"Oh, Christ, will you shut up? What I do is my business. Please, *mo-ommm*." Tiffany rolled her eyes, then slumped over crossed legs and huffed.

"She's barely going to graduate," Roxanne told us. "I work two jobs while she sits in the park and drinks."

"And guess who's having more fun," said Tiffany.

I held up a hand. "I have some questions for you, Mrs. Funk."

"Ms. Battle. Funk's her name," she said, jerking a dry thumb at her daughter.

"O'Shanter's my name, dimwit," Tiffany countered.

"Okay," I said, my temper rising by the second with this ungrateful little shit. "Ms. Battle, where did you live prior to here, in Phelan?"

"Santa Susanna. Why?"

"And did something happen to Tiffany eight or so years ago?"

"My God..." Tears sprung to the woman's eyes, the pain of those eight years ago still fresh.

"What's the fucking point of bringing that up?" the she-beast asked.

"Ms. Battle?"

"Yes." Roxanne swallowed past a lump in her throat. "Excuse me. Yes. Tiffany..."

"Jesus, mom."

"Tiffany was...she went missing."

"Yes, ma'am. We know. I'd like to get back to that, but

first I want you to know why we're here, and why we were following Tiffany."

"Tam," the girl corrected.

"You know what?" I said, inches from rope's end. "You want Tam, you want the respect, show some yourself."

She rolled her eyes and glared at the wall.

"We're here," I continued, "because we're investigating a series of murders, and..."

"Murders?" Roxanne sat forward and rested her fore-arms on the table. Her hair, frizzy and parted down the middle, looked unwashed and lifeless. The outfit she wore said she worked as some kind of nurse or caretaker, the thin white stretch pants and the printed top was the standard uniform in hospitals and care facilities.

"Yes. And it seems..." I took a deep breath and tried for a better way to say it. I couldn't find one. "It seems the common trait the victims have is that as young children they were abducted, held for four days, and then released. It seems that this guy, or an accomplice, is targeting those victims as adults, and he targets the ones who have been in trouble." I looked at Tiffany. "We don't know why. We think he might have access to police records, or in some other way he's keeping track of his victims, and then coming after them at their most vulnerable, which being truant, being a runaway, and hanging out in the park will make you."

Tiffany glared at me. "Blaming the victim, now. Great."

"I don't think that's what they're doing," said Roxanne. "They're simply saying..."

"Oh, for the last time, you fat, fucking bitch, shut up! You have no idea what you're..."

I was out of my chair so fast no one had time to stop me. I grabbed the back of Tiffany's chair, pushed it back and held it balanced on its back two legs. Out of the corner of my eye, I saw Alex raise the back of his hand against the chest of one of the deputies attempting to stop me. I stuck my face two inches from hers. Her eyes got big, and her breath came in spurts. I could smell the pot and the booze and the cigarettes and the waste she was making of her life, made clear to me in the five minutes I spent sitting in this stale room engulfed in her bad juju. Enough was enough.

"I have sat here and listened to you and that mouth all I'm going to. You are sitting in a room with your mother and four cops who know a bit more than you do, so you're going to keep that filthy mouth of yours shut and listen. You don't, and I'm going to toss everyone out, take my belt off, and teach you some manners."

"You pervert! You...you can't do that. I'm eighteen!"

"Then act like it. You show your mother some respect and try on some self-respect while you're at it. Your life is in danger, and as bad as that fire was, it saved your ungrateful, miserable life. Shut your foul mouth and do what you're told. Do you understand me, or do I send mom and my partners out for coffee?"

She stared at me wide-eyed. I pushed the chair back until she was almost horizontal. Her hands gripped the edge of the seat, and a gasp escaped the tough mask she wore.

"Do you *understand* me?"

"Yes," she whispered.

"Yes, what?"

"I hear you. I'll listen."

"I am not joking with you, little girl. Do not test me."

"I kn—know." Now tears sat in her eyes, and she wasn't so tough anymore.

"I'm guessing you have something to say to your mom." She nodded and I righted the chair.

"S—sorry, Mama," Tiffany said. Roxanne looked at her

daughter, then at me, stunned, tears sitting in her eyes. The mother was doing it alone, and she had no one to help her fight the little shit. The fight had gone out of Roxanne a long time ago. I guessed it had been a while since the kid called her mama.

"Is there someplace you can go, preferably out of town?" I asked Roxanne.

"I...I have two jobs, she has school...how?"

"All right, listen to me now," I said to Tiffany. "What I am saying to you is serious. This guy has killed off those previous victims who've gone...astray, okay? You understand what I mean?"

"Yes," she whispered. "I think so." I liked that. A little fear was good.

"One went into prostitution. Dead. One fell into drugs, among other things. Dead. You getting me now?"

She nodded.

"And these were all kidnapping victims, like Tiffany?" Roxanne asked.

"Yes, going back to 1988."

"Oh, my God. You're kidding."

"I wish I was. Other victims of the abductions have gone on to lead productive lives, no trouble, no police records, and he hasn't bothered them." I glared at Tiffany. "You hearin' me? You sensing a pattern here?"

"Yes."

"What happened to you when you were little was shitty. It sucked. You have reminders and lasting thoughts and feelings about that. I know. I get it. There are resources, places to go to get help, and it won't cost your mother a dime. Help for you ain't in some park smoking dope and sneaking vodka or flunking out of school a month from graduation. You're going to get it together now. You're going to help your mom find another place to live, you're going to graduate from high school, and you're going to be a good citizen. You get me?"

"I...what about...? Am I safe?"

"No. Your little friends, the ones from the park? You move in a pack with them. And you *stay sober*. Getting drunk leads to bad decisions, and you are in no position to be making bad decisions now. It's not a moral judgment, this time. It's life and death. You choose which you want. Walking down the goddamn street alone in the dark is stupid. Don't do that anymore. Stay out of the park at night." To the deputy, I said, "Talk to the school. Make sure she's safe while she's there."

"We can do that."

Back to the girl. "And these guys can always toss your butt in a cage if you can't handle freedom. It'll hurt less than if this lunatic gets hold of you."

"Shit," she said. "I mean..." She swallowed past a lump in her throat. "Sorry."

"You work two jobs," I said to Roxanne. "What do you do?"

"I work at Wal-Mart from eight to five, then I take care of an elderly woman through an agency from seven to midnight."

Christ. "You hear that?" I said to the girl. "Figure it out, and do the right thing, or the next time I see you, it'll be on a steel bed in the morgue."

Roxanne didn't flinch. She knew I spoke the truth.

I WAS READING the fire incident report aloud to Alex the next day when Preston McConnell came in.

"I was messing around and...I know you didn't tell me to, or anything, but I was just curious about maybe other cases of missing kids, and the four days thing..."

"Slow down," I said.

"Yeah, right," he gulped. "Well, so here's the thing: between nineteen-eighty-eight and nineteen-ninety-five six kids went missing in California, all girls, all aged ten to twelve."

"From where?" Alex stood and came over to my side, and I took the paper Preston had in his hand.

"That's the thing: all over. See? And the other thing is, none were ever returned—not in four days, not in...*ever*."

"Carlsbad, Fresno, Riverside, Redding, Yucaipa, Bakersfield..." I looked at Alex. "Up and down the state." His eyes went to the whiteboard.

"That's our break," he said. "That's the break we see in our dates."

I did a quick mental calculation. "The sister is in college, and then living life during this time. She's not there anymore to keep him in line. He's killing them, Alex. In those seven years, he's killing those kids. Of the twelve we know about, he almost killed them, too, with the underwear around the neck, but something stops him."

"His conscience."

"...thy name is Beverly."

Alex and I spent the morning researching each missing child, and then calling every department associated with the investigations.

All were still missing.

———

I SAT across from Tariq Williams while he devoured a

cheeseburger. His face had filled out since I'd seen him last, over a month ago. The lines around his eyes, the bags from lack of sleep and worry, were gone. Bill Grayson had taken Tariq into his home immediately, and within days found a foster family for him. Hank Petra, the social worker, expedited it all, despite his overwhelming caseload. He would personally supervise the short stay in the foster home until Tariq's aunt could take him in November.

"How you holding up?"

"Okay," he said between bites.

"Miss your mom?"

"Yeah. A lot."

"You like your foster home?"

"Yeah, it's okay."

"They nice to you?"

"Yeah." He took a bite big enough for two people.

"You can call me anytime. You know that." I paused. "You know...if things aren't going right."

He nodded as he polished off the burger and started on the fries. "Thanks for the burger."

"You're welcome."

Thoughts of Tiffany Funk came to me as I watched Tariq. He'd been through a lot but managed to show appreciation for a burger.

"This place, where I'm at? Got four other kids," he informed.

"All foster?"

"No. Two they own. Girls." Pause. "They white."

"Yeah?"

"Yeah." Pause. "Other kids? They Korean."

"Yeah?"

"Yeah." Pause. "Girls."

"All girls?"

"Yeah." Pause. "I'm outnumbered."

"Nice kids?"

He stared at me like I'd grown horns. "They *girls*."

"Right, okay. Girls, Tariq, not aliens."

"Right." He rolled his eyes, gulped half his coke, and burped. "S'cuse me."

I fought back a grin. "You the oldest?"

"Yeah. They kids young, like five, six. Then the other two —one's ten, the other's twelve, somethin'—sisters, I think. Not sure."

"The oldest," I shrugged. "Big deal, that."

"Yeah? How you figger?"

"I dunno, maybe these people look to you to watch over, take care of what's theirs when their backs are turned." I shrugged again. "They trust you, maybe."

He sat back, leaned an arm over the back of his chair, proud. "Yeah. Maybe. I can hang wi'dat."

"Good." He seemed happy, relatively speaking. I hoped so. "So, Dr. Gennaro got you in to that fancy school, and she said you did well."

"Yeah. It was good, you know? Nice people, learned a lot. I got a problem, you know, they check in, I check in."

"That's great. Dr. Gennaro's proud of you, Fourteen. So am I."

"Yeah. Thanks. She says I could call her Karen. You think that's cool?"

"Of course, if she says it's okay. Karen says she's going to let you work in her clinic over the summer."

"Yeah."

I let that linger for a while. "You like Dr. Gennaro...*Karen*?"

"Yeah." He raised an eyebrow. "You?"

I laughed. "Yeah, I like her all right. She's on your side—we both are."

"I know. I 'preciate it, you know?"

"You don't need to say that. We don't care about that. We—Karen, Mr. Grayson, Mr. Petra...*me*—we just want you to have the things you should have. We all have our jobs, and yours—your only one—is to do good in school."

"*Well*. Do *well* in school."

I smiled. "You're correcting *my* grammar?"

"Yeah, yeah. I know. I'm a work in progress, 'ight?"

"'Ight." He chuckled. "You've been through a lot, but I think your mom would have wanted you to work your butt off so you can have a good life for yourself when you're older. You got good grades before she got sick, right?"

"Yeah. She kick my ass if I di'nt—sorry."

"It's fine, just not around the ladies, huh?"

"Sheeit." He took another gulp of his coke and burped again. "I'm outnumbered."

"Keep quiet and pay attention to the ladies, my man," I said. "You just might learn something. Let's get, kid. Gotta work."

"Can I come?"

"Not this time. Maybe another time, okay?"

His eyes got big. "No kiddin'?"

I looked at him with new eyes. He was a bright kid, raised by a tough mom who left him too soon. Didn't know anything about the people in his life, but I knew this: he was hungry for attention. His big brown eyes held the promise of youth and the pain of the shit life dealt out. He had a chance, but it would take work.

"Yeah. We'll talk about that. 'Ight?"

He chuckled. "Sheeit. 'Ight." He eyeballed me sideways. "*Homes*."

NEEDING A COUPLE OF EXTRA HANDS, we were given two detective-first-grades to help us out on this case. Their assignment? Work the files on these missing girls from '81-'90. I wanted a common theme, an eyewitness who saw something that made more sense to us than it did to investigators twenty-something years ago. I wanted a break.

33

_____

*T*he Stone. It was a few hours after our shift ended, and we both needed to be home, but such was police work. Sometimes decompressing in a bar was easier on the family than doing it at home. I still had to be careful with that. My situation was still new, and I didn't expect Karen to understand this part, or put up with it for long once she did.

"The fire was arson," I said to Alex as I drained my beer and signaled for another. "They're still sifting through evidence."

"You think it was Beverly Shay, as a warning to the girl?"

"I don't know. That is pretty over the top. Harsh warning, but it was effective."

"Yeah. I thought you were going to come unglued on that girl."

"I almost did."

"The look on the deputies' faces when you went after her...like a mix of jealousy and nerves. I could tell they wanted a piece of her, too, but, you know...the job, and all."

"Imagine talking to your mom like that?" I said.

"I tried it on a couple of times. Never fit. If I ever went to that extent with my mother, my father'd have to come home from the construction site so he could peel me off the floor for another beating. He didn't put up with any shit from us against our mother, and she was no stranger to the left hook, either."

I chuckled. "Yeah. I remember the time I called my mother a cocksucker."

"Oh, my God. What are you, crazy?"

"I didn't know what it meant. I was, like, eight. I'd heard it around the neighborhood. So one day, she said no to something, so I called her a... I said it. Anyway, she gets this look on her face like I'd just thrown up on her, and I turn and see my father standing in the doorway."

Alex chuckled. "Oh, man."

"Yeah. Suddenly I'm counting the knots in the hardwood floor while he polishes his belt on my ass. Of course, after it was over, I ran right to her."

"Yeah, I did that, too," Alex said. "No matter what, my mother could always make me feel better."

"So, later, she says to him, 'You know, he didn't even know what the word meant'. The old man said, 'Well, he does now'."

"Yes, sir." Alex laughed. "I feared my mother, and God, in that order. No question."

"My parents were more predictable than God. I feared God. Then I feared Guiliana Pastorre."

"Yeah? Who was she?" Alex signaled Mac for another beer.

"She used to beat me up. She was twice as big as I was and mean. She had this flat face and a big mole on her cheek. She'd get me behind a bush or a building at school, and I'd come home with bruises all over my arms and legs."

"And you didn't hit her back?"

"Hell, no. She'd tell on me and my ass'd be raw for a week. She finally moved away, got fat, got married, had a brood of kids. Bitch. Good riddance."

"And you couldn't tell anyone about it, 'cuz she was a girl, right? You didn't want anyone to know you got your ass kicked by a girl."

It felt good to share like this with my best friend. He got it. He understood. "Yeah."

"You are a fucking pussy. Grow a pair." He got up and walked to the bathroom, and I escorted his beer to the nearest trashcan.

"Nice try," he said, taking my beer after seeing that his went MIA. It was filled to half, and he drank it down, then clapped me on the shoulder. "I'll see you tomorrow."

"Yeah. I'm going to talk to Mac a minute, then I'm out, too." I paused. "I'm back with Karen."

Alex sat again. "Yeah, I thought I detected a glow. I'll listen in while you give my wife the gory details next time you see her. Meantime, I'm glad as hell, John. She is good for you."

"Yeah."

"Yeah." Alex stood, gave my shoulder a squeeze, and headed to the door with a phone at his ear.

I gave Mac the eye, and he came over. The bar was quiet for a Thursday night. He wiped the area in front of me and spoke.

"So, apparently Laborteaux is involved in some hairy shit," Mac said, picking up right where he left off a week or so ago. "Worse, I hear, than Rampart."

Rampart was the biggest scandal to hit the LAPD, ever. It involved the CRASH unit and officers run amok. Drugs, gangs, framing gang-bangers; it was all bad. I couldn't imagine worse.

"All I know is, he's got that north end of the valley locked *up*. The gangs, weapons, drugs, the porn trade—especially the porn trade. He's got his hands in all of it, and making fuckin' *bank*, John."

"He killed Mark Gonzales."

"Yeah? Well, Gonzales ain't the only one. He's not afraid. He ain't scared of nothin'. He's a sociopath, and no one has a clue."

"Yeah. People have a clue, they just can't catch him at it." I finished my beer and laid some bills on the counter, significantly more than the beers were worth. "Keep your ears open but be careful. I'll find out another way if you get nothing. Don't take chances, and don't talk to anyone else."

"I won't, John."

"Thanks, Mac. Seriously."

I walked out into the cool night and thought about calling Alex, telling him the latest. I knew how he felt about my obsession over Laborteaux, but when a man knew a thing, a man didn't want to let it go, even if he was the only one who knew it. I had time, and I was lucky. Time allowed for the right thing to be done the right way. I would not get Laborteaux today, or tomorrow. But one day the fucker would go down, and I'd be standing over him.

"Sweetheart," I said into the phone when she answered.

"Hi, love," she whispered. "How was your day?"

"It was a day. Where are you?"

"On the balcony with my feet up. I have a bottle of Amarone breathing and water boiling on the stove. Where are you?"

"On my way."

"Good. Will you stay tonight?"

"Sure. I'll stop home and get clothes. I had lunch with Tariq today."

"You did?"

"Yeah. He's a good kid. I was wrong about him."

"Eh. I don't know about that. Taking it one day at a time is a good idea. Was he happy?"

"Seemed to be. I'll tell you all about it when I get there."

"Okay, love. I'll greet you at the door with a glass of wine."

"Do it naked, please."

"Of course. See you soon."

"Hey." Wind whistled through the phone and her slow, steady breathing had me wishing I were already there. A breeze picked up off the ocean and the salt air reminded me of how her body captured and held only the purest of scents, and how that elixir owned me every time I buried my face into her skin and inhaled the subtle nuances of her refined, unadulterated womanhood. "Hey, baby."

"Yes?"

"I love you, Blue."

"I love you, too, Johnny. Hurry home to me."

I hung up and walked toward home, feeling hopeful for the first time in a while, yet brewing underneath was that weight I carried like an extra limb, and it was a weight I needed to unburden to Karen before we moved into this any further. I had a past, and my past was colored gray, a gray I harbored in my world of black and white. My world was a world of right and wrong, fat and thin, yes and no. I didn't have a lot of maybe in my world, no *well, sometimes* moments. Not ever. So, this burden I carried, this crime I committed long ago to avenge my father... it would always be there, it would always sit with me. Some days...most days it sat well. Other days, like on days when I needed to

be the best of me, for myself, for Karen, even for my partner, the burden weighed extra heavy. I needed to know
how she felt about this. I needed to know if Karen
Gennaro could be with me, knowing I could spend the rest
of my life in prison if the wrong people found out, or dead
in a bad, painful way if the other wrong people found out.
And just morally. She saved lives; she didn't take them.
Could she look me in the eyes every morning and love the
man I was, the man I am, burdened, tainted, imperfect,
and hypocritical? I blew a man's face off because he killed
my father and I did it wearing a badge. Where's the heroics
in that? Where's the proud moment I can look back on
when things turn to shit and proud moments are all I have
left? How can I ask this woman to love me, trust me,
believe in me when I'm just as bad as the fuckers I put
behind bars? We'd discuss it when I got to her place, and
then I'd know.

I came to Speedway, an alley that cut north in a one-way
through the heart of Venice and separated one block of
apartment buildings from another. As I started to cross, a
man on a bicycle appeared from the shadows.

"Hey. You Simple Man?"

I squinted into dark. "Yeah."

"Trouble." He turned the bike and headed north down
Speedway. I watched him go in that slow way that forced
him to cut the bike in and out or he'd fall over. He turned
back and saw I wasn't following.

"Trouble," he said again and circled back toward me.
This didn't feel good. I pressed my left arm into my side,
feeling my holstered KelTec PF9, then lifted my phone and
spoke to Siri.

"Call Alex." I ventured down the alley. The guy on the
bike looked back to make sure I was following.

"I'm sorry, Big Swinging Dick, but I can't take any requests right now."

"Goddammit," I hissed. I lifted the phone up as I walked and tapped Alex's cell. Karen. She did that. She probably grabbed my phone while I was in the shower, and had a nice five minutes with Siri, my cell phone's answer to a secretary. "Call me Big Swinging Dick," I pictured her saying, and Siri responding, "All right, I will call you Big Swinging Dick." The woman would pay dearly for retraining my personal phone assistant to say shit. Not cool. Definitely not cool. As I walked on, Alex's voicemail came on.

"Speedway, north toward the numbered streets. Something's up." I said to his voicemail, then I disconnected and called his home. When Lisa answered and said he wasn't home, and she couldn't reach him, either, I got pissed.

"I need him." I hung up and dialed the emergency dispatch number as I followed the guy on the bike. I introduced myself when dispatch answered and asked for a patrol car at my general location. I ended with the informative, "I have no fucking idea what's going on. Send a car."

The bike circled in front of me. "Trouble," the guy said again. I followed him down Speedway, passing a building under construction. No lights, no cars, no people. The guy turned right twenty-five yards ahead of me and disappeared. I stopped walking and tried Alex again.

"I don't know where the fuck you are, but get to me," I whisper-growled into the phone. The phone went into my pocket and out came my PF9. I moved forward toward an occupied building, dim lights shining down on parked cars under an overhang; that was it. I made a right and entered into a narrow passageway separating two buildings, one abandoned, one under construction. A temporary telephone pole had been erected, offering little room to pass on either side, yet the bicyclist managed. He sat on his bike on the other side of the pole.

"Trouble," he said. Then he turned and rode down the passageway and disappeared out the other side.

The pole was misshapen, looked like another pole was behind it a little off center. I squinted, getting used to the dark. Then I saw it. Someone was standing up against the pole. I raised my gun and stepped back. My eyes focused on the details.

It was Tree Top. A steel spike had been run through his chest, attaching him to the pole. He'd been beaten. His eyes were swollen shut, his jaw was twisted and out of alignment, the left side of his skull sported a huge gash, and his right arm hung at an odd angle.

"*Guffsnaps*," he gurgled, bloody bubbles of air coming out of the hole around the metal object that pierced his chest and held him in place.

"Fuck, Toppy," I said. As I approached him, he managed to shake his head.

"*Gffff—shhhrp!*"

I turned, gun in hand, to make sure nothing was behind me, then I pulled out my phone. I had no idea what to do for him, and I knew I couldn't save him. I also couldn't leave him. I lifted the phone to my mouth, pressed the home button, and waited for the beep, my personal invitation to order Siri around. I saw Tree Top's reaction a second too late, and then everything went black.

34

I was outside. It was cold and wet. The heavy weight of canvas pressed me into the floor. I smelled paint, turpentine, and nail polish. I lay on a ridged floor; I heard the rev of an engine.

I lay supine in the bed of a truck. I slid as the truck turned, and then again. My hands were tied. My ankles, tied. My head ached. I shrugged the canvas down until I could see. It was dark, damp. It had rained, and the bed of the truck was wet. The canvas, wet.

"*Nnnnufschreps...*" A finger poked against skin rubbed raw, every nerve, every pore was on fire.

"*Eeergravlox...mov...moo...movingnotmovingnotmoving... HEY SIMPLE MAN! HEY!*"

A finger poked me again.

Simple man. Just a simple kinda man. I could smell him; beach and that murky cheese smell of the unwashed. And blood. I smelled blood.

"Hey." Poke. "Hey s-s-s-s-s-simple m-aaaaaa-n."

A car engine revved. Pot holes. Bounced up. Got air and I was tossed back. I must have been sitting up. I could make out the silhouette of a man, bearded, long hair, white tee, long pants, no shoes. He poked me again.

HEY SIMPLE MAN! HEY!

Shut up.

Hey.

SHUTUPSHUTUPSHUTUP!

The silhouette fell over the wall, disappeared.

Hey!

I said shut up!

POP. One.

POP. That's two.

I passed out.

MY ARM ACHED, my chest ached, one eye stung and I couldn't open it. The blood running into my eye was from my head. It was throbbing, and the damp around the rest of my hair that was dry, confirmed I was still bleeding.

Someone had been with me until recently. He poked; he spoke. Then someone tried to stop him from doing that.

Shut up.

SHUT up.

A gun. Two shots. Remember two shots.

Remember.

I pressed my elbow against my waistband. The under-the-waistband holster and my off-duty weapon were gone.

Two shots. Five left.

My gun was used to shoot whoever it was riding with me. I was as familiar with the sound of the PF9's report as I was with the soft whispers of my woman.

Karen.

Hurry home to me.

"Shit. Shitfuck."

I lay on my left side. I lifted my head, focused, got my bearings. Middle of nowhere. Dark, shadow-trees, the smell of earth and rain and fennel and sage and land. The subtle smell of water evaporating off stone. I don't know how long we drove; don't know how many times I went in and out of my head. I raised my chin and tried to see behind me. I saw one head in the driver's seat, nothing in the passenger's. One person. And me. I'm a big man, and I know one person could not have lifted my dead weight into this truck. Fucker had help, and his help just went over the side of the truck bed. That left me. And him.

My hands were bound in front of me. Plastic ties dug into skin. I rose on my left elbow and looked around. My head throbbed. I couldn't focus. Everything was blurred. I found an edge—any edge. I pressed the plastic tie that spanned my wrists down against the edge, and I rubbed. All I needed was a sharp spot, a worn spot, a weathered, rusty spot, and the tie would go. It'd go. I worked the wrists and tested the tie around my ankles. Tight. I caught the heel of one shoe on the ridge of the truck bed, and I pulled back. The shoe came off my heel. I shook my foot until the shoe came off, and then I kicked the other one off. With my shoes off, maybe I could slip a foot out. Feet tingled and pricked as circulation returned, then they went numb again.

He would stop the truck eventually. I didn't have long.

I slid back and forth. Winding road. Bright moon. Large mountainous boulders in the distance. I'd been here before. So had Alex.

I twisted my right foot until the top was facing my left ankle. Plastic dug into my skin; the sting, the air chilling against ankle, raw and bleeding. I twisted my right foot, working it loose. My calf cramped up. I stiffened against the pain. I pulled my right heel out of the tie, and after a few more twists, my foot was free. I pushed the tie off my left ankle and I turn back for a look at my captor. I heard music. He was moving his head to the beat. He seemed relaxed.

That would be his first mistake.

I balanced on my left elbow and looked around the truck bed. A plastic shopping bag, tied at the top, something inside. I gripped the top and tore it open with numb fingers. Medication; a prescription for something. I could not read the name. The ride was too bumpy. It was too dark. Medication was important, and the medication had a name, a script number. It could be traced.

I lifted the bag to the edge of the truck and tossed it over the side. Whatever it was, it was no more. If it were important, it would matter. It would get a reaction. Emotional enough, and I could take advantage of that. Maybe someone would see it, driving down this dark road. I tried to dump the canvas over the side, too, but it was heavy, and there was too much of it. I kicked it off me. I knew that kicking at the tailgate would bring me too much attention too soon, and I'd never get it to go down anyway. I slid forward as brakes were applied, and then I slid to the right. He was making a left.

Into the turn I took a chance. I threw my right leg over the edge of the truck bed and pushed myself up with my forearms. Pain traveled through my body from my toes to the top of my head. I half-straddled the edge until I could push up off the wheel well. When he accelerated into the turn I pushed myself over the side of the truck. I landed hard on my right, and the inner edge of the rear bumper slammed against my knee as my captor drove on, oblivious. The pain took my breath, but then the adrenaline kicked in and I rolled through mud until I was off the road. The truck stopped, red lights bright against a dark quarter-moon night. The driver's side door opened, and a pair of boots settled to the ground. I got to my knees and forearms, the pain searing as I put weight on my knee. I pushed up hard and groaned as I pressed into the mud with my toes and straightened.

"Ah, come on now. Come on now. You don't want it this way, fella." I took off into the brush. I ran through high weeds and basketball-size boulders. My stocking feet were little protection. No matter.

"Come on now."

Pop. That's three.

I heard him behind me.

People don't tell you how hard it is to run when you can't use your arms for momentum.

"This is not the way to go, fella."

Pop. Four bullets spent. Three to go.

Closer now. I looked back. He was having the same trouble I was, maneuvering over weeds, rocks and ruts in the earth. His advantage was balance. He had arms—and my gun.

"Mistake," he shouted behind me. "Big mistake, making me mad." I picked up speed. A wall of rock loomed ahead of me. If it had a backside, I'd find it. If it didn't, I couldn't see around it, so I'd most likely be trapped. I kept my eyes on the wall, the boulders above appearing to hang by an invisible thread. And then I was airborne, big toe and top of foot accepting the full impact of running man against rock. I fell on my face. I turned on my back as he reached me, and I kicked out, aiming for anything, any part of his body to slow down the inevitable. He moved closer and the impact of his heavy boot against my left cheek sent me over on my side, my back to him. A kick to the kidneys, another to the hamstring...

Thunder only happens when it's raining...

Players only love you when they're playing...

A large hand hooked between the tie that bound my hands, and he dragged me behind him. The plastic tie cut into my skin and I felt the cool trickle of blood run down my arm. My exposed lower back scraped over the ground against rocks and weeds and thorns. He dragged me over something small, dark. He was crazy strong. In his desperation to subdue me, he had dropped the gun. I kicked out, maneuvered my legs, and captured it between the bottoms of my feet. Seventeen and a half ounces. I would not be able to hold on to it for long.

"Didn't have to be this way, fella. Did not have to be like this, nope. I am not a violent man."

He dragged me across the dirt road from the weeds. At the back of the truck he pulled out some thin rope, looped it through the section of plastic tie that spanned my wrists, then looped it around the tow hitch.

"Don't do this," I spit out. "Don't you fucking do this, Mardigan. I'm a cop." I pressed the gun into the ground, covering it with my foot.

"I know you are, fella. You're also in my way." He tightened the rope, and I hung off the tow hitch sideways. "You're about to find out what I do with people who get in my way."

He got into the cab of the truck, and I set the gun between my feet, soles together. He put the truck in gear and proceeded down the dirt road. The ground was muddy in places from the rain. The fire under my right side grew hotter as my skin made contact with the earth. He hit a bump in the road and I flew into the air, landing facedown. The gun was no longer between my feet. At least he didn't have it. I lost a sock, and the other was halfway off. The tops of my feet were raw from dragging along the ground. I fought to keep my face from riding the dirt road where tires, only tires belonged. I lost my pants.

Women, they will come and they will go...
When the rain washes you clean, you'll know...
You will know...

WHEN I CAME TO, I was inside. It was dark.

It had been a long night.

I had been stripped and hosed down.

Gotta be clean. Gotta get you clean, fella.

My hair was still wet. My head throbbed. I was scraped up. The hard spray of water, icy cold, brought all those numb nerves to the surface again, and right now there wasn't a spot on me that didn't hurt.

I am not a violent man.

I was on hard ground; felt like concrete. A garage, maybe, except there was no car smell. I smelled, instead, moisture, like a sidewalk that had just been hosed off. I was upright against a wall. I was wearing thin pants and t-shirt. I had socks on my feet—not the ones I came with, since I lost them somewhere between bump one and pothole sixty. A blanket rested across my lap. My hands and feet were unrestrained. I was attached to the wall by a large chain covered in rubber hosing. It was around my neck.

These were the facts, as I knew them. Here's more:

There was a large knot at the back of my head at the base of my skull. Sticky-tacky oozed from a gash below the knot. My left cheek felt tight, sore. I remembered being kicked in the face.

I was tossed down and hosed, after being dragged behind a truck. This I remembered. I drifted through layers of consciousness, jerking awake if I leaned too heavy on the restraint around my neck.

The Stone, with Alex. Mac, talking about Mason Laborteaux. Karen. Told her I'd see her soon. Followed dude on a bike down Speedway.

Tree Top.

It was all I remembered about before-now.

Tree Top. He wasn't going to make it; of that I was sure.

He knew too much, like Henry McLaren. They were in the way.

Like me. Like Alex.

Alex.

A door opened and low light streamed in. A hand felt the wall and a dim light came on overhead.

"Well," he said. "How are we today?"

Branch Mardigan was bald, and in fact had no hair that I could see, anywhere. No eyebrows, no eyelashes, no five o'clock shadow, no faint growth of hair around his crown. No arm hair. Nothing. His face was raw, red, welted, scarred. Marked. The rest of his exposed flesh, the same. He winced at some unseen pain. A strong chemical odor came off him. He wore white, loose pants and a white t-shirt. White socks. Through the open door I saw a clock on the wall. 9:20.

How are we today?

Morning. The room. Dark walls, gray concrete floor, still wet in places. A one-by-one-foot drain was in the middle of the floor. The door he came through was the only way in or out of this room. On the ceiling, a plain white ceiling fan with a light. A long table sat against a wall, and on it, jars. Dozens, filled with nuts and bolts and screws and washers and nails and marbles and hair ribbons and cellophane wrapped candy. Above the table were pictures tacked to the wall. Some were in color, some black and white, some taken from newspapers and magazines, but all were of girls, young girls. On the wall opposite, a twin bed, made. A white blanket covered my lower half. A metal bucket next to me, shiny and new.

Me. White crew socks, off-white thin pants, like pajamas, white t-shirt.

Kidnappers don't know that the best chance of a successful escape occurs in the first fifteen minutes after abduction. Adrenaline is high, there is confusion, the participants haven't yet settled in to the inevitable. Chances go down dramatically after the settling-in has happened. This man looked settled.

Killers don't know that every minute they allow their victim to live decreases their chances of successfully killing them. I have been allowed to live for approximately twelve hours. He didn't want to kill me, or he'd have done it already. This would be his undoing.

"I've seen better days, Mardigan" I said. "How you doin'?"

35

"*Y*ou complicate things for me." He said this with a smile. His teeth were spaced evenly. All of them. *Wince.*

"You look like you're in pain," I said.

"Enough about me, Detective Testarossa. Let's discuss you."

"Okay." I cut my eyes to the open door, and what lay beyond. He walked the few feet that separated me from freedom and closed it.

"Okay. Good. Now, then. I have no desire to kill you. Let's put that out there right quick. I'm not a violent man."

I looked at my wrists, felt the throb in my head, my lower back, my face. "Good to know."

"Your cooperation ensures freedom. See?"

"Sure."

"Would you like to sleep in the bed instead of on this cold floor?"

"Sure."

"Sure," he mimicked. "Good." He crouched down in front of me, just far enough away so I couldn't kick him in the throat. "I've shown you a kindness by not binding your hands, haven't I?"

"Sure."

"They look sore. I'm real sorry about that. You were in my way, see?"

"What are you doing?"

His smile faded. "Beg pardon?"

"What are you doing?" I raised my arms in a shrug. "Molesting them as little girls wasn't enough, was it? Now you're coming back for more."

"Ah. You are a good detective. The intel on you was on the money. You're smart. You're thorough. You *care*." He pursed his lips, mocking me.

"So, why?"

"Why am I ridding the earth of the dirty little girls? That should be obvious. They come to me so pure, so innocent, so...childlike."

"They're childlike because they're children. And they don't come to you; you take them."

"They needed me." He raised his hand in anticipation of an argument. "Now, before you comment or pass judgment, let me just say for the record that I prepared them, got them ready." He stood. "So, when *it* happens to them, they're... ready. If society would calm down, take a step back, and just let *be*, they'd learn that children are sexual beings and..."

"Shut the fuck up." I needed freedom and three minutes alone in a room with this animal.

"You're right, Detective. Enough talk now. I have things to do. Sit tight and don't cause me trouble, and you'll be back with your people before you know it."

What killers don't know is that we learn a lot by listening. "I need to go to the bathroom."

"Ah. Well, there's a bucket there. You'll figure it out. Just don't fall forward." He laughed as he closed the door behind him with a snick. I was alone again.

I pulled against the neck collar. There was some slack between where the chain attached to the collar and where it attached to the wall, and there was room around my neck. I tried to pull the collar up and get it over my head. There wasn't that much room after all. I could feel a heavy silver chain that was covered in rubber hose material. I was able to turn my head until the wall behind me stopped movement. The chain felt like one piece and was attached to something hard behind me—not the wall. It felt like a brace. I grabbed the collar and moved it up, trying to go along with it. I slouched down as far as I could, and the collar joined me. Next, I leaned forward until the collar stopped me by cutting off my airway. I got as far as it took to create a twelve-inch space between my lower back and the wall. I turned my head and looked up, and behind me. The collar was attached to a common slide rail.

You'll figure it out.

I pressed my back against the rail and tried to push myself up. The rail dug into my back, already scraped raw. I slumped to the ground and turned on my right side so that my right arm and shoulder were pressed against the rail. Unfortunately, my head was, too, as I pushed in to gain momentum. The edges of the rail dug into all the sore spots, and I realized another place where I was cut and bleeding. That's when I noticed blood on an otherwise pristine shirt. I turned on my left side and felt around the rail, grabbing for leverage so I could pull myself up. My fingers found the thin metal edge at a depth of about an inch. My thick digits couldn't find a hold, so I grabbed the whole rail and, pressing my left side hard into the metal, pushed through the floor until I was semi-upright. The edge of the metal railing sliced into my upper arm like a razor. My legs rebelled and my knees buckled. I grunted and pushed through it.

I was up. Good enough.

I used the time wisely. The collar wouldn't allow me to turn enough so I could study the rail system, so I stayed perpendicular to the wall and let my peripherals take over. A simple metal piece attached to a stud in the wall, the other piece I recognized as a simple vertical blind railing system. The notched rod was set in the middle of the attached piece, and if this was a vertical blind system, the thing that attached the collar to the rod was plastic.

Okay.

I turned until my back was against the wall and I studied the room. Two steps up to a door that opened into what looked like the main house, from the quick glimpse I got while the door was open. Ahead of me, a wall that stopped about three feet from the ceiling and was attached to the sidewalls of the room with brackets. The ceiling was open beyond the wall, and for about three feet on my side before a ceiling began, a fan and light were set in the center. Along the wall where the workbench sat, a piece of painted plywood covered a roughly two-by-two-foot section. A window, possibly—next to the collage of little girls.

I was in a garage, attached to the house. The wall was an attempt to hide the garage door, or to discourage use. The restraint system I was attached to wasn't the only one in the room. There were two places along the wall near the workbench where large eyebolts had been secured into the wall. There was a large one in the concrete floor next to the drain. There was also a large one in the ceiling between me and the fan. None looked like they were meant to keep an adult secured for long.

More good news.

Unable to hold out any longer, I pulled the metal bucket toward me with my foot and tried to determine stream range since I couldn't look down. Most of it went in the bucket. I was pissing red. My lower back hurt.

It was good to stand but it was damn hard to do, so I was in no hurry to sit down again. I did for an hour or so before Mardigan came back for another visit.

"Well," he said as he closed the door behind him. "You've done your business, I see." He stared at the floor in front of me. "You missed a little."

"I'm not exactly mobile."

"Yes, well..." He took the bucket and left the room, returning a few minutes later with a white plastic bucket and a long-handled scrub broom. He dumped the contents of the bucket on the floor where I 'missed', and scrubbed in hard, quick jerks.

"These things happen," he said, his voice vibrating in rhythm with the scrubbing. "Gotta be clean. Can't have this." When the floor was back to his liking, he took the bucket and broom back into the house, leaving the door open. I heard water running, the kitchen being right inside the door. He returned with the same white bucket and tossed the contents over the area he'd scrubbed raw. The sharp smell of pine cleaner burned my eyes before it dissipated with the water that flowed toward the middle of the floor and then down the drain. The cold humidity coming off the wet ground drove a chill through me.

He looked at me and smiled. "Well...you'll get the hang of it. Nothing to be ashamed about."

"Can I have some water?"

"Water? Sure. Oh, you must be thirsty. Some food, too,

would be nice, huh?" It was like he was talking to an invited guest. "I'll be right back."

I watched the water trickle toward the center of the room, the lilt of its final descent into the drain to an unknown destination oddly soothing. The sound reminded me of the small fountain I'd installed on my patio a few months ago, lulling me into numbness after a hard day, accompanied by a scotch or two. This was not that.

Mardigan returned, tossing half a dozen plastic water bottles on the floor next to me, along with a box of granola bars and six Clementine tangerines.

"Your generosity is overwhelming," I said, meaning it.

"I'm not all that bad."

"No, you're great. You abducted little girls, molested them for four days, reasoned to yourself they liked it, then came back for more years later. Since I'm a homicide cop, it's the coming-back-for-more-years-later I'm interested in most."

"I understand that." He sat down on his haunches like a peasant in a rice paddy. His smile was invasive, his teeth bared for a feast, eyes dead, yet so fucking alive I wondered if I was the one gone.

"I imagine in your line of work," he went on, "you see people a second, sometimes a third time around. I mean, maybe you see a certain criminal and he's not so bad, but you sense that could change. Then you see this same criminal again, maybe years later, and you find you were right. Then, maybe you see him a third time, and you're thinking, 'Jesus, what do I have to do to get through to this guy?' and it is maybe that third time where you say to yourself, 'There is only one thing to be done because this fool simply will not learn'. That ever happen to you, Detective?"

It had. I walked a false path with a nest of vipers for ten

years before I got my revenge, and every day was worse than the one before. But that was one confession I'd keep to myself.

"I usually come on the scene after they've passed that third phase and killed someone, Mardigan. What are you getting at?"

He stared at me for a moment and nodded, like we'd come to an understanding at last. "No one's safe. You get me? The bad ones are out there, and they are not safe."

"Who? Who's not safe?"

"Girls." Mardigan looked down at hands chafed and red, dangling between his knees. "With boys it's different. They aren't in much danger that I have seen. But girls..." He looked to the ceiling, tears welling in his eyes. "Alone, without someone to protect them, and he will come. He will come like a shadow, and then they are lost."

"But *you* came. *You* took countless little girls and did unspeakable things to them. The monster you're talking about is you."

"No, Detective. The monster I'm talking about is long gone."

Turns out he had a son, but no one ever saw him. Rumor was he was in some sort of institution. Kid had problems.

"How do you know the monster?"

The odd grin and the eyes raised in surprise sat frozen on Mardigan's face. His smell was overwhelming—ammonia, pine cleaner and something underlying, a sweetness, thick and cloying. His clothing, loose and flowing, strained in places where hard muscle belonged. His almost sixty years were not evident in the places age should show up, yet this man had lived a hundred lifetimes, every one of them a nightmare. I'd seen it in too many eyes, both alive and dead. The room was cold, and an icy chill ran down my back. My head ached; my legs ached. I wanted to lie down.

Mayor was beaten to death. No evidence. No nothing.

"I know the monster, Detective, because I lived with him."

My mother told me once that she learned more about me while she was driving me and my friends around in the car than at any other time. For some reason we believed that a cone of silence was lowered over that backseat once the car started moving. She said we talked like she wasn't there. Criminals believe that once they have their victim restrained, held in place, safe from rescue, anything goes. The victim often times becomes the confessee, and the criminal believes he has nothing to lose, or all will be forgotten in the end—whatever the end is. But like a mother behind the wheel of a car filled with boys, the words live on. They are remembered.

Branch Mardigan drew the door closed behind him and I heard the distinctive click of deadbolt lock into jamb. And then I heard two beeps, high-pitched and quick. And then his footsteps, fading.

Beep.

Beep.

I studied the closed door. Small, white wires rested against the outside edge of the white molding around the door, then disappeared between the door and the jamb at the dead latch and strike plate. I followed the wires up and around the door, then across the wall where it met the ceiling, and down the length of the room. The wires continued along the façade wall and then they came back toward me along the wall above the workbench. Half way, the wires took a turn south and came straight down, disappearing between the workbench and the wall. A metal pot sat on the floor in front of the workbench. I couldn't see the wires, but I'd have bet a few paychecks they were attached to that pot.

A pressure cooker bomb—simple and very effective.

The room was rigged. In case he got caught, in case someone came along uninvited—police, maybe. In case he needed to destroy a victim in a hurry. They'd open the door and anyone inside the room, gone. The fool who opened the door, badly damaged. Without knowing for sure, I guessed Mardigan had the garage door on the other side of the façade rigged, too. My new worry now was that he remembered to turn off the trigger before he entered the room.

I grabbed the front of the collar with both hands and yanked hard, trying to loosen it from the rail. I yanked and twisted, the front of my neck slamming against my fists with each attempt. I sat down, spent. My head pounded, and with every movement of my eyes, my neck, every wince that pain brought, brought it again a hundred-fold. I studied the room. I saw now that the walls I believed were painted dark were covered almost completely by three by three sections of foam padding. A few inches of white wall could be seen in between the sections. The ceiling, the walls, and all exposed hard surface except the floor were covered with the stuff. It absorbed sound.

It muffled the screams of little girls.

The hose came again in the middle of the night. Didn't like what he saw, didn't like what he smelled. I was chilled through, in the way only a fevered person can be. I fell in and out of dreams, and at various times I saw someone standing in front of me. That person stood in front of me now. It was Jesus.

36

To a soul not in his right mind, it could have been Jesus. But, of course, it wasn't. Beverly Shay seemed to glow above me in flowing pants and tunic, her wavy hair framing a face that was angelic, and the way the shadows played there, at least for me, here and now, she looked to be sporting some facial growth. No wonder drugged up, psychotic homeless people thought they were seeing Jesus. It was more about the aura than anything else. I saw it, too.

"This is about as bad as it gets," she said, almost to herself. I cracked open an eye. "You're ill." Without turning away, she continued. "He needs to be in that bed and we need to get him well. You need to stop with the hose. Have sense."

"Okay, I'll stop with the hose, but he stays right there."

"And how long do you think you can keep him like this before he starts working himself loose. Have—sense."

I groaned as I straightened into almost upright. The door was open again, and unnatural light filtered in from the kitchen. The clock said 8:20. It was night again. They stood over me, one looking over the other's shoulder with wonder, like I was a rare bug under glass. I was dry, and I was warm again—as warm as someone with the chills can be. The full effects of what I'd been through—the knock to the head, the kicks, the leap over the side of the truck, more kicks, and then being dragged for however far—was beating a new tune, a rhythmic pulse that kept time with my heart, each beat like a new kick to the kidneys, a new smack to the head.

I heard a cry. It was soft, young, afraid. The wonder on their faces at the creature before them changed to panic at the cry heard by more than just them.

"Go," Beverly hissed, and Branch disappeared, closing the door behind him. I didn't hear a beep this time. He was cognizant enough to realize his sister had to get out eventually, and he wanted her to do it in one piece.

Yes, I remembered now. The room was rigged. Right, stew pot...no. What the hell was it called? I looked toward the workbench. It was still there, out from under the table, out in the open where it would do the most good if called upon.

Pressure cooker.

Yeah. They seemed to make pretty good shrapnel bombs. And it didn't take much to set them off.

"Understand," she said. "My brother..." She took a deep breath and tried again. "My brother has had it bad. Very bad."

"What's...what's wrong with him, with his face?"

"Mmmm. Well, sadly those are chemical burns—bleach, acetone, whatever the latest quirk and form of trickery he can find on the Internet to help him with his condition."

"Alo-something."

"Alopecia, yes. He's had it since he was young, fifty years

or more. No one knows why people get it. For my brother, I think it was stress."

"What stress?"

"Living with our father."

"The monster."

"Hmmm. Some—my brother—would say that."

"He was the mayor."

"You've done your homework. Yes, he was the mayor."

"And a monster."

"We all have a public life, and we all have a private life. We all deal with the matters of life, the good and the bad, differently."

"How bad was the bad?" I asked. When she didn't answer, I said, "It'd be nice to know why your brother did... does...the things he does."

"Must there be a reason?"

"There usually is."

"Not always. Sometimes a kid is just bad, a mess...fucked up."

"That's his story? *Just bad*? *Just fucked up*?"

"Uh huh. Doesn't make for a good crime novel, I know, but he wasn't abused, he wasn't neglected."

I stared at her through my fevered fog, and it hit me. *They needed me*, Mardigan said. *I prepared them, got them ready.*

They're not safe. No one's safe.

"It was you," I said, my voice shaking through convulsive shivering. "The mayor hurt you." Beverly Shay shook her head, pain deep-set in her eyes. "That's why your brother murdered him."

"No. He was an extremely unhappy man with a troubled son and a spoiled, unhappy wife. Understand, he committed his fourteen-year-old son to an institution because he tortured house pets and put his hands down little girls' panties." Beverly Shay sat cross-legged in front of me and settled in.

"Fiona Shay was the only black woman on Mayor Mardigan's staff. My mother performed a function that made his life easier. She was a highly intelligent woman. She spoke, and the mayor listened. He fell in love with her. He couldn't help himself. When she became pregnant, he could have sent her away, forced an abortion, any number of things. He was the mayor. It's not the president, but he had pull. He was popular at the time. Instead, he left his wife. It took a long time, but I remember the mayor's house, all the rooms, hiding behind false walls. Mardi didn't take it well. He was always good to me; don't misunderstand. He never took his anger out on me."

"Mardi?"

"My brother. It's what everyone calls him. Mardi started coming around shortly before our father died. My mother tried to explain to me about the hospital. I didn't understand. When I finally met Mardi, I understood."

"Understood what?"

"Why he was in the hospital. It didn't help. He didn't get better, he just got better at it."

"Hurting children."

"Yes. He hid his illness behind lots of charm and intelligence. He learned how to hide what he did."

"No hair, no DNA, using objects."

"Yes, to all of it."

"And where do you come in?" I asked. "What part do you play in all this?"

"Not a good one, not one I'm proud of."

"He hurt you, didn't he? It wasn't the mayor; it was your brother."

"No."

"Deny it all you want. Someone hurt you, and the buck ain't stopping with you. Change that. Right now. He's inside with a child. I heard her."

"I'll do anything to protect him, and I have. I've saved some—" She looked up to the heavens in search of the word that would make them remain objects rather than children in her sick mind.

"Say it. They're *children*," I hissed. "Human beings. You can't even acknowledge that. If you did, you might have put a stop to this a long time ago, regardless of what happened to you."

"You're not wrong." She stood. "I tried to keep him close. I opened the shelter so I could keep him close to me."

"Did you know that he continued this while you were off living your life, but these girls he never returned, never let them go?"

"I suspected."

"You did, huh? Well, you're just as bad...as bad as he is."

"You're shivering. Here." Beverly Shay pulled the blanket up around me. "You need to be in that bed." She sat back on her haunches. "And I am not as bad as he is but understand —I have to help him. I *have* helped him."

"You want to help some more? Stop him. Get that kid out of here and home, where she belongs. Don't let him ruin one more life."

"I will. I will do that."

"Do it now."

She nodded. "He's good, and so sweet. He's just got...troubles."

I shook my head. Oddly, I found her more reprehensible than I found him. "He's not sweet, Beverly. He's a pedophile and a killer."

"Oh, don't say that."

"Come on. You're an educated, compassionate woman, and you've let him run wild. You've spent your life trying to save him from himself, but now you need to save those he hurts. He's sick, and he's dangerous. Keep him away from that kid, Beverly, and you'll have helped."

"Stand down, Detective. He will kill you. Do you hear me? He knows about you, he knows who you love, he knows where you live. He will destroy all that you hold dear. He's hard to stop, and I'm the only one who can do it, so you just lie low."

"He won't hurt me, Beverly, you know why? I'm smarter and I'm tougher. Keeping me alive gives him more time. He kills me, it's over for him—and you. Believe that. You want to save him, do it now, because if you don't it will be too late."

"You have no idea."

"No. He doesn't. And you don't. Your chance is now, and it's the only one I'm giving you."

"A lot of words from someone who's attached to the wall by his neck."

"You're starting to lose my sympathy, Beverly."

"You can't stay here like this. You can't." She smiled down at me. "I'm going to bring you some soup."

When she left, I stood up and started yanking at the chain around my neck. If I made too much noise, one of them would be back, but I didn't care. I yanked and twisted. It wasn't about me anymore. They had another child in the house. The soup never came, and that gave me as much time as I needed to plan. And while I planned, I yanked and twisted that chain around my neck. The apparatus used to hold me was not supposed to hold a two-hundred-pound adult. It wouldn't be long before I was free. I think at the beginning, Mardigan's plan was to kill me, but something stopped him. Maybe it was the truth I told; maybe it was Beverly Shay. In the end, keeping me alive long enough for me to pull myself off this fucking wall would be this asshole's undoing.

After enough yanking and pulling on the attachment to risk bringing one or both of them back in the room, I took a break. This was not going to work. I lifted my arms with the idea to gauge how far above my head the tracking system ended, since I couldn't see. My right arm screamed in pain and then a steady throb set in. I felt around my shoulder area with my other hand and felt a knot, like the shoulder was separated or dislocated. I kept it glued to my side at the elbow and felt above me with my left hand. That throbbed, too, but not as much. I was able to reach the open top of the rail with my hand. It felt like I needed another foot or more.

The metal bucket next to me was about fourteen inches tall. I kicked it over with my foot. Urine from a previous piss trickled out. That would annoy Mardigan when he came back in, and it would distract him. That gave me an idea for later.

I overturned the bucket and balanced on one foot as I placed all my weight on the bucket with the other and pushed myself up. If the bucket slipped out from under me now it would make a racket, and possibly snap my neck. I tightened and held steady on my right leg. The knee that the bumper caught as I flew over the side of the truck buckled and I started to go down. I tottered on the bucket as I pressed my body against the railing, the metal cutting into my back. I pressed hard, determined to stay on my feet, and when I felt steady again, I reached above me with my left hand. The top of the railing hit my head dead center. I'd need another six inches or so before I would be high enough to slide the attachment up and out of the rail system. The thought of getting down off the bucket and then getting up on it again after I figured things out wasn't happening. The only thing that would get me off the bucket now was a visit from my nutty captors. I didn't have a lot of time.

I looked around for something else to stand on to give me some height. This was not your average garage, with boxes of nothing piled on bags of useless. There was nothing in here, except a bed—useful had it been at my side —a pressure cooker bomb, and a workbench with a lot of useful shit, if only I could get to it. I wasn't going anywhere until I could get myself out of this harness.

I stood on the bucket for a long time, thinking, switching legs to give that banged-up knee a break. I studied the room, memorizing it. Once free, I'd not have a lot of time. Where would I go first? What was my plan? What would I need at my disposal to overpower these people?

How long do you think you can keep him like this before he starts working himself loose?

Mardigan wasn't thinking; or maybe he was momentarily distracted by a cooler head—Beverly's. She was right, of course. The longer they let me remain here, the quicker I'd get loose. It was only a matter of time, and for some reason, they were giving it to me. The child inside the house gave them something else to think about besides me.

The clock outside this room read 8:20 last time I looked. An hour or more had gone by already. One of two things would happen within the hour: I would get free or I'd be killed. I thought about Karen, at her place waiting for me. I had been on foot, a five-minute walk home to pack up a few things, then a five-minute drive to her place. I pictured her pacing along her balcony, waiting for the call up to announce me. Ten minutes; thirty. An hour. A day. Alex would have gone to her already, and she sat now with the realization that something had gone very wrong. She was worrying. Alex was on this, too; I could feel him. Maybe it was on the news. Maybe not, depending on strategy. You go through the academy, but there is no way they can prepare a cop for this. The military guys, the ones who did their time in service to their country before coming to the Department knew better than I about this shit. Captivity, isolation, the threat of torture or death. They knew what to do; they'd been trained for this. What I did know was that all the psychological shit needed to have happened earlier—that's where they get you; that's where you become their bitch. Give the prey no time to formulate thought, make a plan, talk too much. Yeah. Mardigan and his sister had made a big mistake, and it was time now to capitalize on that.

I leaned for a moment against the restraint around my neck. I needed to focus the cramping pain off my legs for a moment—the one I was standing on and the one that was hanging loose in the air. I placed my hands flat against the wall behind me and dug my fingers into the foam material that covered the walls of this room—to muffle screams.

"Moron," I chastised myself as I found the edge of one of the foam panels and pulled. I didn't know if the stuff was glued on or nailed in. Didn't care. I pulled until I came away with half a two-by-two hunk in my hand. I stepped off the bucket; didn't want to. Getting back up would not be pleasant. I set the foam piece on top of the bucket, knowing that once I stepped on it, I'd have no more height than without. I tore off the other half and then went to work on another one. They'd notice all of this when they came in, of course. By then I'd be free, I hoped.

I managed to get enough of the stuff off the walls to

make a decent pile on top of the bucket so that when I stepped up, and then stood on my toes, I'd be able to move the attachment on the restraint to the top of the railing—barely. After the third attempt I tipped the bucket over and I went sideways. My feet dangled off the ground as I hung by the restraint around my neck. I saw stars, and then my eyes went black. I grabbed at the restraint and held it off my neck until I could slide the twelve inches or so to the ground. I sat in defeat as the oxygen reached my brain again.

Then I grabbed the bucket and threw up.

TIME WAS MEASURED in short dreams as I moved in and out of consciousness. In one moment of lucidity I gathered the foam and brought the bucket close. I heard footsteps coming toward the door. I stuffed the foam behind my back. The light went out and a beep sounded, indicating the trigger for the bomb had been set. Then footsteps retreated. Tucking me in for the evening. How sweet.

I thought about the kid, somewhere in that house, and what was happening to her. I could not sit here any longer. In the pitch dark I stood, threw the contents of the bucket near the door and upended it. I got to my feet, set the foam atop the bucket and then planted my left foot. I pushed through the cramp in my calf as I lifted and then held my weight steady as I rose onto my toes and tried to move the attachment up and out of the rail. It was halfway out when I teetered again on the bucket, but this time I held my balance, and when I tried again, the attachment slipped out.

I was free.

37

I had a decision to make. I could not see a thing. As much as I thought I memorized the layout of the garage, in the black of night I could not trust myself to make my way to the workbench, where a whole lot of loot could be gathered to do damage. Had to see it to do it.

Now what?

I stepped off the bucket and felt around the wall next to me. I gathered up the foam pieces and tried to piece that puzzle back together on the wall to my left. Some of it stuck, much of it fell to the floor. I stuck the remaining pieces behind my back to cushion against the sharp metal railing. I righted the bucket, sat and ate a few granola bars and drank two bottles of water. I also pissed. Branch Mardigan was strong, and I needed something that would incapacitate him, if only for a moment. I thought I had a good handle on what that would be. I was still cold, still hazed out from what I could only guess was a concussion, plus the fever, which was a good one. I rarely got fevers. When one came along, it made an impression.

I listened for footsteps, for cries, for voices. I closed my eyes and tried to retrace the route here, tried to estimate how long I spent in the back of that truck, tried to bring back the muscle memory of the twists and the turns, hoping, wishing I had an idea of where we were so once I got out of here, I'd have a direction to go. The boulders I saw in the dim light of night, that first night, were familiar, and they looked like the mountainous terrain in and around Chatsworth, where we spent time with former Sheriff Steve Pauling. It felt like the drive was longer than it would take to get to that particular area, but I was in and out of consciousness. To avoid detection, he could have taken canyons and surface streets. I remembered another thing: the truck, which was white, according to DMV records, wasn't white when I was being dragged back to it after my escape attempt, nor did white register as I was being dragged behind it. If that was the case, Alex was looking for the wrong truck.

The one thing I did remember was that, from the turn off the main road where I jumped, to where the truck finally stopped—here—had not been far: the length of a football field, maybe two lengths. I had not been dragged far. In my haze, and given Mardigan's anger, I expected that incident to go farther than it did, and in fact, I didn't expect to survive it. That I was dragged over a short distance reduced injury and trauma and, most importantly, told me I wasn't far from a main road—less than a mile.

The next time I opened my eyes, still standing, I could see a trace of light coming from under the door to the house. I heard footsteps. I grasped the chain that used to connect to the slide railing behind me, and I slid myself down to the floor, making sure the chain came with me still resting against the railing. The light came on, nothing more. But not for long.

I groaned as I stood and limped to the workbench, every bone, every muscle aching, and my knees so stiff I could hardly stand.

The jars filled with nails and bolts and marbles and other things had not been an illusion. A few jars were empty, and I knew their contents were residing inside the pressure cooker. I thought for a moment about disengaging it, but I had great respect for the bomb squad people, and I was smart enough to stay away from shit I knew nothing about. I left it. It would serve me later.

I took off my socks and filled them with the contents from the jars. I opened the narrow drawer under the workbench and found locks and plastic ties and leather restraints. I pulled them all out and returned to my prison, shoving my contraband under a blanket. As an afterthought, I shoved a couple of Clementines in the socks. The more the merrier. I positioned myself against the wall and made sure the collar matched up where it needed. Then I waited.

Time passed, and I drifted in and out of sleep. I passed the time staring at the wall of pictures above the workbench, trying to spot a familiar face. Loud voices behind the door brought me around, and I positioned myself against the railing. The door flew open, and Branch Mardigan missed both steps as he barged in, almost stumbling over himself. When he hit the floor, he slipped on the contents of the bucket I'd tossed in the middle of the night. The stench of vomit was reignited and Mardigan screamed as he realized what he'd landed in.

"Ack! God...Jesusshitfuckgoodammit!"

"Problem?" I asked. He looked ready to pass out.

"What did you do?" Mardigan hissed. Cameras. I never thought about that, never thought I was being watched. The scene just didn't feel that sophisticated. I'd misjudged. I'd underestimated. But why had he waited so long to come in and confront me? I'd been back in place and semi-conscious for a while, so why now? It was now or never. I set myself, ready to pounce.

"What the fuck did you motherfucking do?" He stood in front of me, arms outstretched, a wretched look on his face, simmering in rage and disgust, trying to decide if he wanted to clean up or get his question answered. What the fuck had I done? So much...

"Mardi."

Beverly Shay stood behind him. Mardigan was pale and sweating and on the verge of collapse. She regarded him with mild amusement, then her expression changed to sympathy.

"C'mon, honey, let's get you..." Beverly Shay reached for him, intent on getting him freshened up, but he jerked away from her and turned his fury on me.

"There was a bag in the back of the truck," he hissed, his eyes wild. "Where is it?"

Ah. So that was it.

"There was a bag with some prescription medications for Mardi. It isn't there." Beverly Shay spoke as if she were discussing the weather—detached, unemotional, while her brother hissed and sputtered in front of her.

"Why is he sweating?"

"He's diabetic." Beverly pulled a piece of candy out of her pocket and unwrapped it. "Here. And go in the shower. Now, Mardi."

Mardigan popped the candy into his mouth and closed his eyes as whatever relief it gave washed over him. *The bag.* The bag in back of the truck, the one I grabbed and tossed over the side, out of spite, out of desperation that maybe if Alex, or others, happened along, it would serve as a clue, like a piece of bread on the trail to grandmother's house. Insulin. Prescription numbers would lead to an address.

Hold it together.

The smell coming off him now was sickly sweet, mixed with puke. Sweat poured down his face in shiny rivers. His hands shook. I recalled what Karen said about the smell of diabetics.

"I'm going to have to run out," she said.

"No, you can't," Mardigan hissed.

"They're not looking for me, they're looking for you. I'm taking the girl with me and I'm dropping her outside of town."

"The fucking hell you are!" he said.

"Let her take the kid. Do one thing right, Mardigan."

I didn't see him move until I felt the back of his hand connect with my face, and I had to brace hard against the railing so I wouldn't fly off to the side and give away my secret. A heavy boot connected with my side, followed by excruciating pain and a dull crack as something broke inside me.

I'm not a violent man.

"Stop it! Goddammit, stop it!" Beverly Shay grabbed at Mardigan's arm and pulled him away. I gasped as the pain shot through me, and I pressed myself hard against the wall so I wouldn't slump over. "I am going to get you what you need. You are going to sit out there and drink your juice and take your blood sugar every few minutes."

"I will not die like this," he fumed at me. "Not like this." He reeled, and I saw him steady himself to deliver another blow with his boot. So did Beverly Shay.

"I said stop it, Mardi, right now!" She grabbed him and shoved him back. He almost went down. "Go to the table and do like I said. I'll get you cleaned up and I'll be back." She pushed him up the two steps and turned to me.

"Make this end," I gasped. "Get help. If you don't, he will not live through this, I promise you."

"You are in no position to make threats," she hissed.

"I'm telling you what will happen. Bring back a cop, or he dies. And you'll die with a fucking needle in your arm. I promise you."

She closed the door behind her, and I heard two beeps. Great. Mardigan was in no condition to think, so if he opened that door without disengaging the bomb, Alex will have goulash for a partner. I slumped forward and went down on my right side, struggling for breath, for clarity, for a moment when the pain dulled just a bit. I got to my feet. Every breath was like the pierce of a knife. I pulled the bucket closer. I heard a car start, and as that sound disappeared, I heard hard footsteps coming for me. I listened for a beep, heard it, and took a breath as he opened the door and stumbled down the steps. He was still covered in vomit, and insane with rage. This was it.

"I underestimated you," he said.

"Because I'm not a ten-year-old girl."

"You're funny, you know that? You're there, attached to a wall by your neck, and I'm here."

"Stinking like cotton candy and sick while your blood sugar flops out of control. Tell you what, Mardigan. Turn around with your back to me, get down on your knees, lace your hands behind your head, and I'll let you live. Don't, and I'll kill you."

His laugh started out low, and then it broke loose into hefty, mouth-open guffaws that caused him to toss his head back and hold his belly like Felix the Cat.

Whenever he gets in a fix

He reaches into his bag of tricks...

Despite his condition, he seemed to have energy for this. I jerked away from the wall and grabbed the bucket. I tossed the contents over him while he was still in full belly laugh.

You'll laugh so much your sides will ache...

He sputtered and coughed, looked down at himself, then up at me. And then he screamed. He screamed and he slapped at himself like he was on fire. His penchant for cleanliness, his need for control in all areas, but especially that one, where dirt and piss and shit were sometimes not in anyone's control, was his undoing. He grunted and screamed and spun in a circle, looking for the bucket and pine cleaner that didn't exist, and while he did that, I came up with the two socks that were filled with nuts and bolts and nails and marbles and tangerines, and I swung for the fences. He went down on his knees and I swung again, hitting him across the temple. Mardigan spat at the ground in front of him, trying to get the taste of my piss out of his mouth. He lunged for me and caught me at the knees, bringing me down. I came up with a right, catching him full in the face. I rolled away from him, the shards of pain in the side causing me to cry out. I got to my knees as he lunged for me again, and I caught him with a forearm across his left cheek. He went down, blood pouring from his nose and mouth. He got to his knees as I got to my feet, and I brought the sock down across the back of his neck and swung the other one up between his legs. He screamed out and fell onto his back. Without shoes, my feet weren't the weapons his were, but they were all I had. I brought my heel down hard, and I heard his nose crack under my foot. I did it again and felt his mouth crash against his teeth.

I flipped him over on his belly, and I went for the restraints. I grabbed two plastic ties. They were too short to go over both wrists, so I pulled his hands behind his back, tied one around one wrist, then slipped the end of the other one through that, and then around his other wrist, and secured him tight. Then I grabbed a leather restraint and tied his ankles. I dragged him to the middle of the floor and slipped another leather restraint between the ties on his hands, then secured it with a padlock to the eyebolt sticking out of the floor next to the drain. Then, because I could, I reared back and smashed my fist into his face.

"That's for all the little girls who didn't have the strength to do it, you fucking low-life piece of shit."

He lay on his side and groaned while I went to the wall above the workbench and I took all the pictures down. I would find these girls. I climbed the two steps, closed the door behind me, and pressed the red button. At the sound of the two high-pitched beeps, he screamed his fury into the silence.

I held the two filled socks in my hand and walked down a short hall, the clock on the wall just inside the kitchen reading 9:30, but it was not an hour from the last time I'd seen the clock, it was twenty-five.

I searched for a phone in all the places a phone would be kept. Nothing. The clock's second hand moved at a normal pace, and had I not seen that, or heard the ticking, I would have believed it to be broken. It always seemed to be 9:30, but maybe I just dreamed that.

A half-finished glass of orange juice and a sandwich on white bread sat at a vacant seat. The floor throughout the house was cement, something en vogue by design, yet I believed Mardigan did it for a different reason: easy to hose down, easy to hide the blood. The drains in the floor strategically placed confirmed my theory. The kitchen cabinets were smooth white lacquer, the counters a hard-smooth material that resembled the floors. The appliances were white and utilitarian. To the left of the kitchen, opposite a short dividing wall, was the living room. It, too, was not furnished in the usual style. Iron outdoor furniture with simple olive-green cushions took the place of couch and chairs.

I grabbed a plastic drugstore bag off the table and slipped the pictures from the wall inside. Moving through the house, I opened the first door I came to—a bathroom, done in minimalist style like the rest of the house. Bath toys sat along the rim of the tub, and then I remembered: there was a child in the house.

I slammed open every door until I came to the last room on the left. I heard the small whimper of a child behind the locked door. I stepped back and kicked out with my foot. Pain shot up through my heel and the door splintered at the jamb. I rushed the door with my body, and it flew open.

The room was done in pink and lime green, the twin bed covered in poufy pink ruffles and flowers. The room was twice the size of the others. Lucite boxes of bright beads, lanyards, costume jewelry, crayons, markers, paints and clay lay neatly stacked along one wall. A wooden dollhouse five feet tall dominated a corner. A mirrored vanity with a silver and mother-of-pearl brush, comb and hand mirror sat neatly on a polished surface. Everything a little girl could want was in this room, and if the little girl never had these things, this was a room that would keep her here, at least for a while.

She sat on the ruffled pink bed, her knees up under her chin, her eyes red and hollow. She jumped when the door flew open and scooted back against the padded headboard when I entered.

"Hi, sweetheart," I said, trying to keep my voice level,

despite the need to get out quickly. She'd been through enough—what, I did not want to imagine. I had no idea how I looked, but by the look on her face I must have been a horror.

"My name is John, and I'm a policeman. I'm going to take you out of here." I watched her face scrunch up and huge tears leak out of horror-filled eyes. Her cry was silent.

"Shhh..." I said as I approached the bed. "You're safe now, honey. We're going home, you and me." I smelled like piss and puke and general dirt, but the little girl flung herself at me and wrapped her arms around my neck anyway. She was a small girl, thin and lithe. The curves, the budding breasts, the attitude—it would come, but it wasn't here yet. I winced as her spindly legs dug into my sides, but I wasn't about to let her go.

"I got you, darlin'. Shhh. Are you hurt, sweetheart? Did he hurt you?"

"No," she cried into my neck.

"Okay. Okay, good." The relief that single word brought was overwhelming, and my eyes burned with emotion. "What's your name, darlin'?"

"Violet," she whispered.

"Okay, Violet, here we go. I want you to do exactly as I say, and I don't want you to be afraid. You're safe now. Understand?"

"Okay." She sobbed into my neck as I carried her out of the room and down the hall. I entered the living room at the same time Beverly Shay did. She dropped her bag on the floor.

"Where's Mardi?"

I put Violet down and set her back into the hallway. "Stay here." I turned and rushed Beverly Shay as she came into the living room, past the outdoor furniture, the plastic tables that could easily be replaced after a big mess, past the Lucite boxes with books and magazines underneath like preserved relics, past a green glass-based lamp with no shade, past a swooped sculpture of some unknown creature, the only bit of personality in the room. That she grabbed and swung it at me. I ducked, and my fist came up under her chin, sending her over the plastic end table with the green glass-based lamp, over the Lucite boxes with true-crime novels and issues of Rolling Stone underneath, and into the bare wall, primed only, so that blood and evidence could be quickly erased, painted over like the horror never occurred. She landed in a heap, and as I grabbed Violet up and headed for the door, she came onto her knees.

"What did you do?" she growled. "What did you do?" And then she did what I hoped she'd do: instead of coming at me, she went to the garage, and instead of moving toward the door, I rushed into the hallway, all the way to the end, and back into that pink and lime-green room. I closed the door and covered Violet with my body as the blast shook the walls. A scream from Beverly Shay cut through the dead silence that always seems to follow a blast, and as I rose with the girl in my arms and exited the room, Beverly Shay staggered into the living room with pieces of her brother clinging to her face, her body cut up, gashes bleeding. One eye was gone. She staggered toward me and I shoved past her with Violet in my arms.

"Close your eyes, baby," I said. "Don't look." As I opened the door to freedom, Beverly Shay collapsed against the iron couch with the neutral cushions. The stains could be washed away, surely. What she was, and the condition of her brother, would never change.

I stepped out onto the porch and into the dark night. No lights, a sky full of stars and no moon. In my semi-feverish state, I'd have to figure out where we were in order to get us out of here.

"Don't let me go," Violet said into my neck.

"I got you, baby. I got you." As I took the last step off the porch, a flood of bright lights hit me, and then I felt the barrel of a gun pressed against my ear.

"Don't you fucking move."

The air was dry, but the smell of outside, of earth, of this particular area, was familiar, and oddly soothing. The rain of however-many days ago was a memory, the dry, loose dirt under my bare feet sliding through my toes with little effort. The floorboards creaked under someone's heavy foot. The bright lights caused my head to pound, and a kaleidoscope of colors swirled in front of me. The socks, filled with heavy things meant to stun, swung against my gut like a pendulum in the breeze. The plastic bag that held the history of innocence was secured in my fist. The thin t-shirt and pants I'd been given to wear offered little protection against the chill that swept over me, and the barrel of the gun pressed against my head opened an old wound. I felt as trapped now as I did the night I was lured into an alley, and dropped my guard as I watched Tree Top, nailed to a pole, fight out a warning to me before he died. As trapped as I felt, I knew this was different. This was not the end. It was the finish, but it was definitely not the end.

"Hold it. Johnny? That's my partner. John? Get that fucking gun off him." I heard Alex, the panic, the concern in his voice. And as he came out from the shadows and walked in front of the headlights from the SUV, the child was removed from my arms. She screamed, and in that blinding light her arms reached for me, her mouth curled in horror, because to her this was not over. She begged me not to let her go, but I did. Someone else took my sock weapons out of my hand. Alex stood in front of me dressed in black. His eyes were tired and ringed in black.

"Took you long enough," I said.

"I had shit to do. What?"

"Well, I appreciate you making the time."

And then I blacked out.

38

I worked my way up through the dark, the weight of being under water holding me down. I fought it. I fought *up*. The antiseptic smell hit first, that rich fear of being somewhere I didn't belong sliced me sideways. Swim up. Swim. Up. Up.

NOW HERE I GO AGAIN, *I see the crystal visions*
I keep my visions to myself

I OPENED my eyes to a dimly lit room, the tube snaking out of my arm and up to a plastic bag hanging above my head, the smell of alcohol and rubber, a clip trapping my right index finger, and a screen to my right showing spiky lines that moved told me that, A) I was alive, and B) I was in my favorite place in the world: a hospital.

To my left, ten bare toes painted pink curled into the sheet that covered me. I followed the trail over a smooth, bare ankle, up tanned shin to white denim, then over a pair of bent knees to the hem of a pink sweater resting against alabaster skin two inches above the waistband, up across flat plains of stomach to rising mounds—two of them—beneath a V of flesh before the angles of a long swan neck and the soft contours of the most beautiful face God ever had the grace to create came into view. And the only thing I missed looking into were her eyes. They were closed. In sleep, Karen Gennaro was the most beautiful woman I have ever seen. It was the only time her face stayed the same, and it was the only time I felt I knew her best.

I lay my hand over her feet and caressed them awake. Her head came up with a start, and she pulled her feet off the bed and stood.

"Hi, babe."

The face that was so serene a moment ago was now contorted into concern mixed with a feeble attempt to hold back emotion. Seeing this face killed me. Knowing I caused it did the deed slow.

"Stop this or I'm kicking you out."

"I'd like to see you try." Karen placed a cool hand against my cheek and then she bent over and kissed me, her lips gentle against mine.

"I'm looking down your sweater, Doctor Gennaro."

"Feeling better I see." She turned away and dabbed at her eyes.

"Hey." I tugged at her arm. "I said stop that." When she turned back to me, it was with her chin high and her eyes dry.

"How are you feeling? Do you hurt?" she asked.

"I'm not feeling much of anything. You got me high."

"*I* didn't."

"Where am I?"

"Parkman, in the valley."

"So, you didn't get me high."

"Nope. Not allowed."

"But you're world-famous."

"Not in here."

"I'll speak to someone about that." I moved her hair off her face and over a shoulder. "You're very pretty." She closed her eyes and shook her head. "How do I look?" Karen kept her eyes closed, and I saw the beginnings of tears again. "That bad, huh?"

"Not so bad," she whispered.

"Starting at the top, what's wrong with me?" I asked.

Karen lowered the railing on my left and sat on the bed. "You have a concussion, you have a gash at the back of your head that they closed with butterfly bandages, and one on the right side of your head that took twelve stitches. You have a separated shoulder and kidney contusion. Your urine is clear."

"It wasn't before."

She nodded. "You have a cracked rib, number twelve—one of your floating ribs."

"Ow."

"Mmhm. You have multiple contusions, your back and your legs are..." Karen closed her eyes again and took a deep breath.

"That's my girl."

"Oh, shut up. You're torn up pretty good, John."

"Not very clinical."

"I'm not feeling terribly clinical. Alex said...Alex said you were...you were dragged behind a truck." She held my hand and looked down. "Your wrists and ankles are cut where you were bound."

As she went down the list, I added it all up, and decided it all hurt. And had I not been a little high, it would have hurt worse. "Come here." I moved a little to my right, lifted my left arm and pulled her down next to me. She lay on her side and rested her head against my chest. The simple movement took my breath, but as she settled next to me, her touch restored it.

"Loving a cop isn't easy," I said.

"So I've heard."

"And do you listen?"

"Usually not. And being a cop is harder than loving one." She raised her head, sending shards of pain down my side. "And who are you to tell me who to love?"

"No one, apparently. Get back down here before I pass out. And don't move again."

"You're just dying to see this all end again, aren't you? Is it the chase you like best? I'll let you chase me for the rest of our lives, but I'll be damned if I'm going to let you walk away from me. You can be a real sonofabitch, Testarossa. Nevertheless, I have no intention of giving you up." She raised her head again. "Got it?"

"Got it." I eased her head back down against my chest. "Move again and I'll whack you like a catholic school girl."

"I've still got that plaid skirt somewhere."

I chuckled, and it hurt worse than if she'd taken a flying leap on top of me. "I may be high, Gennaro, but that's something I won't forget."

I sat in a high-backed chair while Alex sat in the bed with the head raised almost straight up and down.

"The body of Dennis Hillman got us started," he said. "His body was found off the road near Santa Susanna Pass. We didn't hear about it until the next day, and the only reason why we heard about it was because one of the sand sleepers who saw what happened to you told us that Hillman was among Mardigan's helpers."

"I was out of it, but I knew he was there in the back of the truck. He knew me. And then we stopped and he wasn't there anymore, and then I heard the shot."

"Yeah. It was your gun Mardigan used. Then it was like following a trail. We found a grocery bag with prescription insulin and some deodorant. Then we found your gun, your pants with your wallet still in the back pocket, your socks... like a trail to grandma's house."

I nodded, remembering. Out of all that happened, being dragged behind the truck was the worst of it. "How far was it from the turn in the road to the house?" I asked.

"About a quarter mile."

"That feels about right." I shifted on the chair.

"Mardigan was a mess, John. What the hell happened?"

"He had the room rigged. Shrapnel bomb using a pressure cooker. He engaged it every time he left the room, I'm guessing in case he's caught. He gets one last kill before he's taken to the fuckin' nut farm. That whole garage was made into a dungeon, restraints and eyebolts built into the floor. It's where he held them, where he did his dirtiest work."

"What I'm asking is, how did it get reengaged after you left the room."

"I have no idea."

He bit back a grin and shook his head. "I saw the bedroom."

"Yeah. How's the little girl—Violet?"

"She's fine. He never touched her. Maybe you were too much of a distraction."

"Or, Beverly Shay talked him down. How is she, by the way?"

"She's alive."

"Yeah?"

"Yeah. We're waiting for her to get clear on a few things, like choosing life over a needle in her arm." Alex heaved himself out of the bed. "Get your ass well. She knows where the bodies are buried. She also started that fire at Tiffany Funk's place. Her good deed for the century." He walked to the door, and before he opened it, he turned back.

"Just so you know, Captain Brennan—Dana Torrance—was on point through this whole thing. When you went missing, she held a press conference, talked about her ordeal. We got to you quicker because of her."

I nodded. "Thanks, Alex."

"One more thing." His eyes met mine. I'd never known Alex to be particularly sentimental, but the expression on his face spoke a language I'd never heard, at least from him. "Those were the worst days of my life. In the future, I'd appreciate it if you waited for me before venturing down dark alleys. I feel better having your back. Just a quirk of mine."

His words took root in the one hollow place I had left in me, the one spot I'd reserved for the healing, a place where all the shit could accumulate, and then maybe one day, with some time, some love from a good woman, and a return full-time to the job I loved, I could purge it, like week-old trash.

"How long was I gone?"

The walls of the room were taupe, erring toward green. I'd been disconnected from tubes and finger clips since nine a.m. that morning, preparing to go home. The bed, raised high, still had the blue gel pad I laid on to ease the pressure on my back, which was still raw. The room was big enough for two beds, yet I'd roomed alone. The light of day was the only illumination offered to this room, the fluorescents triggering headaches I didn't need, on top of all the other stuff I had going. Alex was dressed for work in a light gray suit and an indigo shirt, his gray and blue tie pulled loose at his neck. Twirled around three fingers of my left hand was a satin ribbon of the deepest purple. During my time here, Violet Hemingway visited me, along with her family. I was in and out, still fighting fever, and according to doctors, an infection, yet I remembered her visit, her presence. And I remember taking the ribbon and wrapping it in my hand. Violet was fine, untouched. Another survivor.

DREAMS OF LONELINESS LIKE A HEARTBEAT, drives you mad
   In the stillness of remembering
   What you had, and what you lost
   And what you had
   And what you lost

"FOUR DAYS, Johnny. You were offline for four days."

EVERYONE but me thought I needed care, and so that's how I wound up at Karen's. She threatened to take a few days off, and I balked. Giving in was easier, which I always figured out too late. I was out of work for the time being, and there was talk of me seeing the department head doc before I could return. The extra attention, and the belief that I needed to get my head clear weighed heavy. During my marriage I was less conscious of making my wife crazy with this career I chose. I kept it off her by stopping at The Stone Cantina three or four nights a week and letting it all go there. I knew Karen wouldn't stand for that, and oddly enough, I had no desire to worry her like that. I wasn't going to burden her with my workday, either. And being at her mercy while I healed didn't sit well with me. I was out of sorts, restless. By day three I was snapping at her.

I sat outside on her balcony overlooking Marina del Rey, Palos Verdes and beyond. She rigged the already-cushioned chair with extra padding, and I found I could sit for ten minutes without wanting to get up and walk around, which the doctor said was good to do. Whatever. Karen came out carrying a tray with a pot of tea, two cup-and-saucers, a china creamer and matching sugar bowl. I watched her pour the tea and then prepare it like her grandmother used to, with milk and sugar. I loved it this way, and it never tasted right when I did it myself. She handed me the cup and saucer, and the first sip soothed me more than I expected.

She took a sip herself, and then set her cup on the table between us.

"If you're waiting for me to tell you what happened," I said after the silence went on too long, "You'll be waiting a while."

"Fine."

"I just need a little time."

"I understand."

It wasn't and she didn't. I chuckled into my fancy teacup.

"If you weren't laid so low I'd throw something at you," she hissed. "I know what you're thinking."

"You do, huh?"

"Yes. Taking care of you makes you weak in my eyes. Sharing your hurts and your burdens makes you less of a man, somehow."

"You are way off base."

Karen leaned forward with her elbows on her knees. "We let each other go once, for all the wrong reasons, yet you were always with me. The way you've chased me, ridden roughshod over me and called it foreplay, tells me I was with you, too."

"You were," I confirmed.

"And two weeks ago, while you were buried inside me, you told me you weren't letting me go again; you told me you wanted more than a night. Your feelings on the matter were pretty clear."

I felt weary. "That hasn't changed. I'm not talking about my work. Period."

"Why not?"

"Because you don't want to know.

"Yes I do."

"This isn't up for discussion."

She was quiet for a long time, and then she stood. "Fine. Great." Again, it was none of the above. My phone rang.

"It's Alex," I said. Karen shot me a final look and went inside. I listened for a long time, mumbled a few words to my partner and hung up. I stood and steadied myself with the heavy shillelagh, gifted to Karen by a famous Irish rock star she pieced back together after an auto accident.

I watched her stomp around her bedroom through the open door. She moved between the bed and the closet, putting folded laundry away.

"I have to meet Alex, then I'm going home," I said from the doorway.

She did one of those laugh/cry things and muttered, "Go."

I followed her into the walk-in closet and came up behind her. I snaked my arms around her middle and pulled her back against me.

"Hey, Blue," I said in her ear.

"It's fine. Go."

I turned her to face me. "Don't say it's fine when it isn't, and please don't make this a thing. You want what you want, but it's something I can't give to you now."

"I want to help you," she said, her whispered words hanging on a sob. "That's all."

"You help me by being here, being with me, and being available when I do want to talk. Come stay with me at my place. Please. That's how you can help me." I took her face in my hands. "I love you."

"That's not up for debate," she sniffed.

I ran my hands over her backside and gave it a solid swat. "Huh. I think the proper response is, 'I love you too, Daddy'."

Her mouth flopped open in shock and then a laugh exploded, unhindered by the last five minutes of discomfort. She held my face and kissed me softly, letting her mouth linger over mine long after the kiss was over. "I love you, too, Daddy," she whispered.

"Yeah, baby."

Her hand lingered at the back of my neck and her mouth moved to my ear. "I think I just had a little orgasm."

"Hold that thought. I'll be back soon."

"You aren't serious."

"You'll be gentle."

"Dear God."

39

The air vibrated. It wasn't the wind that decided to kick up for no reason. It wasn't the diggers and mini earthmovers standing at the ready in case extra help was needed. It wasn't the silent tears of uniformed rookies and veterans of years in a life like this, a job like this, where the sins one human commits against another never gets old, never numbs, never stunts the heart. No. It was none of that. It was the souls. They came back, and they hovered over their unnatural home, confused, angry. Some wept. A black cloud settled over the open graves, undulating as if the pain were simply too great to carry.

The bodies had been buried on the property where Branch Mardigan and Beverly Shay held me for four days. They held others, too. Many, they never bothered to return to their families. Beverly Shay cut a deal, and then she talked. She would grow old in prison, but she wouldn't die on the taxpayer's dime. That was the deal.

Earth had been moved in baby steps, and the odd mounds that covered the property were flatter now, the non-native flora and fauna that grew out of them torn away and scattered to the wind. Remains were excavated and laid out on white sheets—nine so far. Some were decomposed beyond recognition; most were skeletal remains. All were small. The dirt mounds had been replaced by mounds of white sheets. The property looked like a battlefield.

Too many Jane Does to fathom at this moment, because there were many mounds still intact and waiting to be taken down a few notches. The setting sun reflected off the San Fernando Mountains and cast an amber glow over the scene.

Alex shifted next to me. "How many so far?" he asked.

"Nine."

"Nine." I watched him force a swallow past the lump in his throat. He was noting the size of the remains and thinking of his kids now. So was I. Where had they all come from? We had pictures, and we were matching them with missing persons reports. Some we could not match. It would all take time. This was far from over.

I closed my eyes and listened to the howling, the rage at life taken too soon. The muted chatter was fear-laced. None had moved on. The wind kicked up again, and a twist of dead leaves hovered above a mound higher than the others, the dirt new, fresh. Nothing lived on that mound; nothing grew. Not yet. The leaves settled with the dying wind, and then rose toward heaven. The black bird stood on the mound, its gray beak raised proudly.

I will see them home now, it said. *I will see them home.*

40

*I*t was almost dark. I threw on a pair of sweats, went out to the kitchen, poured a scotch, and went out to my patio. The sun was going down over the houses across Linnie Canal, and the surface of the water glowed amber. My life with Karen Gennaro less than a year ago was filled with the joys and the little lies of a new relationship, and then it abruptly ended when I got stupid. It was time to have a relationship now, and the kind she wanted involved sharing and honesty. I was not ready to talk about the last four days, because I had other issues—issues that could haunt us for the rest of our lives, issues that might make her decide I wasn't the man for her after all. I needed to get the big stuff out in the open, let her know who I was, before I talked about being held in a room for four days by a maniac. That was nothing compared to this.

She was here when I got home, as I'd asked her to be. As I led her to the bedroom she balked. She thought I was kidding. I sipped my drink, sore but content in the knowledge that it all worked—for both of us.

The door opened behind me and she came outside in one of my dress shirts and a smile—until she saw what was in my hand.

"A scotch. Seriously, John?"

"I haven't had a pain pill since last night. Please, let me have some pleasure."

"I let you have some about an hour ago."

"You did, and I thank you."

"You weren't a hundred percent, but you did amazingly well."

"Thank you for that, too. Pour yourself something and come back out here. I need to talk to you."

"All right." When she came back, a glass of red wine in hand, she sat next to me and stared at the water. "Beautiful."

"Yeah. Could you see yourself here?"

"I go where you go."

"I like your place, too. When we get married can we live in two places?"

"That's a lousy proposal."

"When I propose, baby, it's one you'll remember."

"Is this really what you wanted to talk about?"

"No."

"I didn't think so. You tend to pace verbally when you want to discuss something you don't want to discuss."

"You're sassing me again."

She laughed. "Yes, well..."

I took her hand. "I want this to work. I don't want to live without you. You're the most important thing in my life. Going forward, I'll be good to you, Karen. I will. I'll be the man you need me to be."

"I know."

"And, I heard you earlier. I'm not the best communicator, but I'll work hard to make you happy in that regard."

She kissed my hand. "Enough blowing smoke up my ass. Talk to me."

"After I tell you what I need to, one of two things will happen: We'll either talk about a life together, or you'll walk away from me."

Worry creased her face, and then disappeared. "There's not a third option?"

"No. I know what I want and the only thing keeping me from that is you."

"All right."

"There are some things about my past that you need to know, baby."

She tucked a leg under her and kept hold of my hand.

"My old man was a cop. You know that."

"Yes."

"He had the day off one day, so he walked me to school then stopped for a bite to eat. When he came out, he was murdered—shot in the head, point blank range. Mob hit. He was working them—the mob—and got in too deep. He probably did some things the department had a problem with, but the bottom line is they didn't get him out in time, then once he got hit, they made him look dirty to save face. I did some time working OC."

"What's OC?"

"Organized Crime, out of Brooklyn. They—the department—thought that the 'like father, like son' angle would get me in close to them, too. It worked. We made some arrests, and they pulled me out before I got too deep—learned their lesson, I guess. I left New York, came here, and married Marisol. After I moved here...shortly after...Giancarlo, my grandfather died.

"The red-head."

"Yeah, the red-head. I went home for the funeral. I still

had friends on the force. They looked out for my family, for me. Some were still with the Organized Crime Unit I'd worked in. They kept me in the loop." I let that stand a while, not sure I wanted to continue.

"While I was in New York for the funeral, I got in touch with Sonny Vitello, the head of the crime family. I hadn't seen him in a while, and I don't know why he agreed to see me unguarded, but he did. I killed him. I killed Sonny Vitello, for my father. I earned his trust and when the opportunity came, I blew his face off, so that his mother couldn't view him at the wake. He took my father from me, and from my mother. I became judge, jury, and executioner, and I took him from his wife and his mother—and his children. I killed him." Something splashed in the water, and I squinted in the dark until I could find more words.

"I'm not sorry. I feel no remorse. I'm probably supposed to, but I don't." I paused. "You asked me once if I'd ever killed anyone. I didn't answer then. I'm answering now. Twice. Once on the job, and this."

Karen's face was unreadable as she let go of my hand and stood. She walked to the edge of the patio with her back to me. Whatever happened, happened. She had to know my story before we could continue. This was something that could come back to bite me—us—one day, and she needed to know, needed to be prepared to fight the fight with me, or not. She was in the life saving business, not in the life-taking business. I didn't expect her to understand this, not for a minute.

A good amount of time passed before she turned around and sat. Her face had changed. It was hard, certain and not at all afraid. She was leaving me. This was not for her. I got it.

"Who else knows?" she whispered.

"My priest."

She nodded

"Karen..."

She shook her head and held up her hand to silence me. "There will come a day when you will need to tell someone else about this, and when you do, everything you are now will be gone—your career definitely, and your freedom most likely. You'll do this because of who you are." She took my hand. "And then again, maybe you won't. But I don't want that to be because of me. Whatever you decide, I want to do it with you. Losing your father, and then taking revenge for that loss has defined you. You work hard at a job that you love like no one else I have ever known, because of that. You're the cop you are, because of that. You are the best of the best, because of that. Make taking that life matter, Johnny. Don't stop being who you are." Karen leaned over and rested her head against my shoulder.

We all pay for our sins eventually. I wondered if I had already paid enough. Losing Mark Gonzales, choosing a job that never allowed me to see the light at the end of the tunnel, a job that never gave me closure, or the satisfaction of saving lives, a job that tore at my heart each and every day, my inability to grow scar tissue making the pain as unbearable as the very first time. Was that the penance I was to pay? Was the career I'd chosen enough to make up for it all?

I never spent a minute regretting ending Sonny Vitello's life. Did that make it worse? Did that ensure that the favor would be returned to me someday, that something precious would be taken from *me*? Was this life I was leading *enough*? And did I have the right to involve another person in it for the long haul? With remorse and sorrow comes redemption, but I felt none of those things. I tried to make up for it in other ways, by being an honest man, by doing my job the right way, so that *less* lives were lost. And I took care of the people I loved. I would take care of Karen. I prayed that whatever else was coming would come just to me, and not to her. I'd well-earned the penalty of being alone for the rest of my life, and any decent man in a situation like this would simply live his life alone, taking women to his bed when the urge demanded it, committing to no one. But I loved this woman. And I would not survive without her. I was in so deep with her that there was no escape. Not for me, at least. Was that my penance—to love someone beyond all reason, only to lose her too soon? Or was I being forgiven, and that was why she was with me now?

I did not know the answer, but one day I would.

THE DAY GREW warm off a chilly morning. I sat at an outdoor café on the Walk nursing a beer. The injuries that covered most of my body were beginning to scab, and with that came a lot of itching and general discomfort. I was off the walking stick. That, alone, made me feel better.

Each night, Karen covered the injuries with salve to prevent drying and scarring, and on a rare night, in my bed, I'd gather her against my side in the dark, stare up at the ceiling, and tell her about my four days. It helped to do it in the dark, because I could pretend it was the light fixture I was addressing instead of my woman. She needed to hear it, and I suppose I needed to say it. And to her credit, she mostly listened. But the idea that I'd brought it on myself through hubris and carelessness was hard to admit, and it was a weakness I didn't want to share with anyone—most of all the woman I'd sworn to protect. If I could be that stupid, that arrogant to traipse down a dark alley after some jackass on a bike, how could I be depended on to keep her safe? She didn't see it that way, but I did. And that's all that mattered.

I had a few sessions left with the department head shrinker before I went back to light duty and possibly some investigative work. That wasn't easy either, talking to some doctor who held my future in his hands—in this case, her hands. She was helpful, overall. Still, I wanted to be done with it.

I stood when Captain Dana Brennan walked in after speaking briefly with the hostess and spotting me. She took a seat and had what I was having.

"You did it in full uniform," I said of the press conference she held while I was holed up in a dungeon garage.

"I'm a cop first. People needed to see that."

"You're a cop second and third, too. You don't play the victim well, if at all."

"Not at all," she said, tapping her bottle of Corona against mine. "So, you have some issues with someone in Foothill," Brennan said, getting to the point of our lunch.

"Cop named Mason Laborteaux." I gave a brief history, then got more detailed about the day at the house in Palms.

"And you heard two distinct reports," she said, referring to the gunshots I heard that day.

"Yeah."

"How did he do it, do you think? With cops all around, you're saying he took the gangbanger's gun, shot Gonzales, then took his own and shot the banger."

"Yeah, except he fucked up. That's how Laborteaux wanted it to look, but what he did was shoot the kid first with his duty weapon, then took the kid's .22 and shot Gonz.

I distinctly heard the deeper gunshots first—the shot from Laborteaux's gun."

"And when I look at the report, I'll see all the right bullets in all the right bodies?"

"Yeah. Look into the distance of the two shootings. From where the kid was laying, a .22 couldn't have done that much damage to Gonz. If the kid shot Gonz, he would have been closer. And Laborteaux would have been farther from the kid than the wounds on him indicate."

"You've done your work."

"Yeah. Laborteaux's partner, Sebby Castro, lied, saying he was there in time to see Labby shoot the kid, and Gonz was already on the ground. Not true. And now Castro is mouthing off about a side gig Labby's got going on." After getting her word that this would go no further, for now, I told her about my conversation with Mac at The Stone. And then I told her what happened at Big Tommy's place, to his girls.

"I'm going to look into this, and it's going to take some time. I may not find anything, John. I may end up agreeing with FID."

"I know. I doubt it, but I hear you."

She nodded. "Another thing: the up-highs want to look in to how Mardigan met his maker. Any thoughts on that?"

I shrugged and shook my head. "Room must have been rigged."

Dana Brennan stared into her beer. "So, you'd like that kind of talk to cease."

"I would"

"Done."

"Thank you."

"When do you get back on the job?"

"Soon. I have a few more sessions with the BS doc, and then I can come back for light duty."

"Good. You have more to do on this case." She stood. "I'm sure they'll let you finish things up."

"Yeah," I said. "It's the finishing up that'll be the hardest."

EPILOGUE

The blender whirred, cracking ice and melding good tequila and fresh lime juice from the tree on my patio. I pulled a beer out of the cooler and grabbed one for Alex. He stood on my small dock while his three kids settled themselves in the Johnboat.

"Ready, *Nino*," Bryan called.

"I'm coming." I bent down and kissed Karen on the cheek as Lisa handed her a margarita.

"I'm not sure I've ever seen you with a drink," I heard Lisa say to her.

"Because I'm usually on call," Karen said. "I'm taking the week off."

"Yeah, you are," I smiled down at her. "Okay, now," I said to the assembled boaters. "He is in charge," I said to the little ones, pointing to their responsible older brother. "Stay seated and no fooling around."

"And stay in front so one of us has eyes on you," Alex added.

"I'm feeding the ducks, see, *Nino*?" Celeste said, cradled in a neon green life jacket and holding up a bag of duck kibble.

"Me, too," echoed Stevie, wearing the same outfit.

"Just don't stand up to feed them," Bryan reminded. "I don't feel like jumping in to get you two." At eleven, the kid was beyond his years, and despite his protests, he'd kill himself protecting his siblings.

"Okay, off with you now." I untied the rope, tossed it in the boat and gave them a shove with my foot.

"Stay where we can see you," Lisa called out.

"We know," all three kids yelled back.

"*Nino*, when's dinner?" Stevie asked.

"Sometime while we're still sober is the plan, my man," his father answered.

"Papa, can I sleep over *Nino's*?" Stevie shouted as the Johnboat caught the slow current of the canal and took them toward Grand.

"Me, too," echoed Celeste.

"No, only me," argued her brother.

I turned to Karen, who only shrugged.

"Don't worry," Alex said. "A bomb won't wake him once he's down, so your high-pitched screams won't bother him a bit. He likes French toast for breakfast. Want the other two?"

"Alex, stop it," Lisa said.

"You're a prick," I said.

Alex watched his kids drift away down the canal, and I wondered what it would be like to have three and not be able to give them back at the end of the evening, or the next day. I loved his kids, but they weren't mine. I got to love them and then return them, like rental cars. While Alex and I watched the kids drift down the canal, the ladies continued their conversation behind us.

"How's he doing?" Lisa asked.

"Fine," Karen said. "On the mend. All the physical stuff

healed nicely. He's dying to get back to full duty." She had more to say, and she would once my ears were closed.

"How are you with all this?"

"All right," Karen said, the brave face to her tone fooling no one.

"Don't expect much," Lisa said. "When I started dating Alex we were still in college, and by the time he entered the Academy we'd been married a short time. Back then it was exciting. I wanted to know all about his day, and he wanted to tell me. I remember during his field-training period there was a get together for all the spouses of the new officers, and they told us how things would change. I didn't believe them."

"How do you mean?" Karen asked.

Both Alex and I turned around, curious ourselves. Lisa looked at her husband as she spoke. "How could something as exciting as being an LAPD officer change a man? He'd be changing lives for the better. In my view, he had a chair next to God because of what he was doing. Now, I don't remember the exact words..."

"When was this?" Alex asked.

"You weren't invited. None of the officers were. Just their spouses." Lisa turned to Karen. "They said there would be changes; anger, and cynicism and distrust. All the things these men and women are now, they said, will change. And it did. I've seen it."

Alex moved inside the gate.

"Don't start justifying," she said to him with a raised hand. "I'm not criticizing. You are still the man I fell in love with, but you're different." Lisa turned back to Karen. "Every time I hear someone say, 'I hate cops' or 'I don't trust cops', I want to say, 'Just one day. Just one day in their shoes, and you'll know hate; you'll know distrust'."

Alex was hearing this for the first time, by the look on his face.

Lisa grabbed Karen's hand. "Don't ask him how his day went. He doesn't want to tell you. He doesn't want to relive it, or soil you with the shit he has to see every day. Don't ask. Just be here for him when he gets home. You want to really do right by him? Do that. There. I've said it." Lisa turned to me. "I'm sorry. I've had a few margaritas."

Karen caught my eye and I gave her a wink. Her mouth hung open—shock? Embarrassment? I did not know. I owed Lisa Ortiz big for this one. She said everything I couldn't, and better.

Alex walked over to his wife and crouched down in front of her. "Did I just hear you say 'shit'?"

"I'm afraid so. My quota for the year." She kissed him on the mouth and handed him her empty glass.

"No more for you," he said. "My ears will bleed with what you'll say next."

"Get going," she answered, gesturing toward the blender. He took Karen's glass and filled both. I heard sirens in the distance and as they got closer, I wondered how this subject managed to stay in the background during my first time around with Karen. Maybe because the relationship was so new, and happened so fast, we avoided the minutiae we were both determined to tackle this time around. I didn't expect Karen to understand completely. I wasn't sure I did.

"John? Oh, John, thank goodness." I turned to meet the worried eyes of Esther Horowitz. Attached to her was Lou Wachley. "Good evening," Esther said to everyone. "So sorry to interrupt, but something terrible has happened: Erin Willits is missing, John, since last night. She never came home from school. The police are with Sara now," Esther said.

Cruise Mom. Erin Willits' mother. Alex and I exchanged a look. Words were not necessary.

"Get the kids to the front of the house," Alex told Lisa. "We'll be right back."

I didn't have to ask how or where or when. I knew where Erin Willits was, either by her own choice or someone else's. I saw the lust in his eyes and the shame in hers that night in the yard after the Neighborhood Watch thing. They made for strange bedfellows.

Alex and I talked with Sara Willits, who knew of her daughter's schoolgirl obsession with Daniel Amir. So did Mrs. Amir. I told the uniforms all I knew of Amir and the night I saw he and Erin Willits together, and then I turned Esther and Lou over to them. They had more to say than I ever would, and they'd have more fun saying it.

"*I frutti proibiti sono i più dolci*", I said to Alex as we made our way back to my place. The sun was down, and we had women and kids to feed.

"What does that mean?"

"Forbidden fruit is the sweetest."

"A-fuckin'-men to that, bubba."

Three days later, Erin Willits' body was found under her house. She'd been raped and beaten. A silver hoop earring caked with dried blood and torn flesh was clutched in her fist. Daniel Amir was in the wind, but we'd find him.

This is what we do. This is who we are.

ALSO BY JD CARY

Testarossa

4 Days

ABOUT THE AUTHOR

JD CARY BEGAN WRITING FAN FICTION, AND THAT EFFORT MORPHED INTO THE FIRST NOVEL, *TESTAROSSA*, WHICH WAS ORIGINALLY PUBLISHED BY KRILL PRESS IN 2010. IN 2013 *TESTAROSSA* WAS REPRINTED UNDER THE BOOKSPAN/DIRECT BRANDS IMPRINT AND RETITLED *A DEADLY LEGACY*. IT WAS RE-RELEASED IN TRADE PAPERBACK UNDER THE CROOKED LANE BOOKS BANNER IN SEPTEMBER 2015.

NOW, GOING BACK TO ITS ORIGINAL NAME, YET RE-EDITED, *TESTAROSSA* WAS RE-RELEASED INDEPENDENTLY IN 2019.

JD LIVES IN LOS ANGELES WITH AN ADORING FAMILY.

facebook.com/JDCaryAuthor